Readable Writing

Revising for Style

H. Wendell Smith

Wadsworth Publishing Company
Belmont, California
A Division of Wadsworth, Inc.

English Editor:
Kevin J. Howat

Production Editor:
Deborah M. Oren

Designer:
Paula Shuhert

Copy Editor:
Russell Fuller

Signing Representative:
Diana Rothberg

Printed in the United States of America
2 3 4 5 6 7 8 9 10—89 88 87 86 85

ISBN 0-534-03278-8

Library of Congress Cataloging in Publication Data

Smith, H. Wendell
  Readable writing.

  Includes index.
  1. English language—Rhetoric. I. Title.
PE1408.S593   1984   808'.042   84-3582
ISBN 0-534-03278-8

Preface

Easy writing's vile hard reading.
Richard Brinsley
Sheridan (1751–1816)

For most of us, reading is an everyday thing. We can hardly get through a day without it. We read for information. We read for directions. And we read for pleasure.

We usually want our reading to be effortless. When the reading is "hard," we give up quickly; to puzzle out a meaning is just too much work, and there are plenty of other ways to spend our time. Anyway, hard reading is likely to lead us in wrong directions, to mistaken conclusions. And, of course, hard reading is "vile"; it spoils our pleasure.

So when we get on the other side, the writer's side, we have to remember that it's the writer's job to make the reading easy, readable, informative, and fun. After all, our writing is wasted if readers don't understand, if they get the wrong ideas, or if they "give up" because the reading is difficult or dull. We want what we write to be easy to read—and worth reading.

When we turn Sheridan's well-known line around, we find another version: Easy reading is hard writing.

Writing, when it makes good reading, is carefully planned and thoughtfully finished. It is smoothed and tightened in revision. And it is meticulously edited. All the planning, writing, revising, and editing—the whole process—takes a lot of hard work.

No, readable writing is not easy. But why should we want it to be? There's little satisfaction in doing easy work; it's the hard jobs that challenge us. And when the result satisfies, when the finished essay is readable and worth reading, it's also worth the tears and sweat.

The First Draft: Raw Material

Someone has wisely said that there's no such thing as good writing; there's only good *rewriting*. In other words, we can expect to write well only if we are willing to write *again,* to rewrite and rewrite until what we've done becomes easy to read.

The real writing is always the *rewriting*.

So most of this book is about rewriting, *revising*. We look closely at the ideas we have written and consider how to make them readable and worth reading. Almost nobody produces readable writing at first try. The first draft of an essay (the most common form of writing done in college) is likely to be a sketchy and unorganized searching for things to say. It is by no means a finished product, and it does not pretend to be. We'll do well to think of our first draft as a way of discovering what we want to say, a way of gathering the raw materials to be later shaped into the real essay.

The Introduction takes us through that adventure, the search for raw material and production of the first draft. We'll learn to search our minds for ideas. We'll learn to hook ideas quickly and capture them in brief, not worrying at this stage about whether they are good or bad. We'll learn to discover a useful *purpose* for our writing, letting it guide us as we organize. We'll see how to turn our list of ideas into a step-by-step plan and how to work that plan into a useful first draft.

We'll find that we can write that first draft without worrying over details. All we have to do is *write;* we don't have to *be right*. After all, the first draft is supposed to be raw material.

Then, with the first draft in hand, we are ready to begin the real work, the revising. Most of the lessons in this book take us through practical means of revision, ways to bring dead stuff to life, ways to flesh out a bare-bones thought and give it point, ways to put ideas in order, ways to cut through the deadwood, ways to vary our sentence forms, ways to make our ideas clear and give our writing an effective punch—in short, ways to make it readable.

What Makes Writing Readable?

We break the elements of good writing down into eight qualities:

Substance. Good writing has something to say. It presents a reasonable, challenging idea and develops it solidly with illustration, example, comparison or contrast, definition, or other suitable support.

Order. Good writing is orderly. It presents ideas in meaningful sequence. It begins somewhere and leads somewhere.

Economy. Good writing doesn't waste words. It may repeat for emphasis, but it doesn't repeat needlessly. It goes to the point, not around it.

Emphasis. Good writing strikes the mind with firmness and force.

Variety. Good writing develops precise meaning—as well as delights readers—by its varied rhythms and sentence forms.

Clarity. Good writing is clear. It gets its meaning into the reader's mind without presenting a puzzle or an obstacle course.

Consistency. Good writing stays on track. It doesn't shift its point of view or wander back and forth between past and present tenses. When it uses a pronoun, the pronoun clearly matches the noun it stands for.

Appearance and Custom. Good writing is edited. It observes the customs of the written language: spelling, punctuating, capitalizing, and abbreviating. Good writing, in its appearance on the page, leaves an impression of careful work by a thoughtful mind.

From Draft to Finish

We begin with how to prepare and write a first draft, the gathering of raw materials for an essay. The rest of the book is about revision, the real writing. We move through the qualities of good writing, one at a time, learning how to make them our own. The result we look for, at last, is writing of solid substance and readable style—meaningful, orderly, emphatic, concise, varied in expression, clear, consistent, and inviting in appearance.

Using the Book

As we work with *Readable Writing*, let's keep in mind that no book can teach us to write in readable style; only actual writing, rewriting, and more rewriting can do that. We don't learn just by taking quizzes and memorizing points of grammar. We learn by putting the derriere on a chair and words on the paper, again and again.

Some things in life are *important;* others are *essential.* We want to give our time and attention to the important, the things that make life more interesting, not to the mere essential. We'd die without breathing; that's essential. But we don't want to give our time and attention to breathing; it should be done automatically.

This book puts first the *important* things about writing (like inventing ideas and developing an engaging topic with a clear purpose); it puts last the *essential* things (like spelling, punctuating, and capitalizing). But there is no need to follow the given order. In an English class you'll probably follow a sequence of lessons that the instructor thinks will help you best. When you use the book on your own, you can skip about at will to serve your private needs. If you're weak on spelling, Lesson 38; if you want variety of sentences, Lesson 22; if your writing is wordy, Lesson 12; if you'd like the sparkle of figurative language and imagery, Lessons 24 and 36; if you feel writer's block and need help getting the juices flowing, you can turn to "Writing the First Draft," the introduction to the book.

At last, we hope to put it all together in our own writing and find the satisfaction of a readable style, easy and pleasing to read—and worth reading.

Acknowledgments

Expert suggestions by many teachers of writing have made this book more readable in every aspect of style: substance, order, economy, emphasis, variety, clarity, and consistency. I am especially grateful for the helpful counsel of Douglas Butturff, formerly of the University of Central Arkansas, Robert Dees of Orange Coast College, Douglas Haneline of Dakota State College, Eric P. Hibbison of J. Sargeant Reynolds Community College, Harriet Polt Schmitt of Merritt College, Norman Prinsky of Augusta College, and William Woods of Wichita State University.

Further refinements have come from the imaginative people at Wadsworth, particularly English editor Kevin Howat, production editor Debbie Oren, copy editor Russell Fuller, designer Paula Shuhert, and permissions editors Diana Griffin and Peggy Meehan.

It's been a special delight to work with the student essays that appear in this book. For the use of their work (and their permission to misuse it on occasion for teaching purposes), I thank my students at Santa Monica College, including especially Elaine Abramovitz, Joyce Abrams, Mesrak Assefa, John Eric Bergel, Thomas Bignell, Anne-Marie Cosgrove, Julio Fassino, Leo French, Stephan Hofmann, Derek Karnes, Irene McConville, Robert Neman, Hoang Minh Phanle, John Urich-Sass, James Watson, Clayton Williams, Florence Zemborain, and Craig Zimmerman. Their essays have helped to make this book unique.

Contents

Topics for Writing and Revising

Introduction:

Writing the First Draft

Write down the thoughts of the moment. Those that come unsought are commonly the most valuable.
Sir Francis Bacon
(1562–1626)

All of us, we may justly suppose, have known the agony of staring at a blank sheet of paper that we hope will soon bear revelation of our thoughts. We sit, but pen and paper do not cooperate. Thoughts pass through our brains in untold numbers—but we do not write them down.

Some call it writer's block. It is really self-rejection, a fear that the ideas we have are not good enough. We reject ideas and write down nothing until at last the mind, like our paper, goes blank.

Sir Francis Bacon tells us how to cut through writer's block: "Write down the thoughts of the moment." He does not say write down only the *good* thoughts; he suggests that we write down *all* the thoughts of the moment, not caring whether they seem worth the ink. If we take them in our net, if we write them down, perhaps the mind will be encouraged to give us more—and better— thoughts.

Bacon says the thoughts unsought "are commonly the most valuable." We have no assurance, of course, that the brain's next try will bring forth brilliance. But if we write every thought down, the good and the bad alike, we will at least have something to work with, some raw material to be shaped. We may be able to change a "bad" idea into a good one—if we've captured it on paper so that it can't escape into oblivion.

What an Essay Is

An essay is an attempt (that's what the French word *essai* means). Its very name suggests that this form of writing, usually brief, is not an exhaustive discussion, that its writer does not hold its ideas to be the last word or all that can be said on the topic. Still, since it is a *form*, the essay is not mere drivel, either. It has a shape and a kind of completeness.

As we begin to write an essay, then, we need not tremble in fear that our ideas are not perfect. After all, no one is looking over our shoulder as we write. Our first attempt, the tentative *essai*, will not be what we show to the world. It will be what we call the *first draft*, a collection of raw materials to be shaped later. It will be a means of discovering what we want to say.

Step 1: Choosing a Topic

We must first choose something to write *about*—a topic. In college work we are often presented with the topic and do not have to dredge it up for ourselves. We're asked to write about what we've been learning, about history or politics, a poem or book, a theory in science. And often we're asked to write about ourselves and our ideas and opinions.

If we choose our own topic, we'd better stick to things we know something about. If an instructor assigns a topic, then we'd better keep our essay directly on that topic and not let it wander. In either case, we need to get started without wasting time staring at that blank sheet of paper.

The old advice is still good: We should write about what we know, bringing as much as possible of our own experience to every topic and making it our own. Firsthand observation, when honest and accurate, draws attention. No matter how limited our experience, it is interesting if *we* are interesting.

We need, of course, to enlarge our experience. If we look into what we have read, into the views of others, and into what we can find of experiment or research, we expand our attitudes toward a topic. And our way of selecting and seeing a topic can be enhanced by looking at it in new ways. We may see a topic as we find it, but we may also see it with a question in mind: What if it were otherwise? There is something to be said for imagination.

We need only look around us for topics. Whatever we see (or hear or touch or read), we may ask some questions about it: *What* is it? *What* is it like or not like? *What* is going on? *Who* is doing it or what has caused it? *Where* and *when* does it happen? *How* is it done? *Why* is it done? *What if* it were different? *What should* be done about it? Any one of these questions can lead to an essay topic.

Step 2: Limiting the Topic

The essay is a limited form. In it we cannot handle a topic that would require extended research or a whole book to develop. At the outset we admit that we are to cover only a small point. To write an essay on "politics" or "music" or "foreign languages" would be impossible, since we could never say all that could be said on such broad topics. Even if we broke the topic "politics" down to "American politics" or "political parties" or "why third parties don't work," we might still have too much to handle in a brief essay. The narrower the topic, the nearer it comes into range.

Let's say we have decided (or have been directed) to write something about learning a foreign language. We may list a few possible approaches:

Why learn a foreign language?

How to learn—by the book or by speaking?

Which language to study?

Where to learn—in school or in the foreign country?

We could go on listing possibilities, but let's say we decide to try writing on the third item: which language to study? What considerations will help a college student decide to study one language rather than another? The topic seems limited enough for us to handle, and we're ready to begin work.

Step 3: Searching the Mind for Ideas

Pen and paper ready, we start thinking about the topic. For about ten minutes we jot down every thought that comes to mind, good or bad. If we have an idea that seems off the topic or "no good," we write it down anyway, just to get it out of mind; once the thought is down on paper, the mind will probably go on to other, perhaps better ideas. The point is to get down as many ideas, whether good ones or not, as we can in the ten-minute sprint.

Handwriting is slow, so we don't write complete sentences; we write only a word or two to remind us later of each thought. For instance, we think, "There are a lot of factors involved in making the choice of a language to study"; all we write down is two words: "Many factors." So we start listing:

Thoughts As They Come	Jotted Notes
Many factors are involved in choosing a language to study.	Many factors
Wasn't Pat going to call me tonight?	Pat
Do I have friends who speak another language?	Friends
Which language would be the most fun?	Fun

Thoughts As They Come	Jotted Notes
Which language do my friends study?	Friends study
Do my parents or grandparents speak a foreign language?	Parents
Why do foreign people talk so fast?	Fast talk
Which languages are taught at my school?	Available
Which language teacher is popular at my school?	Teacher
Pat speaks only English.	Pat/English
What's spoken around my town?	Town
I like that new Mexican restaurant in town.	El Adobe
Maybe Pat and I will go there next week.	Pat dinner
Where may I travel someday?	Travel
Travel is really expensive these days.	Expense
Which language may be easiest to learn?	Easy
Which one may be most challenging?	Challenge
Is any language "required" for my major?	Required
Which language will be most useful in my life?	Usefulness
Which language may I need in my future work?	Job

We stop when the mind seems to have run dry. Looking over the list of jotted ideas, we see a few that have little to do with the topic: "Pat," "Pat/English," "El Adobe," and "Pat dinner." We put them on the list despite their being off the point; to reject them might have stopped the mind from working. Now that we have our list, we can cross off those less useful items. We're ready for the next step in preparing a first draft.

Step 4: Sharpening the Point

We study our list of jottings to find which of our ideas is likely to be the most important, the central point (or *thesis*) of the essay. It will be the main thing we intend to convey to our readers about the topic. After thinking it over, we choose "usefulness": The usefulness of a foreign language is the best reason for choosing to study it. Now we sharpen that idea, writing it into one sentence.

Choosing a foreign language to study should depend chiefly on its usefulness in your life.

Before going ahead, we consider the idea critically. Is it worth saying? Is it more than merely obvious? If satisfied that it makes a worthy point, we decide to use it as our central idea, organizing all the other ideas so that they lead to that point. We're ready to go ahead to our next step.

Step 5: Arranging Details

After we have chosen our thesis, we may think of a few more ideas that help to support it. We think of some new ideas about choosing a language to study: "travel possibilities?" "study overseas?" "a job overseas?" We add them to our list. And we decide that some of the ideas we have listed do not particularly relate to or help to support the thesis; we cross out "many factors," "teacher," and "expense."

Next we determine a useful order for the remaining ideas on the list, deciding to begin with the least important ("fun") and work up to the one we've chosen as our thesis point ("usefulness"). We number all usable items in what seems to be a reasonable order:

omit—~~Many factors~~	omit—~~El Adobe~~
omit—~~Pat~~	omit—~~Pat dinner~~
5—Friends	2—Easy
6—Friends study	14—Challenge
1—Fun	4—Required
7—Parents	15—Usefulness
11—Fast talk	9—Job
3—Available	10—Travel
omit—~~Teacher~~	omit—~~Expense~~
omit—~~Pat/English~~	12—Study overseas
8—Town	13—Job overseas

If it seems to help, we can now rewrite the list in numbered order so we can get a clear idea of how the essay will develop from idea to idea:

1—Fun	6—Friends study	11—Fast talk
2—Easy	7—Parents	12—Study overseas
3—Available	8—Town	13—Job overseas
4—Required	9—Job	14—Challenge
5—Friends	10—Travel	15—Usefulness

Having thought more about it as we've worked, we decided that idea 11, "fast talk" (Why do foreign people talk so fast?), is not relevant to the point of the essay; we decide to cross it out. Now we are ready to begin writing.

Step 6: Considering the Tone

Now that we've given considerable thought to the topic, we need to give some to our readers. What kind of people do we expect to reach with this essay?

Since it's about a special sort of college study, our most likely readers will be college students who, like us, may be thinking about beginning to learn a foreign language. The phrase "like us" is important: Our topic being what it is, we want to consider our readers as our equals, sharing our general interests, attitudes, levels of knowledge, and failings. If we have our readers in mind as we write, we will be more likely to choose words that "talk their language." That is, our writing will tend to take on an appropriate *tone*.

We must also consider our attitude toward the topic. How shall we approach it? Are we serious about choosing a foreign language, or is it just a joke to us? Are we going to consider it logically, scientifically, or lightly and with a sense of humor? Can we be both serious and lighthearted? We decide to try this last approach, remembering that we aren't stuck with it; we can later change to another if we want to.

Step 7: Getting Started

We can now write a paragraph of introduction. We want that paragraph to catch the reader's attention, present the topic, suggest our attitude toward that topic (serious yet lighthearted), and establish the tone, or *voice*, of the essay.

We may even begin with a tentative title:

Choosing a Language to Study

1   Nowdays you find that the people you must live with all do not
2   speak your language. In many neighborhoods you hear the sounds
3   of unfamiliar languages. It must occur to you that for several reasons
4   it may be wise to study some foreign language. But which one to
5   choose? Should you just stab at one in the college catalogue and start
6   attending class? The choise really deserves more attention.

It's a beginning. At this moment we don't worry about how good a beginning it is; we know we can change it, improve it, even discard it later if we want to.

Step 8: Completing the Draft

Not stopping to be critical of our beginning, we go ahead, writing a sentence or two to cover each of our jotted ideas. (We have numbered the ideas in the right-hand margin.

7   Perhaps you'll pick the language that is fun. Or it may be a   *(1)*
8   good idea to stick with the one that's easy. Common sence tells   *(2)*
9   you to look into the college catalogue to see what's available, or *(3)(4)*
10 the one that is required for your major.
11   If a friend of yours speaks a foreign language at home maybe   *(5)*
12 you should go for that language. It would be fun to talk with
13 him in it, and maybe get some help on homework. If you have   *(6)*

14 friends allready taking a language class, you may consider going
15 that direction for companionship. And if there is a foreign lan-
16 guage in your own family background, maybe it would be wise
17 to choose, for your roots.   *(7)*
18   If one foreign language is spoken much around your town,   *(8)*
19 it may come in handy when you get a job, since talking to cus-   *(9)*
20 tomers or clients in their own language could be a plus value.
21 If you are looking forward to travelling to some inticing country, *(10)*
22 to know it's language could help. And is there a possibility of
23 maybe going to school in another country? Why not learn the   *(12)*
24 language first? Perhaps knowing a foreign language could lead   *(13)*
25 to a carrier overseas and you'd better choose what is spoken were
26 you'd like to work.
27   Maybe you should choose to study a language because you
28 see a challenge in it, a way of prooving to yourself that you can *(14)*
29 learn it and use it to expand your mind.
30   In conclusion, having fun is nice but doesn't pay all the bills.
31 Friends are great, but they should not be copied blindly, and
32 that language of your family's background may not lead you to
33 the carrier you hope for. So the practicle reasons for chosing a
34 foreign language may prove best, after all. Considering what
35 you want to make of yourself, choosing a foreign language to
36 study should depend not on trivial or passing factors but rather *(15)*
37 on its usefullness in the achievement of that goal.

Our first draft is completed. If we have time, we put the draft aside for a
while so that we can go back to it later with a fresh, objective mind. When that
time comes, we are ready for revising.

Step 9: Revising the Draft

Now the real work begins. Until now, we've been gathering raw materials,
putting them in some kind of order, giving them some preliminary shape.
Now it's time to turn those raw materials into a finished product.

We read the first draft carefully, giving special attention to its point, its
substance. Is our central point challenging? Is what we've written worth our
time and the reader's? Does the essay have a clear purpose? Are there parts
that should be rearranged or cut out? Are there examples that can be added,
words that should be changed, sentences that should be clearer? As we continue studies in this book, we'll be discovering many more guidelines for revising essays. Right now, these directions and the example essay will help us get
started.

As we carefully read the first draft of "Choosing a Language to Study," we
try to "listen" to how it sounds as well as to what it says. As we go, we correct
spelling, punctuation, and word usage. Here are some of the things we mark:

- We change "Nowdays" to "Nowadays" (line 1).

- We question "live with" (line 1), because it suggests only our own family; we change it to "live *among*."

- We feel uncomfortable about "all do not speak your language" (lines 1 and 2); after all, some of the people *do* speak our language. We decide that "do not all" would be better.

- We notice repetition of the word "language" (lines 2, 3, 4); we circle the word, reminding ourselves to put the idea some other way.

- The words "several reasons" (line 3) make us ask, "What reasons?"— and we make a question mark to remind us to fill in some reasons.

- Moving along, we change "choise" to "cho<u>i</u>ce" (line 6).

- We decide that "certainly" or "surely" will be better than "really" (line 6).

- We put a question mark over "attention" (line 6) to remind us to find a better word for the idea.

- The essay mentions a lot of points, but it doesn't show many examples. Can we find examples for what makes a language "fun" (line 7)? Can we name examples of languages we think may be "easy" or hard to learn (line 8)?

- We change "sence" to "sen<u>s</u>e" (line 8) and correct other spelling errors as we find them. Is "travelling" right with two *l*'s (line 21)? Should it be "<u>i</u>nticing" or "<u>e</u>nticing"? Should there be an apostrophe in "it's" (line 22)? Does "carrier" mean "career" (lines 25 and 33)? Does "were" mean "where" (line 25)? Shouldn't "prooving" be "pr<u>o</u>ving" (line 28) and "chosing" be "ch<u>oo</u>sing" (line 33)?

- Do we need the phrase "In conclusion" (line 30)? We cross it out.

- To make the essay more interesting, we decide to follow up on the "roots" idea (line 17); we add "flowers" to stand for "career you hope for" (line 33) in our final paragraph.

- The phrase "in the acheivement of" (line 37) seems long-winded; we change it to "in achieving," correcting the spelling at the same time.

- Listening to the tone of the first draft, we find that it's a bit preachy. "You do this" and "You do that," it says to the reader. The *you* approach may be causing that tone, so we make it *we* instead, putting ourselves and the readers in the same boat.

- The title is a bit flat. We decide to make it more attention getting. And we are ready to write another draft:

A CHOICE OF TONGUES

1   We discover more and more that we are not alone in

2   the world, that the people we must live among are not

3   all in our family, of our town or country or race. Nor

4   do they all speak our language. In many neighborhoods

5   we hear strange sounds, the sounds of unfamiliar

6   tongues. To satisfy ~~curiousity~~ *curiosity*, to get along with

7   people, to fulfill ambitions, it may be wise to study

8   ways of speaking other than our own.

9   But the many languages we hear around us give us

10   pause. Which should we take up? Shall we just stab at

11   one in the college catalogue and start attending class?

12   Surely the choice deserves more directed thought.

13   Impulse urges us to study a language that is fun;   (1)

14   we have fanta*s*dies of colorful fiestas, wondrous sushi

15   bars, afternoons in Gay Paree. Another impulse, our

16   lazy voice, says study one that's easy to learn; we've   (2)

17   heard Spanish is easier than French, which is easier

18   than German, which is ~~not so tough as~~ *less formidable than* Russian or

19   Japanese. Common sense tells us to look into the

20   college catalogue to see what languages are available   (3)

21   and which is required for our major.   (4)

22   A friend speaks a foreign language in his home;   (5)

23   maybe we should go for that language, for the fun of

24   speaking it with him--and maybe getting some help on

25 homework. If we have friends already taking a language   (6)

26 class, we may consider taking that class for companion-

27 ship. And, if there's a foreign language in our own   (7)

28 family background, maybe it would be a wise choice--

29 roots, and all that.

30   If one foreign language is spoken most around our   (8)

31 town, to speak it would be handy when we get a job.

32 Knowing how to talk to customers or clients in their   (9)

33 own language would be an asset. And if we look forward

34 to traveling to some enticing country, a knowledge of   (10)

35 its language may help. ~~We may even decide to go to~~

36 ~~school in some foreign country, and it may be good to~~   (12)

37 ~~learn something of the language first.~~ Perhaps speaking

38 a foreign language may lead to a career overseas, so   (13)

39 we'd better choose what is spoken where we'd like to

40 work.

41   ~~One possible reason for choosing a language is~~

42 ~~that we may see a challenge in it, a way of proving to~~   (14)

43 ~~ourselves that we can learn it and use it to expand our~~

44 ~~horizons.~~

45   When all possibilities are weighed, fun is nice   (1*)

46 but doesn't pay the bills. Friends are cherished but   (6*)

47 are not to be blindly copied. And our roots may not   (7*)

48 produce all the flowers we hope for in life. The

49 practic~~le~~ᵃˡ reasons for choosing a foreign language--

50   traveling, expanding, making a living--may prove best   (12*)

51   after all.   Considering what we want to make of   (13*)

52   ourselves, choosing the foreign language to study

53   should not depend on trivial or passing matters.   The

54   choice should depend chiefly on which language we think

55   will be most useful in achieving our life goal.   (15)

---

*These ideas are picked up from early parts of the essay and echoed here as a kind of summary before the thesis point (15) is cinched.

We have completed our second draft. As our marks show, we have read it over carefully and marked some changes and corrections:

- "curiosity" for "curiousity" (line 6)
- "fantasies" for "fantacies" (line 14)
- "less formidable than" for "not so tough as" (line 18)
- "practical" for "practicle" (line 49)
- We decide that the sentence about "going to school" in a foreign country (idea 12, lines 35–37) and the paragraph about "challenge" (idea 14, lines 41–44) do not add much to the essay; we cross them out.

We are nearly ready for our final step.

Step 10: Submitting the Essay

Before we submit the second draft (or third or fourth if we've found more improvements to make), we want to make the paper attractive to the eye, with wide margins where the instructor may write suggestions. If the changes and corrections we've made are not too messy, and if we'll have an opportunity to revise again later, we may submit the essay as is. But if this is to be the only submission, we'll want to make the paper look as attractive as possible, even if we have to recopy or retype. We check for general appearance, then submit the essay. (In Lesson 42 there's more on preparing the manuscript for submission.)

Revising for

Substance

He who has nothing to assert has no style and can have none.
George Bernard Shaw
(1856–1950)

An essay is readable evidence of a mind at work on ideas. It is a piece of writing that represents an honest attempt to discuss those ideas in a meaningful, interesting way. If the essay does not show evidence of thought, if it is not honest, if it is not meaningful and interesting, it is a sheer waste of paper.

To be worth reading at all, a piece of writing must be "about" something that will engage the minds of readers: It must have a topic. Almost any topic will do, since it is the writer's way of seeing and handling it that is interesting, not the topic itself.

Topic, of course, is not enough. The essay must have a purpose, a reason for being. And it must have a point, a central thought worth considering. All the better if it makes that point by giving readers a real sense of life—real people, real things, real experience.

What we're saying here is that an essay must give readers something solid to consider. It must have substance.

Engaging Topic

For most of us who sit down to write a college paper, the first problem is deciding what to write. Even when the topic is assigned, we still have to make a choice among many ways of going about the job. The approach is often the hardest part; it requires that we determine our purpose, then go about the writing in an engaging way.

Selecting a readable topic to write about means forming a triangle of mutual interest: ourselves, the subject matter, and the reader. As writers we must be genuinely interested in all three.

Interest in ourselves is a prime essential. What we write about cannot matter unless we ourselves matter. We care about who we are, what we know, what we believe, how we think. We care about the quality of our inward lives, our experiences, reactions, emotions, dreams. We try to see ourselves as others may see us. The objective view means taking life seriously but always with a sense of humor; it means not self-love, but self-respect.

Interest in our subject matter is another point of the triangle. More often than not, what we write about will be something from the world beyond ourselves, so we cannot be merely self-absorbed. To keep the mind alive, we must have a genuine interest in that world. The range of our interests and concerns determines, in large part, who we are and how interesting we will be to others.

Readers are the third point of the triangle. We need to be considerate of readers' needs, respect their attitudes, recognize that they too have inward lives, experiences, reactions, emotions, and dreams. We select a topic because we think they, as well as we, will find it interesting. What we write about must engage the readers' minds.

Writing from Experience

The world teems with limitless fascination: people, places, situations, things to see, to touch, to hear, to taste, to smell. And all of them—ideas to think about, fear, and laugh at, pleasures to enjoy and share, pains to learn from and appreciate, accomplishments to admire—all are the potential stuff of writing.

We may ask questions of whatever we experience: *What* is it? *How* does it fit into life? *What's* its value to us? *What if* it were different? *What* is going on? *Who* is doing it or causing it? *What* may be its results? *Where* is it happening? *How* is it done? *Why* is it done? *What should* be done about it? Answers to such questions can lead to many essay topics.

Since most topics have been written about for centuries, we need to recognize that it's not our topic but our way of looking at it that will make the essay worth reading. Our personal view of things can make any topic our own. We need to bring to it illustrations from our own experience, examples from the real life we see around us.

Considering the triangle of the writer, the topic, and the reader, we may think of dozens of possibilities for getting into an essay. But we can't write *all* about friendship, *all* about music, *all* about taxes, or *all* about our favorite sport. We need to narrow the topic to what we can comfortably handle in that brief form, the essay.

Limiting the Topic

Once we've set out to write an essay about marriage, readers may expect us to cover every aspect of that complex experience. That's why a general topic like marriage doesn't work well as an essay topic; it has to be limited to a much narrower field, one that can be reasonably covered in a few paragraphs. So we need to think how to cut broad topics down to narrow ones. Let's look at some broad topics and see how they can be brought within the range of an essay:

The generation gap
    Changing attitudes toward sex
        *Two views of "living
        together"*

Animal training
    Obedience training for dogs
        Teaching your dog to "stay"

Successful enterprise	Human relationships
Starting your own business	*Meeting prospective mates*
Opening a small car wash	*How I met Chris*
Having a sense of humor	Religious rituals
Making people laugh	*What prayer does*
How to write your own jokes	*What* amen *means*
Learning to cooperate	America's energy problem
Joining a group enterprise	*Producing nuclear energy*
My year in a kibbutz	*Risks of nuclear production*
A day's work in a kibbutz	*An error at Three Mile Island*

Each of the general topics would be beyond covering in a brief essay. Even the narrower second-line topic would be enough for a book, maybe several volumes. The third-line topic of each set is coming within range, though each may be still further trimmed for best results.

What governs the process of narrowing a topic? In essence it's like opening a large box to find smaller ones inside, then opening one of those to find still smaller ones, and so on until we have a very small box. The smaller the box, the narrower the topic and the easier to cover all its contents in an essay. Let's take, for example, "the generation gap" box. When we open it, we find dozens of possibilities such as differing attitudes of the generations toward music, toward money, toward work, toward sex, toward health. We can select any one of those. Having chosen "changing attitudes toward sex," we open that one and find a number of boxes: views toward dating, courtship, marriage, living together without marriage, sex education. We pick one, "two views toward 'living together,'" and we're set with a reasonably narrowed topic. Or, after opening that box, we may find a still smaller one that would serve better. The aim is to keep opening smaller boxes until we find an interesting topic that still contains enough material to offer substantial discussion.

In truth, there is never too little to write about; there is always too much.

Guideline

 Select a topic that interests you and is likely to engage the minds of others. Limit that topic to what you can cover in a short essay.

Revision Practice: Engaging Topic

At the topic-selection stage of the writing process, what we have to revise is not unreadable writing but unwritable thinking. The first ten items here are thoughts by writers whose minds have "gone blank" on topics. Apply the *what, who, when, where, how,* and *why* questions to any ideas suggested to you by these blank thoughts. Revise the thoughts, pointing up what *could be* chosen as a topic.

1. "It's too cold to think right now. Anyway, there's nothing to say about my life when I don't even have a job and no money to pay the gas bill."

2. "There's nothing on the TV news tonight except ordinary junk and the commentators predicting gloom and doom. Maybe I'd better wait for tomorrow to get an idea."

3. "How can I be expected to write an essay with all this noise going on? This family gives me no privacy at all. I can hardly hear my own stereo."

4. "Thinking up an idea to write about is just too much after spending three hours in classes and five hours on the job, especially after I got bawled out for spilling that soup on my customer today."

5. "If I miss this essay, who'll care? I may not even be in college another semester. It's getting too expensive. Maybe a full-time job would be better anyway. Or the navy. If I enlisted, I might get a free education."

6. "I haven't got any experience to write about. The only place I've ever been to see anything is this dumb town, and it's full of junk and obscene graffiti. And if I quit thinking and go out, I might get arrested again."

7. "Does anyone expect me to write a paper when I'm so upset? Pat hasn't called in three days. All I can think about is the argument we had and how ridiculous it was. I didn't even enjoy winning. Maybe I should call and apologize."

8. "Well, I shouldn't have put this off. The essay is due two hours from now, and I haven't anything to write about. I should have done it last night instead of going 'cruising' with Chris. We didn't meet anybody interesting anyway, unless you count the mugger that ripped off our wallet and purse."

9. "They say, 'Write about what you know,' but I don't know anything interesting. My only skill is playing the guitar, and I had to teach myself to do that. Now I'm teaching Joey to play, too. Maybe I should call him and see if he's finished writing that song for me. But I'd better write some kind of essay first."

10. "I'll bet the professors wouldn't ask us to write so many essays if they knew that some of us have to do all the cooking and washing for a family of three brothers. How could I ever get out and get some experience to write about?"

The next ten items are general topic ideas for writing. Narrow each topic by writing three or more possible revisions, each successively more specific, more suitable for coverage in a brief essay (see the examples for items (11–13).

11. Great inventions
    EXAMPLE: a. Most useful inventions
             b. Labor-saving inventions
             c. Personal robots
             d. How a personal robot works

12. Cults and communes
    EXAMPLE: a. Religious cults
             b. Why religious cults appeal
             c. How religious cults brainwash members
             d. My friend Joe and the Vashni cult

13. Human emotions
    EXAMPLE: a. Unpleasant emotions
             b. Unreasonable fears
             c. How to deal with phobias
             d. How to get over neophobia (fear of new things)

14. Preparing for the future
15. Healthful exercise
16. Psychological pressure
17. Good citizenship in today's society
18. Business enterprise
19. The joys of being a child
20. Learning to play a musical instrument

Follow-up

There are few thoroughly dull days for anyone who's really alive. Any person, event, place, time, or attitude can be the topic of an essay. Make sure that the narrowest of your suggested topics in each case is limited to specific questions, situations, events, or issues.

Purposeful Approach

Some people climb a mountain just "because it's there." But to write an essay just because the assignment is there will not be enough. No professional writes really well if the only purpose for writing is to make money, and we cannot do our best writing if our only purpose is to get a grade. Purpose should always involve what we expect the reader to get from our writing.

Three possibilities present themselves: (1) We expect the reader to be *informed;* (2) we expect the reader to be *entertained* or amused; or (3) we expect the reader to be *convinced,* possibly persuaded to action. It's possible, of course, to write so that the reader is informed, entertained, and convinced all at the same time; more often, though, we set out with one of those as our dominant purpose.

Within each of these purposeful approaches to writing we can put to work some educated guesses about our readers. What do they *want* to know? What do they *need* to know? What do they *already know?* Though our answers must be guesses, they will help us determine our purpose and give us some hints on how to achieve it.

First, let's recognize that we'd best not write for the professor who has assigned the writing. The professor is not in the reader's role but is, rather, like an editor trying to help us in our attempt to reach readers. No, the readers we're talking about are usually a sort of general audience, people somewhat like ourselves—fairly well informed, on the whole interested in life, with an aversion to wasting time unpleasantly or being bored to death.

So we must imagine for ourselves an audience of readers, then write for that audience. For our college work we'd better imagine readers who are fairly sophisticated, a group that will challenge our developing skills.

If we expect to reach those readers, it will hardly do to give them information they don't care to know; to do that would bore them. And to tell them what they already know would waste their time and annoy them. Well, then, what are they likely to want and need?

Readers want to know what we are writing about. They want to see something challenging in it—some reason for reading about it.

And what do readers need?

- to have essential terms defined

- to have complexities explained and simplified

- to have the unfamiliar compared to the familiar and brought into their own experience

- to "see" ideas in concrete examples

- to be shown clear connections among our ideas

- to be shown why our ideas are worth listening to and what the ideas mean in terms of their own lives

All these considerations about readers, what they want and need to know, help us set out with a suitable purpose. They also help us adopt the state of mind we'll need to achieve it, suggesting whether we should choose informal words or formal ones, a staid and serious approach or a freewheeling, easy-going one—or maybe something in between. And they suggest some of the means we may use to carry out our purpose.

Getting Into a Topic

A few simple questions can lead us to interesting, useful ways of handling a topic—purposes for essays.

- When we ask, "What is it?" we may answer with a *definition*. Ron Lovell defines news:

> Those with enough training and experience recognize it instantly for what it is: an event that will affect the lives of more than one person

and be interesting for others to read about or view. An additional element is necessary as well. To be considered news, an event must be reported. The biggest story in the world will not receive that designation if nobody knows about it.[1]

• When we ask, "What's it like?" we may answer with a *description* or a *comparison*. And when we ask, "What's it *not* like," we may answer with a *contrast*. In this passage, Frank Conroy both describes and contrasts:

> The common yo-yo is crudely made, with a thick shank between two widely spaced wooden disks. The string is knotted or stapled to the shank. With such an instrument nothing can be done except the simple up-down movement. My yo-yo, on the other hand, was a perfectly balanced construction of hard wood, slightly weighted, flat, with only a sixteenth of an inch between the halves. The string was not attached to the shank, but looped over it in such a way as to allow the wooden part to spin freely on its own axis. The gyroscopic effect thus created kept the yo-yo stable in all attitudes.[2]

• When we ask, "What are several kinds of it?" we answer with *division* or *classification*. Oliver Wendell Holmes once offered this:

> Certain things are good for nothing until they have been kept a long while; and some are good for nothing until they have been long kept and *used*. Of the first, wine is the illustrious and immortal example. Of those which must be kept and used I will name three—meerschaum pipes, violins, and poems.

• When we ask, "How's it done?" we may answer by revealing a *process*. Essayist E. B. White tells how to start the Model T Ford:

> To get under way, you simply hooked the third finger of the right hand around a lever on the steering column, pulled down hard, and shoved your left foot forcibly against the low-speed pedal. These were simple, positive motions; the car responded by lunging forward with a roar . . . and was off on its glorious errand.[3]

• When we ask, "For example?" we do what readers often do; we're saying, "Give me a f'rinstance." When we respond, the topic gains interest by *illustration* or *example*, as in Shirley Radl's description:

---

[1]Ron Lovell, *The Newspaper* (Belmont, Calif.: Wadsworth, 1982), p. 16.
[2]Frank Conroy, *Stop-Time* (New York: Viking, 1965), p. 113.
[3]E. B. White, "Farewell, My Lovely," in *Essays of E. B. White* (New York: Harper & Row, 1977), p. 163.

When I was pregnant the first time, we celebrated our eighth wedding anniversary. My husband gave me an exquisite pearl bracelet. Six years later I was picking up the pearls in my vacuum cleaner. My son had destroyed it . . . a sad symbol of how two children affected a once beautiful relationship.[4]

- When we ask, "What caused it?" or "What may result from it?" we seek answers that *analyze cause and effect*. Russell Baker humorously considers a cause of a familiar phenomenon:

    Why does the washing machine take two socks and give back only one? Various theories have been advanced over the years, as, for example, that the washing machine eats one of the socks. Arlberg's brilliant monograph, "The Dynamics of Laundry," demolished this theory with laboratory evidence.[5]

- When we ask ourselves, "How can we prove it?" we answer with reasons, with *argument* to support a conclusion. Henry David Thoreau argues that government is not necessary:

    This American government . . . never of itself furthered any enterprise, but by the alacrity with which it got out of its way. *It* does not keep the country free. *It* does not settle the West. *It* does not educate. The character inherent in the American people has done all that has been accomplished; and it would have done somewhat more if the government had not sometimes got in its way.[6]

- When we ask, "What happened?" we discover events and tell a story in *narration*. Here's E. B. White again:

    On the day before Thanksgiving, toward the end of the afternoon, having motored all day, I arrived home and lit a fire in the living room. The birch logs took hold briskly. About three minutes later, not to be outdone, the chimney itself caught fire.[7]

We may use several methods in one essay. We may define, describe, and analyze a topic, or we may tell a story in order to convince readers of a point.

---

[4]Shirley Radl, "One Mother's Blast at Motherhood," *Life*, 19 May 1972, p. 52.

[5]Russell Baker, "The Unipedal Mystery," in *So This Is Depravity* (New York: Cogdon & Lattes, 1980), p. 190.

[6]Henry David Thoreau, "Civil Disobedience," in *A Treasury of the Essay* (New York: Charles Scribner's, 1955), p. 290.

[7]E. B. White, "Home-coming," in *Essays of E. B. White* (New York: Harper & Row, 1977), p. 7.

But for each essay we should have in mind one *central* purpose we expect to achieve.

Suppose we've chosen a topic: "Learning a foreign language." Since learning a language is a process, we may decide to use *process* as our purpose. Or we may develop an essay of *argument* on why learning a language is worthwhile or on whether school lessons and public ballots should be offered in two languages. Purpose determines our approach.

Let's propose another topic: "A life of dependency." We may limit the topic in any of several ways: (1) the male chauvinist's wife, (2) horrors of drug addiction, (3) food stamps as income, (4) pains of being an invalid, (5) elderly parents in the home, (6) people who need people. Each specific topic calls for its own kind of development. Let's suggest some purposes for three of them:

The male chauvinist's wife
    a. *describe* her situation
    b. *tell a story* about her
    c. *convince* readers of need for change

The horrors of addiction
    a. *analyze* the process of addiction
    b. *describe* the horrors
    c. *convince* readers of suggested cure

People who need people
    a. *define* "dependency" relationship
    b. *analyze* causes of loneliness
    c. *convince* readers that "love" may be destructive dependency

Even with a limited topic, we need a clear purpose to determine our approach.

Guideline

Choose an appropriate purpose to guide your approach.

Revision Practice: Purposeful Approach

For each of these topics, suggest two possible purposes for an essay.

1. Keeping a checkbook balance straight
2. Fear of the future
3. Overcoming simple mental depression
4. New life for trite ideas
5. Ability without know-how
6. The rest-home recreation room
7. Meaningful practice of music

8. A visit to the art gallery
9. The movies and four-letter words
10. The night the world began
11. Effrontery as a lifestyle
12. Living for tomorrow
13. A place to end all places
14. Rights as responsibility
15. Political snobbism
16. Progressing backward
17. Building a campfire
18. The video-game arcade
19. Corruption made easy
20. How to be sure of everything

Follow-up

Make sure that the purposes you have suggested are fully appropriate to the topic. Which would best lend themselves to description?—perhaps 6, 13, and 18? Which to storytelling—8, 10? Which to argument to convince?—2, 7, 9, and 12? Which to analysis of process—1, 7, 17? Could any topic on the list be developed with intent to analyze (or classify) its several kinds? Which topics could be treated with irony?

Challenging Point

Having a topic and a purpose is still not enough. We also need something interesting to say about that topic: a central point, or thesis. If the essay is to be readable, that point should somehow challenge the readers' minds, make them "sit up and take notice."

Beginnings are especially vulnerable to vapid, useless sentences. The mind has to get warmed up to the topic before it brings forth its best, and our first paragraph or two may be ordinary, dull stuff that begs for the wastebasket. This beginning of an essay "On Fame" is typical:

> It is quite an interesting subject to discuss how a person becomes famous. Fame can be a desirable thing or it can be undesirable, depending on each person's point of view. A person can become famous in a series of different categories; for instance, show business, politics, sports, and other fields.

It is seldom necessary to announce that our topic is "interesting"; readers will decide that for themselves. The second and third sentences say only the obvious, adding nothing of real interest. Let's consider a few more such unpromising ideas:

There are many different ways of being happy.

Something really should be done about crime.

No two people are exactly alike.

Such statements are *platitudes*, saying only what our readers already know. The justified response may be "yeah, but so what?" Even worse, it may be "who cares?" When we write, we want to turn "who cares?" into "hey, how about that!" What we need is some way of bringing to mind ideas that are not the same old stuff to everybody. We can start by asking ourselves some questions. Whatever our topic may be, we can ask, "What if . . ."

- What if we look at this topic from a different angle, from the viewpoint of a different person or a different time or place?
- What if the topic is not what it seems to be?
- What if we turn the thought upside down?

Our questions may lead us to an attention-getting twist, a new way of looking at old ideas. Writers like George Bernard Shaw and Oscar Wilde, nearly a century ago, drew fame by turning accepted ideas upside down:

Democracy is "the last refuge of cheap misgovernment."
George Bernard Shaw

"A lifetime of happiness! No man alive could bear it: it would be hell on earth."
George Bernard Shaw

"Work is the curse of the drinking class."
Oscar Wilde

"A little sincerity is a dangerous thing."
Oscar Wilde

Essays based on such epigrams would certainly be more interesting than those based on platitude. If we want to make a challenging point, we must be willing to turn ideas over and look at them with new eyes and minds.

The Ironic Twist

When we deliberately say the opposite of what we mean, we use *irony*. That approach gives us another way of turning everyday ideas to good use. Jonathan Swift, author of *Gulliver's Travels*, once offered "A Modest Proposal" for ending the overpopulation and poverty of eighteenth-century Ireland, suggesting that children be bred like cattle and sold as meat:

> A child will make two dishes at an entertainment for friends, and when the family dines alone, the fore or hind quarter will make a reasonable dish, and when seasoned with a little pepper or salt will be very good boiled on the fourth day, especially in winter. . . . I grant that this food will be somewhat dear, and therefore very proper for landlords, who, as they have already devoured most of the parents, seem to have the best title to the children.[1]

Swift clearly does not mean what he says. His "proposal" is a sly parody of what he considered nonsensical proposals then being put forth by the Irish parliament on the problems of the country.

The ironic approach can rescue many a bland thesis.

Saying More or Saying Less

At least four possible ways of saying things offer themselves: (1) We may say just what we mean, no more and no less, using *literal language;* (2) we may say the opposite of what we mean, using *irony;* (3) we may say far *more* than we mean, grossly exaggerating, using *hyperbole;* or (4) we may say much less than we mean, deliberately playing down the thought, using *understatement.* Any of these departures from the ordinary can help to challenge the minds of readers.

Among the masters of hyperbole was Mark Twain, who defined a classic as "something that everybody wants to have read and nobody wants to read." He described one man as "an experienced, industrious, ambitious, and often picturesque liar."

On the understatement side, Jonathan Swift dramatized many points by passing them off as trivial. He wrote that he had seen a woman skinned alive, and "you will hardly believe how much it altered her person for the worse." Alexander Leighton wrote a superb account of "That Day at Hiroshima" without ever mentioning the atomic bomb, and the understatement made a point more eloquent than any exaggeration.

All these approaches to an essay lie open to us. We need only use our minds to look at ideas in uncommon ways.

---

[1] Jonathan Swift, "A Modest Proposal," in *Elements of the Essay,* 3d ed., ed. H. Wendell Smith (Belmont, Calif.: Wadsworth, 1983), p. 448.

Guideline

 Give your central idea a personal twist. Challenge the reader's mind.

Revision Practice: Challenging Point

Revise these thesis statements, many of them platitudes. Try to give each some personal twist, some irony, hyperbole, or understatement to challenge the minds of readers (see examples for items 1–3).

1. Experience is the best teacher.
   EXAMPLE: Experience is a dangerous teacher.

2. Growing up, becoming mature, is an involved process.
   EXAMPLE: Growing up is nearly impossible, but it can be done.

3. Different authors in poetry and fiction see women in various ways.
   EXAMPLE: Fiction's heroines are all alike, from Red Riding Hood to Lady Macbeth.

4. The nature of man is complex and cannot be divided into simple categories.

5. During a lifetime a person makes many crucial decisions about his future.

6. It's a jungle out there, a dog-eat-dog world.

7. Anything that is man-made is artificial.

8. We can hardly blame the victim of a crime for feeling vengeful.

9. If America's poverty problem isn't solved, it will continue to plague us.

10. It seems difficult sometimes to accept reality.

11. One cannot conquer any skill without hard work.

12. Sometimes people just don't get enough privacy.

13. Child abuse is a terrible thing and should be stopped.

14. We often act upon emotion rather than reason. Such action can be disastrous.

15. The earth is fascinating, since it has such beauty to offer.

16. Money is the root of all evil.

17. You can't teach an old dog new tricks.

18. Truth certainly is stranger than fiction.

19. In a nuclear war there would be no survivors.

20. Whatever is worth doing is worth doing well.

Writing and Revising

For suggestions on getting started, writing a first draft, revising the draft, and preparing the essay for submission, review the Introduction. Choose one of the following topics.

Topics for Writing

1. For the first Revision Practice, you have written ten possible topics derived from the blank thoughts of others. Prepare and write a first draft on any one of those topics, following the step-by-step method shown in the Introduction.

2. For the first Revision Practice, you have written some narrowed topics for possible development. Prepare and write a first draft on any one of those topics, following the step-by-step method shown in the Introduction.

3. For the second Revision Practice, you have devised *purposes* suitable to several essay topics. Select one of those topics and a purpose you devised for it. Following the step-by-step method shown in the Introduction, prepare and write the first draft of an essay using that topic and trying to accomplish that purpose.

4. For the third Revision Practice, you have revised a number of thesis statements. Select one of those. Following the step-by-step method shown in the Introduction, prepare and write the first draft of an essay establishing that central point.

Follow-up

Read your first draft carefully, making sure that it has an engaging *topic* sufficiently narrowed, has followed a clear *purpose,* and has established a clear central *point.* Revise if necessary to improve the essay in any of those respects. For a guide to preparing the manuscript for submission, see Lesson 42.

Lesson 4

Concreteness:
The Real Thing

Ideas that we hold in the mind, concepts that cannot be perceived in the real world around us, are *abstract*. They are such ideas as friendship and freedom, anger and amusement, hunger and humility, comfort and corruption. We cannot actually see these ideas; we can only think about them, sometimes hanging them as labels upon things we do see. We see two people laughing together, and we take the scene as evidence of friendship. We see a red-faced man and hear him swear at another; we take those visible things as evidence of anger. We see a child with swollen belly, sunken eyes, and fleshless arms: evidence of hunger. But we do not see friendship, anger, and hunger.

Abstract ideas are difficult to hold clearly in mind. Yet as writers we often want to take those ideas as topics or use them to support a point. And, of course, we want our readers to understand. How can we write readably about abstract ideas?

We can help readers understand by translating the abstract into real things, into things that *can* be perceived in the world around us. If we mention *fear*, we write abstractly; if we show actual evidence of fear—cringing and cold sweat—we write concretely. If we use the word *embarrassment*, we write abstractly; if we let the reader see a blushing face and a hand clapped over the mouth, we write concretely. If we say the sunset is *beautiful,* we write abstractly; if we show the reader its colors and forms, we write concretely. Where abstract statement often fails, concrete image makes an idea easier to "see"; perhaps that's why we so often say "I see" when we mean "I understand."

Example and Illustration

In his essay on what happened after the first atomic bomb was dropped on Hiroshima, Alexander H. Leighton never uses the abstract words *confusion, pain, terror,* and *despair,* but by showing us concrete things and real actions he makes us understand those feelings:

> They were rushing in all directions of the compass from the city. Many were stretcher cases. Some had their hair burned, were injured in the back, had broken legs, arms, and thighs. The majority of the cases were those injured from glass; many had glass imbedded in the body. . . . Most of the people arrived barefooted; many had their clothes burned off. Women were wearing men's clothing and men were wearing women's. They had put on anything they could pick up along the way.[1]

It is trite to say that seeing is believing, but the old saying is worth keeping in mind as we revise our writing. Whatever is too abstract can be given substance by example and illustration.

Other uses for example and illustration come to mind. We often make blanket statements, or *generalizations,* that cover a certain number of facts and judgments rolled into one. It would be burdensome to write without any generalizations at all. But a blanket statement is open to question; readers may not accept it at face value. If we have stated the generalization without offering supporting evidence, our work lacks substance. We need examples that honestly represent that evidence. Discussing the "natural foods" fad, a *Time* essayist uses a generalization immediately backed up by facts:

> The national boom in fresh-from-the-factory natural foods shows no signs of abating. There is hardly a department of any supermarket that does not offer some sort of comestible with "nature" or "natural" on the label. Hershey's Semi-Sweet Chocolate Chips boasts "all natural ingredients." Snyder's of Hanover pretzels are said to be natural, as though just plucked off the old pretzel tree. Mrs. Paul's French Fried Onion Rings? "Only from natural fresh sliced onions."[2]

---

[1] Alexander H. Leighton, *Human Relations in a Changing World* (New York: Dutton, 1949), pp. 27–28.

[2] Frank Trippet, "Little Crimes Against 'Nature,'" *Time,* 11 October 1982, p. 102. Copyright 1982 by Time Inc. All rights reserved. Reprinted by permission from *Time.*

An *illustration* is a brief story from real life, used to give concreteness to an idea. Here's an essay that presents an abstract generalization in its first sentence. An experience from life shows that the generalization is true:

> Our virtues are not always obvious, even to ourselves, and often they appear in us when we least expect them.
>
> My schoolmates always teased me as a coward. It seemed I never had the courage to climb a rocky mountain or even jump from the high board at the pool, and I always stayed away from fights. I felt the tauntings deeply. I was timid, perhaps, but was I really a coward? Each time I turned down a daring chance, I came more and more to feel the reputation justified.
>
> One foggy day as I walked along the river bank, I heard a woman's frantic cry. As I came near her, she shrieked that her little son had fallen into the water.
>
> I looked into the river and could barely see a small figure bobbing up and down several yards out from the bank. I recall no thoughts, only actions and senses. I quickly took off my shoes and jumped into the river. The cold water made me shiver, and I struggled to see the child again on the foggy surface. I swam several strokes, then saw him. I called, "Take my hand!" He was either too terrified or too happy to hear my words. I grabbed for him, then he for me, and I nearly went under as he grasped me about the neck. Without thinking, I struck him. He fainted, and I towed him to shore.
>
> The child's mother hugged him. He revived, and she quickly drew him away toward the road, not looking back or saying a word to me. No reporters interviewed me about the incident, nor did the woman send any letter to my school to praise me for my deed. My friends, I knew, would not have believed the incident had I told of it myself.
>
> But after that foggy day, whenever my friends mocked me as a coward, I felt no pain. The word no longer mattered, for I had met my true self there in that river when I had no time to think.

The illustration, an incident from life, has brought concrete reality to the generalization.

Comparison and Contrast

Another way to bring readable substance to our writing is to *compare* what we have in mind to some experience the readers are already familiar with. Thus we bring their experience to bear upon the topic and make new ideas easier to understand. Suppose we've written, "Being a college student requires money, time, effort, and patience." As it stands, the statement may seem little more than a platitude. We can give it substance by drawing a comparison:

> Going to college is something like being in business for yourself. You need a big investment of money, time, and effort. Like the business owner,

you need patience, and you need to convince others of your worth. You make your profits in terms of learning and can reinvest those profits to learn more.

The comparison fleshes out the bare-bones statement and makes it more quickly understood.

Contrast allows us to make two things stand out because they differ. Stars are hardly seen in the day, for their light is like sunlight itself. But the stars stand out clearly against the night sky. How does San Francisco differ from Los Angeles? How does folk music differ from country-western? How does soccer differ from American football? Readers may learn about both because the contrasts make each stand out. As an example, consider how "the basic American education" according to Russell Baker differs from our usual idea of education:

> By the age of six the average child will have completed the basic American education and be ready to enter school. If the child has been attentive in the pre-school years, he or she will already have mastered many skills.
>
> From television, the child will have learned how to pick a lock, commit a fairly elaborate bank holdup, prevent wetness all day long, get the laundry twice as white, and kill people with a variety of sophisticated armaments.[3]

Our usual belief that "skills" are positive attainments contrasts sharply with the negative abilities the child has learned from television. The contrast helps us to understand Baker's point, his definition of *learning*.

Guideline

Make your ideas concrete by example, illustration, comparison, or contrast.

Revision Practice: Concreteness: The Real Thing

The items contain abstract ideas and generalizations (in the first five they are underlined). Revise them to make each more readable, using example, illustration, comparison, or contrast. Your revisions, of course, will be considerably longer than the originals.

---

[3]Russell Baker, "School vs. Education," *New York Times*, 9 September 1975. Copyright © 1975 by The New York Times Company. Reprinted by permission.

EXAMPLE: Most of us have at least one minor <u>hangup</u>.

REVISION: Most of us have at least one minor hangup, such as pessimism, suspicion of all strangers, or fear of some unlikely disaster.

1. We are all exposed to <u>violence</u> these days.

2. Everyday life is just a jumble of <u>competition</u>.

3. Being <u>sentimental</u> is not much of an advantage when it comes to making important <u>decisions</u>.

4. Ability to tell a competent lie, one that will stick, has both <u>advantages</u> and <u>drawbacks</u>.

5. For years the single woman suffered much <u>unfair treatment</u> by society.

6. We humans are beings of a very special kind in the natural order of things.

7. To put it simply, friends are people you can count on.

8. Civilization has a way of corrupting us all.

9. The limitations put upon us by our energy problems create frustrations for many Americans today.

10. A strong image of self has often been confused with vanity, with narcissism.

11. We are all familiar with the occasional failures of machines that are supposed to work perfectly.

12. Political realities often force the office seeker to be hypocritical.

13. More than once I have suffered the consequences of "telling it like it is."

14. Now and then a citizen really can beat city hall.

15. Optimism is a profitable attitude.

16. Taking good photographs calls for considerable artistry.

17. A pet cat is a test of its owner's tolerance.

18. Every successful relationship is the product of carefully nurtured ingredients.

19. When we were children, my sister's shyness annoyed me.

20. Medicines are made to cure disease, not to prevent it.

Follow-up

Violence, competition, and being sentimental are abstract ideas; how have you made them concrete? Have you shown by example how "we think of ourselves as beings of a very special kind," how we count on friends, how civilization corrupts us, what limitations our energy problems create? Where have you used comparison or contrast?

Lesson 5

Definition
and
Description

To help readers know what we know, think as we think, see as we see, we need to tell them clearly what we have in mind: what things *are* to us and what *qualities* we see in those things. Such communication depends much on a sharing of terms and sensory images, upon definitions and descriptions.

Defining

We sometimes depend too much upon the dictionary to help us define terms. The dictionary, though certainly useful as a guide, is only background for our definitions. It is unwise to quote *Webster's,* though we must take into account what the dictionary says. What our readers want to know is what things are *to us* and in relation to the topic at hand.

In general we define a term by *naming* it and then *classifying* it: "*Slander* [term] is an oral statement [class]." But to name and classify the term will not be enough to make it clear; we must also show how the term differs from other things in its class. Slander is an oral statement "that falsely and maliciously

36

damages another's reputation." To define, then, we must *name, classify,* and *differentiate* the term in question:

Horse sense	is intelligence	that is inborn and practical.
Anarchism	is a political theory	that all governments are coercive and should be abolished.
A humoresque	is a musical composition	that is lively and playful.

Such naming, classifying, and differentiating of terms is *formal* definition, using a method much like that of dictionary makers. Ernest Hemingway uses that kind of definition in his essay "Killing a Bull": "The banderillos are three-foot, gaily colored darts with a small fish hook prong in the end." And, "Before killing the bull he must first do a series of passes with the muleta, *a piece of red cloth* he carries *about the size of a large napkin*" (emphasis added).

That kind of defining looks easy enough, but it requires accurate thinking. We must put the term into a sufficiently narrow class; it would not be enough to classify anarchy as "an idea" or a humoresque as "music." And if the differentiation is inadequate, our definition falls short: If we defined horse sense as a kind of intelligence "that is ordinary and common," we still would not make the point clear. Certainly we must never use the term itself in attempting to define it: "Democracy is a democratic form of government" is useless, a *circular* definition that leaves the term undefined.

Informal, or *extended,* definition goes beyond the formal. Here we are concerned with how the term came to be, how it works, what its consequences are, and especially what it means to us. Here's part of a definition by D. H. Lawrence:

> In the first place, genuine pornography is almost always underworld; it doesn't come into the open. In the second, you can recognize it by the insult it offers, invariably, to sex and to the human spirit. . . . Pornography is the attempt to insult sex, to do dirt on it.[1]

Lawrence's definition is personal and enriched; it goes beyond the formal or the dictionary method.

Describing

Readable description is sensory. It puts into the mind the look, the sound, the smell, the feel, and the taste of things. But good description also goes beyond the senses and establishes judgments, dominant impressions that leave readers

---

[1]D. H. Lawrence, "Pornography and Obscenity," in *The Posthumous Papers of D. H. Lawrence* (New York: Viking Press, 1936), p. 175.

pleased or disgusted, charmed or repulsed, but feeling that they have *experienced* what is described. Here's Mark Twain describing a sunset over the Mississippi River:

> A broad expanse of the river was turned to blood; in the middle distance the red hue brightened into gold, through which a solitary log came floating, black and conspicuous; in one place a long slanting mark lay sparkling upon the water; in another the surface was broken by boiling, tumbling rings, that were as many-tinted as an opal; where the ruddy flush was faintest, was a smooth spot that was covered with graceful circle and radiating lines, ever so delicately traced; the shore on our left was densely wooded and the somber shadow that fell from this forest was broken in one place by a long, ruffled trail that shone like silver; and high above the forest wall a clean-stemmed dead tree waved a single leafy bough that glowed like a flame in the unobstructed splendor that was flowing from the sun. There were graceful curves, reflected images, woody heights, soft distances; and over the whole scene, far and near, the dissolving lights drifted steadily, enriching it every passing moment with new marvels of coloring.[2]

The description gives us much to see: colors, lights, shadows, curves—a visual feast of detail. And the writer enriches his view by figurative comparison in metaphor ("the river was *turned to blood*") and simile ("as many-tinted *as an opal,*" "shone *like silver,*" "glowed *like a flame*") to make us see—through familiar remembered images.

Descriptions of people include the physical features but go beyond them to suggest character in other ways. Mannerisms, gestures, speech, dress, habits, and possessions are all part of personality. Here is Sir Arthur Conan Doyle's description of Sherlock Holmes, in which we come to know Holmes far beyond his mere physical appearance. His habits, his temperament, his stature, and details of eyes, nose, chin, and hands all contribute to a dominant impression that reinforces words like *alertness, decision, determination.*

> He was quiet in his ways, and his habits were regular. It was rare for him to be up after ten at night, and he had invariably breakfasted and gone out before I rose in the morning. Sometimes he spent his day at the chemical laboratory, sometimes in the dissecting rooms, and occasionally in long walks, which appeared to take him into the lowest portions of the city. Nothing could exceed his energy when the working fit was upon him; but now and again a reaction would seize him, and for days on end he would lie upon the sofa in the sitting-room, hardly uttering a word or

---

[2]Mark Twain, *Life on the Mississippi* (New York: Heritage Press, 1944), pp. 62–63.

moving a muscle from morning to night. . . . In height he was rather over six feet, and so excessively lean that he seemed to be considerably taller. His eyes were sharp and piercing save during those intervals of torpor to which I have alluded; and his thin, hawklike nose gave his whole expression an air of alertness and decision. His chin, too, had the prominence and squareness which mark the man of determination. His hands were invariably blotted with ink and stained with chemicals, yet he was possessed of extraordinary delicacy of touch.[3]

The dominant impression is all-important: a central purpose for the description, a single thrust to which all details contribute. The appeal to the senses is primary, with comparison, both literal and figurative, a prominent means.

Guideline

 Define essential terms. Describe people, places, processes, and physical objects.

Revision Practice: Definition and Description

Revise these first five items by adding a formal definition for the underlined terms. Use a dictionary as a guide if you need it but do not quote the dictionary directly.

1. Just beyond the clearing, the Navajo students had built a <u>hogan</u> to show how their ancestors had lived.

2. The winner of the debate had disposed of his opponent's main argument, making brilliant use of <u>prolepsis</u>.

3. After a year at the agricultural college, Edwin came home using words like <u>chresard</u>. We found out all he meant was...

4. One young woman had a severe case of <u>erythrophobia</u>. Her wardrobe and diet were limited by that illness, and she could not watch television except in black and white.

5. The wheels of his compact car developed a serious <u>camber</u>. The tires were wearing rapidly.

---

[3]Sir Arthur Conan Doyle, "A Study in Scarlet," in *The Adventures of Sherlock Holmes* (Norwalk, Conn.: Easton Press, 1981), pp. 11–12.

Revise the next five items by adding an informal definition for the under-lined terms. Though a dictionary may help as a starting point, what the term means to you is the important thing for this kind of definition.

6. It really took <u>guts</u> to avoid getting hooked on what all the gang was doing.

7. Because Fred had no sense of responsibility, he had never known <u>freedom</u>.

8. Though I am not particularly attracted to riches, I know that I would like to become a person of <u>influence</u>.

9. Few kinds of motion are as exhilarating to me as <u>skating</u> on ice.

10. Thousands of actors, both male and female, do believable and enjoyable work. Yet it is something more than skill that makes a <u>star</u>.

Revise the remaining items by providing description, using sensory details and comparisons (literal or figurative) to create a dominant impression.

11. The woman had a rebellious <u>child</u> in tow.

12. His little <u>workroom</u> was crammed with the tools of his craft.

13. It was obvious that the <u>grandfather</u> dominated the family and that three generations of Reillys respected him.

14. Being normally a late riser, I had never been so affected by any winter <u>sunrise</u>.

15. The <u>street</u> that the gang had made its "territory" had everything to make it a less than desirable domain.

16. Teenagers' cars are expected to be gaudy, but this fellow's <u>van</u> was beyond all expectations.

17. The traveler's <u>shoes</u> told much of the story of his wanderings.

18. Once a kind of national shrine, the <u>lakeside</u> now bore the evidence of a score of tourist-ridden summers.

19. The village paper's <u>newsroom</u> was as sleepy a place as the village itself.

20. The <u>woman</u> behind the library desk had the air of having read every book in the place.

Follow-up

Definitions should be brief yet sufficient for the reader to understand. Has each of your formal definitions shown both the *class* and the *differences* from other members of that class? Make sure that descriptions give plenty of sensory detail and that each leaves one dominant impression.

Lesson 6

Reasonable Statement

 $\quad$ **D**espite our intention to write honest, reasonable discussions of worthy topics, in the heat of writing a first draft we may turn out many a sentence lacking in substance. We are, after all, writing in some haste, trying to capture those crowding ideas before they spill over the dam and vanish in the rapids. We have no time then to think carefully, putting every thought to the test of logic. It is only later, when the first-draft rush is over, that we must search our work for the debris of haste, reconsider it, and tidy up.

 $\quad$ Let's take the opening paragraph just above as an example of first-draft material that we must now revise. It was written quickly, and the metaphor of ideas that "spill over the dam and vanish in the rapids" gave its author a flash of pleasure, a thrill of seeing and hearing the water go over the dam to crash below and surge down the rapids. Now we must look at the sentence more carefully. Is the metaphor justified? Is it too farfetched for the topic—words and ideas? Well, no; we'll accept it as within figurative reason. What about those rapids? Do river rapids occur below a dam—or above one? The writer, never having actually seen such rapids, doesn't know for sure; it has to be checked out. And are mistakes and misstatements justifiably called "debris"?

If all these metaphors are consistent and none leaves a ridiculous thought in mind, then we can let them stand.

But when we've written the unreasonable, we must revise. Our readers have to be considered thoughtful people who won't let us get away with the absurd. Here is a passage that readers may question:

> We all make mistakes; they give us opportunities to learn. To make no mistakes would be a misfortune, robbing us of many chances to increase our understanding. Still, we do not want to make mistakes; we want, as much as possible, to foresee our mistakes and do them right.

Is it possible to do a mistake right? Surely the writer means something else, for the concept of mistakes done right is either absurd or paradoxical. Good revision avoids the absurdity:

> . . . Still, we do not want to make mistakes; we want, as much as possible, to foresee our mistakes and avoid them.

Here's another:

> Obviously the old saying "Crime doesn't pay" is true, for it has been around for centuries and is still going strong.

Does a saying become true just by being around for centuries? No, the statement just won't hold up. Many false ideas have been around for centuries, some of them becoming more and more false as they have grown in popularity.

Let's inspect that last sentence. Can an idea become "more and more false"? Aren't ideas either true or false, not "more or less" so? We may defend the statement on grounds that ideas may be "partly true" under certain circumstances, perhaps "less true" under other circumstances. Still, why let the sentence face possible challenge when revision could avoid the trouble?

> Many false ideas have been around for centuries, some of them becoming more *obviously* false as they have grown in popularity.

Here are a few more passages that make unreasonable statements and need revision:

> To finish one's education is important in preparing for a career, since most employers are looking for people who are reliable.

> To be a good friend, one has only to see and enjoy the good side of another person.

> If a politician were perfect, he would make no errors in his speeches. Thus he would be successful in every campaign.

Finishing one's education does not guarantee reliability, and friendship requires much more than seeing and enjoying someone's good side. As for the perfect politician, might not many voters prefer a candidate who is flawed and human rather than perfect? Unreasonable statements often grow from *assumptions*, unexamined ideas that we have taken for granted; they need revision based on more accurate thought.

In the haste of writing a first draft we may use words carelessly, producing the absurd:

> In a marriage the element of trust is tremendous, however nonexistent it may be in some cases.

> There, carved between majestic mountains, stood a creek with flowing streams.

> Kate contained very positive surroundings about herself.

> No unreliable person should be in a respected position such as a politician.

If trust is "nonexistent," how can it be "tremendous"? Is the creek, or only its bed, carved? Does a flowing creek "stand"? Does it have streams? Can a person "contain" surroundings? Is a politician a "position"? The careless use of words produces statements that are not what we wanted to say. Thoughtful revisions may avoid the absurdities:

> Trust is essential to a good marriage. If trust is missing, the marriage is in trouble.

> There, in a bed carved between majestic mountains, flowed a gentle creek.

> Kate had a positive air.

> No unreliable person should become a politician.

When we ask readers to accept the unfounded or the absurd, we lose our readability.

Guideline

Make sure what you say is well founded and reasonably worded.

Revision Practice: Reasonable Statement

Revise these unreasonable or absurd statements. Replace false or unlikely "reasons" with more reliable ones. Use words as accurately as you can.

1. Thanksgiving is always a happy time, because the whole family gets together and eats a lot of good food.

2. A college student who is married is unlikely to do as well in classes as the unmarried student does, since the married student has to work and the single student does not.

3. Today's young people will make good politicians, because they are interested in "participatory democracy," not merely "representative democracy."

4. Gary Gilmore had so little respect for human life that he didn't even respect his own. The same goes for most criminals, who are not executed but go back to society to kill again.

5. It would be impossible for us to solve a social problem that has been around for so many centuries.

6. The "freedom of the press" has the right to print anything they want.

7. Learning dental technology is a very prestigious and lucrative field.

8. Boredom is no problem; the word is simply not a part of my vocabulary.

9. Let's face it; nobody really cares about the problems of illegal aliens.

10. Out in the middle of the harbor stood three huge ships waiting in line for places at the loading docks, like a brood of hens waiting to lay their eggs.

11. Why strive to be understood? Emerson said great minds are never understood.

12. The low achievement scores of American students prove that our schools have failed to do their job.

13. If crime weren't profitable, it would disappear.

14. Nothing worthwhile is achieved without hard work; with it, you can't fail to reach your worthy goals.

15. If we had a real world war of ideas, the best ones would survive.

16. The trouble with society is that nobody today has any ideals.

17. Genuine equality would solve most human problems.

18. We could wipe out poverty if government assured every person a decent living.

19. Computer programing is a field of the future, and anyone who wants to compete in the job world should at least know how to be one.

20. Everybody knows that there's no such thing as getting rich quick.

Follow-up

Are stated "reasons" accurate and sufficient? If number 5 is true, why fight against slavery or other forms of injustice? In number 10, do ships "stand"? If they await loading, are they like hens waiting to lay eggs?

Summary
Revising for Substance

Guidelines 1–6

1. Select a *topic* that interests you and is likely to engage the minds of others. Limit that topic to what you can cover in a short essay.
2. Choose an appropriate *purpose* to guide your approach.
3. Give your central idea a personal twist. *Challenge* the reader's mind.
4. Make ideas concrete by *example, illustration, comparison,* or *contrast.*
5. *Define* essential terms. *Describe* people, places, processes, and physical objects.
6. Make sure what you say is well founded and *reasonably* worded.

Writing and Revising

For detailed suggestions on getting started, writing a first draft, revising the draft, and preparing the essay for submission, review the Introduction. Choose one of the following topics.

Topics for Writing

1. Some places leave unforgettable impressions. Recall a place you have known: a room, a street, an alley, an office, a forest, a beach, a desert. Jot down a list of as many details as you can about that place. Number the details in some reasonable order (such as left to right, high to low). Write a first draft, giving enough sensory detail to make your readers feel impressions like your own.

2. Recall a recent morning in your life. Jot notes of details: what you did and what happened to you from the time you awoke until the time you arrived at work or your first class. Number the details in chronological order. Write a first draft relating the morning's events, trying to make readers experience your attitudes of that day.

3. Censorship is a many-sided moral and political problem. With that problem as general subject matter, devise a narrowed topic, a purpose, and a thesis for an essay. Write a first draft.

4. The Equal Rights Amendment, addressed chiefly to problems of sexual inequality in the United States, failed to win ratification by two-thirds of the state legislatures. With the ERA as general subject matter, devise a narrowed topic, a purpose, and a thesis for an essay. Write a first draft.

Follow-up

As you revise your first draft, consider the concreteness of your treatment: Have you shown your readers real things to see, hear, smell, taste, and feel? If you've written on item 1 or 2, have you left a single dominant impression? Have you used *comparison* or *contrast*? Consider any abstract or personal concepts you have mentioned (such as equality or censorship): Have you offered adequate *definition*? Give special attention to your thesis and any other statements of opinion or conclusion: Are they *reasonable* statements? Make sure each is what you really meant to say. For advice on preparing the manuscript for submission, see Lesson 42.

Review Quiz

Part A: Consider these proposed topics for essays. Revise each to limit the topic, build interest, and increase readability.

1. Being a lifeguard
2. Techniques in playing electronic games
3. Unlikely pets

4. Family gatherings

5. Victims of crime

Part B: Assign a purpose to each of these essay topics, deciding whether to define, describe, analyze structure, analyze process, analyze cause or effect, classify, tell a story, or argue a point.

6. Disabled versus handicapped

7. Taking apart a guitar

8. The first dive

9. Affirmative action

10. Comfortable wheels

Part C: These are flavorless statements of central point for essays. Revise each to present a challenging idea.

11. There are many things you should do if fired from a job.

12. Additives have some strange effects on foods.

13. Rock music has been a phenomenon for nearly thirty years now.

14. Living free is a hard thing to do.

15. Drugs have a tremendous effect on people.

Part D: Revise these passages, providing a definition, description, comparison, example, or evidence (reasons) to bring substance to each. If a statement seems absurd, revise to make it reasonable.

16. Yes, the world does need love, sweet love; consequently, love is not easy to come by when so many people have so many differences.

17. Although calculators save time and reduce errors, we should all get away from calculators and practice our math skills without them.

18. Now I have realized what I really like and what I want to do. I have natural leadership ability, and I am a good organizer of work. So I am a business major.

19. Americans are creating many advantages for themselves. Our mortality rate is much higher than it was two hundred years ago when it was only about fifty years old.

20. People laugh at things they can relate to or at something they do every day.

Part E: Read this first-draft essay critically, then consider the questions and suggestions for revision that follow it.

1   SOME WORLD PROBLEMS

2   A universal compassion would probably resolve many

3   problems that the world faces today; however, this is an

4   impossible task. Overpopulation, prejudice, and ecological

5   balance are some major problems; nevertheless, these

6   problems are not unreachable.

7   Prejudices are the attitudes based on favorable and

8   unfavorable stereotypes; moreover, if society were more

9   open-minded, caring, and less harsh on others, people would

10 communicate better.

11   The lack of birth control leads to overpopulation, but

12 many steps are being taken to provide the needs for those

13 seeking it. As a result of the high cost of living, the

14 overpopulation rate is decreasing.

15   Long before there was man, there was nature, and its

16 survival depends on us. Conservationists, along with most

17 people, are trying to preserve what is left of the world,

18 because the scars on nature are just beginning to be

19 noticed.

20   Although these three problems are not the only ones

21 that need focus, with that much more concern on them the

22 world will be a better place for everyone.

Questions and Suggestions for Revision: Consider all these questions and suggestions before you begin to revise the essay; then take up each in turn as you revise. Add appropriate material where it seems needed for substance. The numbers here refer to lines of the essay.

1 Is the title appropriate? (See Lesson 13 for what it takes to make a good title.)

2 Does "compassion" need to be defined? Just what does it mean in this context? And how would it solve the world's problems?

4 Why is the task "impossible"?

4 Is "ecological balance" really a problem? Is "imbalance" what is meant?

6 Is "unreachable" the right word? What good would it do to "reach" a problem?

7 Is this definition of "prejudices" accurate and sufficient? (See Lesson 5.)

9 What "others"? Can there be others not included in "society"? Has the idea of prejudice been adequately developed here? Since it is one of the essay's three major "problems," shouldn't the essay discuss why it is a problem and what may be done about it? (This same inadequate development may apply to the essay's treatment of the other two problems as well.)

11 Consider the order of ideas. Since in line 4 the order was (1) overpopulation, (2) prejudice, and (3) ecological balance, shouldn't the essay take up those problems in that order?

13 What does "it" refer to—the lack of birth control, birth control, or overpopulation?

14 Is the slowing of overpopulation caused entirely by the high cost of living, or is that cost merely a contributing factor? And is overpopulation really decreasing throughout the world or only in our country? What is meant by "overpopulation *rate*"?

16 Since nature was here before us, why does its survival depend on us? Isn't it more likely that our survival depends on nature? Is it true that "most people" are trying to preserve the world?

18 Is "because" appropriate here?

21 Is "focus" the right word? Is "on" the right word? Will the world be a better place for everyone as the result of "concern"? Won't it take some real action to solve the problems that have been mentioned? What kind of action may be suggested?

Follow-up

Read your own revision critically, considering its order and development of ideas. Though it may still not be a great essay, does it seem to be an improvement over the original? You may find it helpful to exchange essays with another student and discuss the variations. Why are both revisions more readable than the original?

Revising for

Order

Good order is the foundation of all good things.
Edmund Burke
(1729–1797)

Disorder makes for confusion, an enemy of readable writing. If an essay is readable evidence of a mind at work on ideas, then the essayist has arranged those ideas in an orderly way to make them understandable. Ideas relate to one another, and the relationships must be clear.

Orderly writing does not always appear in a first draft. It is possible to organize our ideas before we write, to outline what we want to say, but more often we begin writing without a clear plan. Our ideas come to us haphazardly, and we set them down as they come. The first draft is often only a collection of raw materials, far from finished work.

It is in revision that we shape the raw materials into an essay. Having selected and narrowed our topic, we arrange the materials according to a purposeful design: What do we want the essay to say, and how do we want it said? What will be suitable to the topic and to the audience—as well as true to our own attitudes? It often takes a considerable rehashing of ideas to get them into an arrangement that satisfies: an orderly design.

Within the essay, details are best understood if they follow a reasonable order, if they move as the eye naturally moves from place to place or as the mind perceives things as larger or smaller, more important or less so. Concepts of space, time, size, and importance all have appropriate arrangement. And as the mind works to classify or divide, to analyze a structure or a process, or to search for causes and effects, order in large part determines readability.

Orderly Design

In practical experience the essay, as a form of writing, does not have a set form, a rigid design. The form grows from the material itself and our individual treatment of it. Still, the essay will engage and hold readers' interest only if it clearly creates an expectation, develops along a path easy to follow, and at last satisfies.

It seems almost too obvious that a readable essay must have three parts: beginning, middle, and end. Yet most essays in first draft do not reflect that orderly plan; often they are all middle, their ideas confused and without appropriate emphasis. Revision brings the ideas into readable order so that each of the three parts does its special work.

The central job of the *beginning* is to create an expectation in the readers' minds: to introduce the topic, suggest the main point, and establish the point of view and tone. The beginning sets a direction for readers to follow.

The *middle* of an essay moves readers along the path, amplifying the central idea in keeping with our purpose. The job of the middle is to hold attention by clarifying essential points and building upon the readers' expectation. Support for the central point is developed by marshaling details: definition, description, example, illustration, explanation by comparison or contrast, presentation of steps in a process, or reasoning to back up an argument.

The *end* of the essay must satisfy; that is, the end must gather up all loose threads, summarize, reemphasize, and bring the essay to a finish. The word *finish* is crucial here; a good essay doesn't just quit but has a finish to it, like a fine piece of woodwork.

Arrangement of details is of primary importance. It is usually a good idea to save the best or most important for last, so that interest rises from beginning to end.

Here's an essay that needs to be revised for order:

The Eternal Handicap

1   The majority of us are fortunately not afflicted by a major phys-
2 ical handicap. There are, however, other kinds of handicaps that
3 plague and debilitate us. Prejudice ranks high on the list in this cat-
4 egory, as does fanaticism. Both, unfortunately, are all too common
5 these days as the numerous international "disputes" and the upsurge
6 of religious cults attest.
7   Brought up in Catholic Northern Ireland, a country tormented
8 by religious and class prejudice, I have had a number of unhappy
9 experiences of both. I learned never to go into town after school
10 unless I changed out of my school uniform. Wearing it branded me
11 a Catholic and invited shouts from my Protestant contemporaries of
12 "Dirty Papist" or "Papist bitch!" (They too were distinguishable by
13 their school uniforms.) My family, too, were not without their prej-
14 udices: My aunt had at one time become engaged to a Protestant boy
15 but because of parental pressure had decided to call it off. Some time
16 later she met and married a Catholic. The family heartily approved.
17 Alas, he turned out to be an alcoholic and badly mistreated her. The
18 surprising attitude in the family was voiced by my father, who put it
19 this way: "Things could be worse; she could've married the Prod."
20   I would be lying to deny my own bitterness over the name-calling
21 incidents. I carried it with me for a long time before shaking it off
22 and during that very negative period was consumed with hatred for
23 my tormentors. Their prejudice, in turn, bred mine. And prejudice,
24 which has a nasty habit of being infectious, is often hereditary.
25   Fanaticism is an extreme form of prejudice. The fanatic is single-
26 minded and obsessed, shutting out all but the obsession itself. His-
27 torically, the ultimate example of fanaticism is the Nazi regime; the
28 Jonestown tragedy is the most recent. Millions lost their lives in the
29 former instance and hundreds in the latter. And what after all is
30 more debilitating than death?

31   My own brush with fanaticism has not been as momentous or
32   grisly. I became smitten by "Beatlemania" in my teens but thankfully
33   have now fully recovered.
34   No race, creed, class, or IQ level is immune to prejudice; it strikes
35   at random. Even the ancient Greeks were subject to prejudice toward
36   the barbarians. Prejudice has been the fuel if not the cause of every
37   war since time immemorial, and in the final analysis prejudice and
38   war are man's great debilitators and eternal handicap.

Revising for order begins with a question: What can be left out entirely?
Details aside from the point of the essay are a distraction; they should be cut.
In this case the material on "fanaticism" (lines 4 and 25–33) seems irrelevant
to the central point and is somewhat confused. It defines fanaticism as "an
extreme form of prejudice" (line 25), yet the detail about Beatlemania (line
32) is much less extreme than that about the aunt's marriage (lines 14–19).
All this material (lines 25–33) can be cut.

Details about the Catholic-Protestant prejudice (lines 7–13 and 20–24),
now separated by the material about the aunt's marriage, should be put together.
The material about the aunt's alcoholic husband, since it is more dramatic than
the childhood name-calling, should be saved for the final paragraph of the
"middle."

Rearrangement will bring the comment about "hereditary" prejudice (line
24) into place as an introduction to the family problem.

Sentences, too, present an order of ideas. The less important should be
subordinated to emphasize what bears directly upon the essay's central topic
or point. Thus the detail about the alcoholic husband (lines 15–17) should be
subordinated in favor of that about the family reaction (lines 17–19).

All the details that extend prejudice from personal experience to the world
at large (and from ancient history to the present time) can be used as part of
the final paragraph of summation, echoing and expanding upon the ideas of
the beginning.

A revised version of the essay puts details in more readable order:

The Eternal Handicap

The majority of us, fortunately, are not afflicted by a major physical
handicap. There are, however, other kinds of handicap that plague and
debilitate us, and prejudice ranks high on that list.

Brought up in Catholic Northern Ireland, a country tormented by
religious and class prejudice, I had unhappy experiences of both. I learned
never to go into town after school unless I had changed out of my school
uniform. Wearing it branded me a Catholic and invited shouts of "Dirty
Papist!" or "Papist bitch!" from my Protestant contemporaries, who were
also distinguishable by their school uniforms. My bitterness over these
name-calling incidents stayed with me for years, and during that very

negative period I was consumed by hatred for my tormentors. Their prejudice fed mine, for prejudice has a nasty way of being infectious.

Prejudice, like certain physical handicaps, is often hereditary in effect, and my family had its share. My aunt had at one time been engaged to a Protestant boy, but because of parental pressure she decided to call off the marriage. Some time later she married a Catholic. The family heartily approved. When, alas, he turned out to be an alcoholic and badly mistreated her, the astonishing reaction of the family was voiced by my father, who put it this way: "Things could be worse; she could've married the Prod."

No race, creed, class, or level of IQ is immune to the disease of prejudice; it strikes at random and in all cultures. The ancient Greeks were prejudiced toward the barbarians. Prejudice has been the fuel if not the cause of wars since time immemorial. It is all too common even today, as our international "disputes" and the upsurge of and reactions to religious cults attest. Prejudice in its many forms is man's eternal handicap.

The essay now has four paragraphs in a clear order, each doing its job: (1) the introduction of topic, thesis, and tone; (2) supporting details on childhood name-calling; (3) supporting details on family prejudice; and (4) summation and reinforcement of thesis, with return to the opening theme of prejudice as human handicap. If the writer chose to add to the substance of the essay, further details on the "international 'disputes' " and rise of "religious cults" might be introduced.

Guideline

As you revise a draft, make sure the essay has an effective beginning, middle, and end, with its ideas in an order that suits your purpose.

Revision Practice: Orderly Design

This brief essay needs revision for order of details. Its sentences have been numbered. In the parentheses, number the sentences in an order you believe will improve the readability of the essay.

THE FAT FAD

( )   [1]Correctly believing that body weight is often a

factor in health, Americans have become a nation of

( )   weightwatchers. [2]There are many fad dieters, yet those

who claim they are dieting don't ever seem to be losing

( ) weight. [3]They generally have bad eating habits.

( ) [4]Usually positive in attitude, they believe they can and

( ) will lose weight. [5]Because of their bad eating habits

( ) they soon regain their loss. [6]Instead of eating three

square meals a day and cutting down the size of portions,

fad dieters eat only some prescribed menu, such as hard-

boiled eggs and grapefruit.

( )   [7]On this spreading weightwatcher scene there are

( ) three kinds of dieters. [8]The two others are the serious

( ) athletes and the obsessive dieters. [9]Unlike the others,

the athletes take their dieting very seriously but not

( ) obsessively. [10]They must be in top physical and mental

( ) shape. [11]Their eating habits are generally good.

( ) [12]Knowing that diet affects the body and therefore the

performance, the athletes follow a balanced diet to

( ) maintain proper body weight and energy. [13]They make sure

they get at each meal at least one food from the four

( ) groups in the "square." [14]Their attitude toward dieting

is sensible.

( )   [15]Obsessive dieters mentally block out all desire

( ) to eat. [16]The eating habits of this group of "dieters"

( ) are dangerously bad. [17]These people may eventually starve

themselves to death.

( )   [18]This extreme attitude has been recognized as a

( ) disease called "anorexia." [19]Its victims may eat only

once a day and then perhaps only one or two spoonfuls.

( ) [20]For most anorexics there is little chance of cure without hospitalization.

( )   [21]Clearly dieting is often--but not always--a

( ) healthful thing to do. [22]Today's Americans are health

( ) conscious but not always health wise. [23]All of us may benefit by taking a close look at our eating habits and determining whether weightwatching is really for us.

( ) [24]Weightwatching is apparently here to stay, whether it is carried on as a fad, an obsession, or a sensible discipline.

Follow-up

After numbering the sentences in an order you find suitable, consider whether any details may be omitted entirely. Then consider whether any details now separated may be combined in one sentence (your revision may have fewer sentences than the original). Is the order of the three kinds of weightwatchers effective? Would it be better to put the athletes, the sensible weightwatchers, last? Finally, write out your revision, making whatever other changes you find helpful. Reread the two versions. Is yours the more readable?

Order of Space, Time, Size, and Importance

Our physical being in the world around us sets a natural order for us. We cannot see everything at once; we must see things as our eyes move among them. We cannot hear sounds at an instant; we must hear them as they occur in the order of time. We cannot even have in our minds all thoughts or images at once; we must consider them one, or a very few, at a time, holding others in memory to be called up as "ordered."

Language, an arrangement of sounds in time or written words in space, can be taken only in small segments, and the arrangement contributes to how we understand ideas. When we write, we try to present ideas in an order that will make for easy, accurate understanding.

Order of Space

Some kinds of writing suggest a natural order. If we describe, we select sensory details and arrange them, moving the readers' eyes from one detail to another as a camera would "pan" about. We move from side to side, top to bottom, front to back, or around in a circle, as the camera or the eye would do. Here is Mark Twain with a description in the words of Huck Finn:

> Phelps's was one of these little one-horse cotton plantations, and they all look alike. A rail fence round a two-acre yard; . . . some sickly grass-patches in the big yard, but mostly it was bare and smooth, like an old hat with the nap rubbed off; big double log house for the white folks—hewed logs, with the chinks stopped up with mud or mortar, and these mud-stripes been whitewashed some time or another; . . . one little hut all by itself away down against the back fence, and some outbuildings down a piece the other side; ash-hopper and big kettle to bile soap in by the little hut; bench by the kitchen door, with bucket of water and a gourd; hound asleep there in the sun; more hounds asleep round about; about three shade trees away off in a corner; some currant bushes and gooseberry bushes in one place by the fence; outside of the fence a garden and a watermelon patch; then the cotton-fields begin, and after the fields the woods.[1]

The eye can move much as the writer wishes, but readable description is likely to follow an orderly progression. Consider a confusing description:

> Her eye had a twinkle of light in the middle of its sapphire. Her feet were small and light as she walked, and her waist was narrow where she had a bow tied around it. Her hair, dark as sable, shone in the summer sun. She had graceful hands. Her shoulders were set square, and her chin, though small, met the breeze like the prow of a tiny sailboat eager for a voyage.

The movement from eye to feet and back to chin is needlessly random. In this case the progression would best be from foot to head, ending with the eye and its twinkle.

Order of Time

Events occur one after another, and as we tell a story the natural order is from first to last. Any wrenching of details from that order is likely to make the narrative difficult to follow. Here is a narrative passage by Jack London, who takes us, in orderly steps, through both time and space:

> I returned to my hut for the shotgun, made sure it was loaded, and went down to the *Ghost*. With some difficulty, and at the expense of a

---

[1] Mark Twain, *The Adventures of Huckleberry Finn* (Norwalk, Conn.: Easton Press, 1981), pp. 260–261.

wetting to the waist, I climbed aboard. The forecastle scuttle was open. I paused to listen for the breathing of the men, but there was no breathing. I almost gasped as the thought came to me: What if the *Ghost* is deserted? I listened more closely. There was no sound. I cautiously descended the ladder. The place had the empty and musty feel and smell usual to a dwelling no longer inhabited. . . . Abandoned hastily, was my conclusion, as I ascended to the deck.[2]

Order of Size or Importance

When we write of things not equal in size or importance, we do well to follow a regular order from minor to major (or vice versa). Such an order is useful when we write an essay of classification or division (see Lesson 9). In an essay on "Territorial Behavior," Desmond Morris classifies human "territories" as *tribal, family,* and *personal*—in order of descending size. The reverse of the principle is used by Wright Morris in an essay titled "Odd Balls"; he considers six of the balls used in games, treating them in order of size from smallest to largest: golf ball, billiard ball, tennis ball, baseball, football, and basketball.

Order helps us build and sustain reader interest. If we start with the less important and move to the more so, we create a rising interest and at the same time let readers know what we think is most important. In an essay about how people react to his own blindness, Harold Krents says they often assume that because he cannot see he also cannot hear; that assumption is annoying. They also often assume he cannot talk; that assumption is insulting. And they often assume he cannot work; that assumption, of course, affects his life most importantly. He treats the three assumptions in order of importance.

This arrangement of details in order of importance is sometimes called *climactic* order; the details rise toward a climax, a final one that caps all the others in rank or importance.

From General to Specific

When a word or term names a large group or class of things, we say it is a general word. When a word or term names just one thing, it is a specific word. *Tool,* for example, is general; *pipe wrench* is specific. Often we have a whole ladder of terms from the very general to the very specific: *animal, vertebrate, mammal, rodent, rabbit, jackrabbit.* It is reasonable to move from the general down to the specific, or vice versa. To mention the terms in random sequence would be confusing.

Reasoning to a conclusion, as we often do in writing, calls for an orderly treatment of ideas. We may start by stating our general conclusion and follow by explaining how we arrived at it, saying, in effect, "It is clear that so and so

---

[2]Jack London, *The Sea-Wolf* (Norwalk, Conn.: Easton Press, 1979), p. 291.

is true, for these reasons. . . ." Another order begins with the specific facts or bits of evidence, withholding the general conclusion until the end.

In this passage Ralph Waldo Emerson follows *deductive* order. He begins with a general conclusion and follows with evidence to support it:

> Traveling is a fool's paradise. Our first journeys discover to us the indifference of places. At home I dream that at Naples, at Rome, I can be intoxicated with beauty and lose my sadness. I pack my trunk, embrace my friends, embark on the sea and at last wake up in Naples, and there beside me is the stern fact, the sad self, unrelenting, identical, that I fled from. I seek the Vatican and the palaces. I affect to be intoxicated with sights and suggestions, but I am not intoxicated. My giant goes with me wherever I go.[3]

Leading from the evidence to the conclusion, Norman Cousins uses *inductive* order:

> The term *conservative* stands for stability as opposed to innovation; for restraint as opposed to daring; for the preservation of inherited conditions as opposed to drastic reform. These ideas are not only compatible with a free society; they have an essential place in it, along with genuine liberalism. True conservatism is opposed to liberalism but not destructive of it. Both conservatism and liberalism serve as the twin structural supports of constitutional government.[4]

Guideline

Arrange details so that the reader can "see" or understand them in a reasonable order.

Revision Practice: Order of Space, Time, Size, and Importance

Each of these passages shows a disorderly presentation of ideas. Revise each, using an appropriate arrangement.

Order of Space

In revising for order of *space*, arrange details as a moving eye would see them—from top to bottom, left to right, or vice versa.

---

[3]Ralph Waldo Emerson, "Self-Reliance," in *Ralph Waldo Emerson's Essays and Lectures* (New York: Library of America, 1983), p. 278.
[4]Norman Cousins, *Human Options* (New York: W. W. Norton, 1981), p. 97.

1. [1]Kirkland is a small town five miles east of Seattle and on the northwest shore of Lake Washington, a beautiful freshwater lake. [2]Many exciting places are within an hour's drive from Kirkland. [3]It is an old town fast developing into a modern one. [4]Buildings are being torn down to make room for more spacious ones. [5]New docks are being built to accommodate the many boats that visit the town. [6]Kirkland has the finest Little League ballpark in the United States. [7]A park is being constructed down by the waterfront. [8]Improvements have been made on the main roads leading to such beautiful places as [8a]Canada, [8b]the Pacific Ocean, and [8c]Snoqualmie Pass.

2. [1]The old man's boots had known mountain and swamp and now were crusted with residue of both. [2]A gray beard was curly and matted, ill-kept like rest of him. [3]His mouth, now never opened, had been lost in it long ago. [4]His shoulders, though stooped, had once been powerful. [5]A mustache seemed but an overgrowth from the beard. [6]What forehead could be seen was deeply furrowed and partially obscured by hair, not growing from his head but in great bushes from his brows. [7]The nose was wide and flat, as if pressed for years against the window of life. [8]Two round patches, on either side of the flat nose, had once been cheeks. [9]Above them hung two sagging pouches. [10]Over one shoulder he grasped a meager bag of gleanings from a dozen rubbish cans. [11]There was, nonetheless, still a twinkle in his eye. [12]He

gave the impression, not a little, of a weary Santa Claus on a sleighless return trip to the pole.

Order of Time

For order of *time*, arrange details with the earliest first, the rest as they happened.

3. [1]Competition is a way of life in America. [2]We Americans have always strived, both individually and among groups, to keep up with--and slightly ahead of--"the Joneses." [3]Settlement of lands on the western frontier was largely a result of competition. [4]Even before the English colonists first migrated to America, their competitive nature had been established in business and social life. [5]Once in the new land they competed with the mother country, at last breaking from it in revolution.

4. [1]My parents have deeply influenced my attitudes. [2]They have contributed to my feeling of independence, and I have learned by their mistakes. [3]They got married while still in high school and had no further education. [4]Now they are seeing all they have missed, and they tell me to live it up and get my education before I get married and have children. [5]Although they are divorced, each of them has done much to mold my way of thinking.

Order of Size

Order of *size*, of course, moves from largest to smallest or vice versa.

5. He had fished in [1]lakes, in [2]streams, and in [3]ponds of many lands, in [4]oceans, and in [5]rivers. He knew what swam in each and what bait would lure it to the hook.

6. [1]We need to get our ideas and feelings clear in our minds without outside interference. [2]For some the need for privacy is intimate and deep. [3]Others fear being alone, as if they exist only in relation to family or group. [4]One feels the need for solitude, while [5]another finds it hard to cope with. [6]But we all need to seclude ourselves at times if only to realize our individuality.

Order of Importance (or Climax)

Order of *importance* usually moves best from the least to the most important or climactic detail.

7. [1]In many ways we Americans are too modern. [2]I feel the best life is away from the big cities. [3]Few deny that our cities are [3a]full of pollution, [3b]plagued by crime, and [3c]overcrowded. [4]Yet some people feel that the excitement and nightlife of the big city compensate for these problems, that business and industry make for progress, and that "progress" is always good. [5]I disagree.

8. [1]We Americans are much too wasteful. [2]We spend our millions for military hardware while our fellow creatures starve, and if the arms are used, we waste lives. [3]We spend our time on frivolity and our cash on smoke and drugs while complaining that we are poor. [4]We lay waste our national brainpower, spending billions on television, movies, and recording stars while we underpay our scientists and meagerly support medical research.

[5]We spend lavishly for busing children to school but decline to pay teachers a competitive wage. [6]We give our children what they ask for, luxurious toys that are discarded in a week. [7]We search for bigger houses with more closet space to store the expensive clothes we have worn but once. [8]We peel the vitamins off our potatoes, refine the nutrients out of our bread, and throw tons of food down our garbage disposals. [9]We waste our land, our water resources, our natural gas and oil. [10]We send millions of gallons of gasoline up into smog as we wait for traffic lights to change. [11]We Americans, if we are to survive, need to watch our waste-lines.

Order of General to Specific

In revising for order of *general-specific,* either arrangement can be followed, inductive or deductive.

9. [1]I have a friend who carries exaggeration to extreme. [2]His stories would do a fisherman proud. [3]In one he tells of his driving a hot-rod through a red light at rush hour. [4]In another he tells of doing a backflip while skiing, even though he is only a beginner. [5]Every time you exaggerate, you are acting. [6]Anyone as good at exaggerating as my friend is should be on the stage.

10. [1]Those who don't need welfare but get it anyway really hurt the ones who do need it. [2]The longer they receive help, the lazier they become. [3]Cases should be more deeply investigated to see whether an applicant really qualifies. [4]My mother worked for

the welfare department. [5]She used to tell me about the many young, able people who ask for free money and get it. [6]Most are just lazy. [7]The welfare system in America is abused. [8]The welfare department itself is partly to blame.

Follow-up

Recheck to make sure you have followed the advice in each category. For order of *space,* arrange details as they appear from top to bottom, left to right, or vice versa. For order of *time,* arrange details from earliest to most recent, as they happened. For order of *size,* arrange details from largest to smallest or vice versa. For order of *importance,* move from the least to the most important or climactic detail. For order of *general-specific,* either inductive order (starting with specifics and arriving at generalization) or deductive order (starting with a generalization and arriving at specific applications) can be followed.

Lesson 9

Orderly Analysis

Much of what we write in college (as well as in industry and business) is based on, or reports the results of, analysis, by which we determine the nature of something by separating it into its components. We may be called upon to write an essay on what a carrot cake is and how to make one, how a single-lens reflex camera is built, how a helicopter works, or what causes spontaneous combustion. Such assignments call for several kinds of analysis.

We may first need to use *definition,* telling what a carrot cake, a reflex camera, or a helicopter is. We have already had some experience with that kind of writing in Lesson 5. And, though definition is not exactly analysis, it does call for orderly use of the mind, for classifying things and distinguishing them from others of their kind.

To handle such an assignment, we may have to determine which sort of analysis is most appropriate to the topic.

Classification and Division

A *class* is a group of things that share certain characteristics. We classify a thing by observing its qualities and grouping it with others that have the same qualities. We observe that a helicopter flies in the air, so we put it in the class with other such things: balloons, blimps, airplanes, gliders, birds, and bees. But we note a distinction: Helicopters are not living things but man-made devices, more like airplanes than like bees; thus, we classify them among mechanical devices that fly, not among living things that fly.

What we've really done is both classify and divide. We have classified the helicopter as a thing that flies in the air, and we have divided flying things into living and man-made ones.

We often write essays of division, considering a class of things and dividing its members into sorts by considering their differences. What are the several kinds of computer? What are several ways of scoring in football? Each such essay would call for careful division of the topic by comparison and contrast. See how Eric Berne classifies people by their appearance:

> We can thus say that while the average human being is a mixture, some people are mainly "digestion-minded," some "muscle-minded," and some "brain-minded," and correspondingly digestion-bodied, muscle-bodied, or brain-bodied. The digestion-bodied people look thick; the muscle-bodied people look wide; and the brain-bodied people look long. This does not mean the taller a man is the brainier he will be. It means that if a man, even a short man, looks long rather than wide, he will often be more concerned about what goes on in his mind than about what he does or what he eats.[1]

Our point in all this is that classification and division both call for orderly thinking and orderly presentation.

Structural Analysis

A *structure* is anything that has physical substance: We can see it or touch it— or at least part of it. The solar system is a structure; so is the chair we sit on, the typewriter we use, the car we drive. In writing a structural analysis, we consider the *parts* of the structure. Readable writing calls, of course, for an orderly presentation of the parts according to some prearranged sorting factor: size, shape, purpose, or location. Thus, if we analyze the solar system, we may present the planets in some logical order, such as their size or their distance from the sun. If we analyze the automobile, we may present its parts from front to back, from top to bottom, or according to some other factor— perhaps distinguishing body from engine and then showing the parts of each

---

[1] Eric Berne, *A Layman's Guide to Psychiatry and Psychoanalysis* (New York: Simon & Schuster, 1947), p. 25.

in some reasonable order. Here's how Eliot Wigginton presents the structure of a wood stove:

> The fire was built in the firebox located on the left-hand side of the stove right under the cooking surface. . . . At the bottom of the firebox is a coarse iron grate through which the ashes fall into the ash box. The soot which rises into the flue later falls back down into the soot tray which is directly underneath the oven. . . . The oven is usually located on the right-hand side of the stove and is heated from the left and top by the circulation of heat from the firebox.[2]

Process Analysis

A *process*, or operation, is a change in relationship among structures. An eclipse of the moon, for example, is a process: a change in relationship among the moon, earth, and sun. A basketball game is a series of changes in relationship among many structures—a ball, ten players, two baskets, and a court. If we were to write an essay on either of those, we'd be writing a process analysis. We would have to present the *stages* of each process, the smaller operations—one by one—that compose the whole process. The readability of our essay would largely depend on the orderly method of presentation. Here's how L. Rust Hills analyzes part of the process of eating an ice-cream cone:

> At each bite you must press down cautiously, so that the ice cream settles farther and farther into the cone. Be very careful not to break the cone. . . . The ice cream should now form a small dome whose circumference exactly coincides with the large circumference of the cone itself—a small skull cap that fits exactly on top of a larger, inverted dunce cap. . . . Because of the geometrical nature of things, a constantly reduced inverted cone still remains a perfect inverted cone no matter how small it grows, just as a constantly reduced dome held within a cone retains *its* shape. Because you are constantly reshaping the dome of ice cream with your tongue and nibbling at the cone, it follows in logic—and in actual practice, if you are skillful and careful—that the cone will continue to look exactly the same, except for its size, as you eat it down, so that at the very end you will hold between your thumb and forefinger a tiny, idealized replica of an ice-cream cone, a thing perhaps one inch high.[3]

---

[2] Eliot Wigginton, ed., *The Foxfire Book* (New York: Doubleday, 1972), p. 192.

[3] L. Rust Hills, "How to Eat an Ice-Cream Cone," *The New Yorker*, 24 August 1968, p. 110. Copyright 1968 by The New Yorker Magazine, Inc. Reprinted by permission of the author.

Cause-Effect Analysis

Another kind of analysis discovers causes—how things come to be. What are the causes of automobile tire wear? What makes a dog howl at a siren? A reversal of this kind of analysis is the projection of effects—what will result from a situation or a thing? What will happen if the world runs out of oil? What will result if aerosol sprays continue to contaminate the atmosphere?

In writing cause or effect analysis we must appeal to reason, first to our own and then to that of our readers. We must make sure that the causes we discover are the real causes, not merely imaginary or "supposed" ones. Are the causes we assign primary and direct causes or only secondary or indirect ones? In an essay on "Mechanic's Logic," Robert M. Pirsig warns us against faulty analysis of cause:

> If the horn honks, and the mechanic concludes that the whole electrical system is working, he is in deep trouble. He has reached an illogical conclusion. The honking horn only tells him that the battery and horn are working. To design an experiment properly he has to think very rigidly in terms of what directly causes what. . . . The horn doesn't make the cycle go. Neither does the battery, except in a very indirect way. The point at which the electrical system *directly* causes the engine to fire is at the spark plugs, and if you don't test here, at the output of the electrical system, you will never really know whether the failure is electrical or not.[4]

All these kinds of analysis demand careful thinking and orderly presentation. The reader's mind must be taken through the categories, parts, steps, or reasons one by one, so that each makes clear sense in itself and in relation to the whole.

Guideline

In an essay of analysis, present categories, parts, steps, or reasons one by one, so that each makes clear sense in itself and in relation to the whole.

Revision Practice: Orderly Analysis

Each of these paragraphs presents an analysis in some disorder. Revise each so that its categories, parts, steps, or reasons are in reasonable order.

---

[4]Robert M. Pirsig, *Zen and the Art of Motorcycle Maintenance* (New York: William Morrow, 1974), p. 110.

1.   The milk, eggs, and flavor extract should be beaten
together. Then add the dry ingredients--flour, sugar, and
spices--which should have been mixed earlier and blended with
the shortening. Pour the batter into three nonstick cake pans
after beating it about three minutes at high speed.

2.   History has provided six kinds of timepiece, more or less
accurate. One of them, the ordinary analogue watch, is still
common today. The town crier helped for a few brief centuries
but was unreliable between hours. The digital clock is a
product of our electronic era. The shadow of a tree perhaps led
to development of the sundial, which always lost its usefulness
after dark. Time was when you could tell the hour by the arrival
or passing of "the 7:14" if you lived in a small railroad town.
The bell in the church steeple did the job in some villages for
centuries.

3.   The best education still boils down to something like the
three R's with some arts, crafts, history, and psych thrown in.
We need to know what has happened on earth before we got here,
and we need to know how our minds and emotions work. To earn a
living, we need some skill in craftwork, like typing or working
with wrenches, pots, wires, and pans. If we learn to paint or
play the flute, we'll have some good times. And it doesn't hurt
to be able to add up the grocery bill and divide the number of
potatotes by the number of eaters at the table. We can get most
of the learning easily once we've learned to read. When we can
write, we can help others learn too, maybe long after we're
gone.

4.   The camp cot is quite a remarkable bed. It is made of a
sheet of canvas almost wide enough for a human body to lie on
comfortably. It has wooden legs, six of them, arranged in three
pairs, each pair hinged together near the center so the two form
an X. The canvas, never long enough, is stretched between two
wooden poles inserted in loops sewn along each side of it. One
pair of legs is at the head of the cot, another at the foot, and
a third in the center to put pressure on the kidneys. Two
shorter wooden poles are inserted in loops sewn at the head and
foot of the canvas, one of the poles for hanging the sleeper's
feet over and one for resting the back of the neck on. The camp
cot was designed for the army so that soldiers would prefer
being awake and peeling potatoes.

5.   The violence on television is deliberate. Television
drama, if it were not violent, would seem too much like real
life. Violence is added to make the commercials, not the
dramas, look like real life. Sex doesn't draw big audiences,
and information makes people think; both destroy the effect of
advertising. When an audience has sat watching about ten

minutes of violence, it is ready for some emotional relief, some cure for the headache, and some shrinking of hemorrhoidal tissue. That's when the really important stuff comes on the screen. Writers put the violence into scripts because they are told nothing else really draws the crowds, not even sex or information.

6.   We have made fine distinctions in the attaching of words to the pathways of our cities and towns. The basic one is the street, the ordinary route of wheeled vehicles and means of keeping buildings apart. A boulevard is a broader roadway, often lined with trees and considered major. Parks and public buildings of an impressive sort are along boulevards. Avenues differ from streets in their direction; ordinarily streets go one way and avenues lie at cross-angles to them. All these are usually straight, except that a boulevard may curve. A court or "place" is usually a short access route between residences, and a "way" is a narrow roadway that meanders. A lane is a little road that usually has just one house--at the end. A road is a motorway that is on the outskirts and usually leads out of town.

7.   Last week I was between a rock and a hard place and thought I'd take a close look at the environment. I got to thinking how I knew the rock was a rock and not a stone, and I decided it was a matter of size: The rock was too big to throw. A few pebbles, smaller than stones, were lying around, like stone's eggs. The rock had some stones nuzzling near it, a bit like the way ducklings tag after their mother. At my left was the hard place, mostly made up of shale and slate, sort of sheeted like the layers of a petrified caramel cake. The rock had a brother, almost the same size but obviously movable; such boulders live loosely, unlike rocks, which stay put. Very few gems are made of rocks, boulders, shale, or slate; most gems are stones and pebbles that have been picked up by lapidaries and polished or cut to look more valuable than they really are.

8.   A banana split has a complicated anatomy. The heart of it, strangely enough, is not the banana but the ice cream, which must always be in three scoops placed in a row, never in a triangle. The banana, split lengthwise, lies in two halves alongside the row of ice cream mountains. Whipped cream is slopped on top of each mountain. The ice cream must be of three different flavors, preferably vanilla, chocolate, and straw-berry. The strawberry is always in the middle. Some fudge sauce is spread over the ice cream before the whipped cream is added, and nuts are sprinkled over the sauce. It is also essential to pour two other kinds of topping on, probably strawberry and butterscotch. A maraschino cherry goes on top of each mountain, and voila!--a masterpiece.

Follow-up

Order of details is of prime importance in this kind of writing. Make sure that a process (1 and 8) has a clear order of steps. Historical events or developments (2) are best related in the order of their occurrence. Structural analysis (4) should move from part to part in order (the "neckbone connected to the collarbone," and so on). An essay of classification (7) or an analysis of division (6) should have details in order of size, time, or importance.

Summary
Revising for Order

Guidelines 7–9

7. As you revise a draft, make sure the essay has an effective beginning, middle, and end, with its ideas arranged in an order that suits your purpose.

8. Arrange details so that the reader can "see" or understand them in a reasonable order.

9. In an essay of analysis, present categories, parts, steps, or reasons one by one, so that each makes clear sense in itself and in relation to the whole.

Writing and Revising

For detailed suggestions on getting started, writing a first draft, revising the draft, and preparing the essay for submission, refer to the Introduction. Choose one of the following topics.

Topics for Writing

1. The polygraph, or lie detector, is a controversial device. Results of its use are not always admissible as evidence in court or elsewhere. With the polygraph as general subject matter, do whatever research you may need; then prepare an essay with *process* as purpose, showing how the polygraph works. Write a first draft.

2. Economic inflation is a virulent disease and a serious political issue. With inflation as your general subject matter, devise a narrowed topic, a purpose, and a thesis for an essay. Write a first draft, being sure to include a *definition* as well as some idea of *process:* how inflation happens.

3. Self-reliance has long been considered an American character trait, yet some say Americans of today have less of it than did those of earlier times. With that thought as general subject matter, devise a narrowed topic and a purpose for an essay (consider *cause* or *effect* as a possibility: Why are Americans becoming less self-reliant, or what will result?). Prepare a thesis and write a first draft.

4. News on television has become a major interest and concern for the American public. With television news as general subject matter, devise a narrowed topic and a purpose for an essay (consider *division* or *classification:* What are the parts of a newscast, or what are the several kinds of news-based programs?). Prepare a thesis and write a first draft.

Follow-up

As you revise your first draft, give special attention to the order of ideas. Does the essay have an orderly overall design? Have you handled matters of space, time, size, and importance in orderly ways? If you have offered classification, division, structural analysis, or cause-effect analysis, are the categories, parts, steps, or reasons in logical order? When you have finished your revision, see Lesson 42 for a guide to preparing the manuscript for submission.

Review Quiz

Read the first draft of "Is Fame Good?" Consider the order of its details; then revise the essay to put them in more emphatic and readable order.

IS FAME GOOD?

( ) ^{1}Fame, despite its many benefits, is a dangerous

( ) thing. ^{2}The famous must be constantly on guard, since

being in the public eye makes them vulnerable to many kinds

of assault upon possessions, self, and family.

( ) ^{3}Celebrities are in constant jeopardy. ^{4}Because they

( )   are often wealthy, they are prime targets for the thief and

      unscrupulous con artist, sometimes for a kidnaper or an

( )   assassin. ^{5}Sometimes a fan will do anything to get close to

( )   an idol. ^{6}An "admirer," meaning no harm, may yet cause much

      pain and loss to the famous by stealing their possessions

      for souvenirs, by actually doing physical harm, or by

( )   tearing off clothing or jewelry. ^{7}Anyone who is jealous may

      attack the famous verbally, spreading false rumor about

      their private or public lives.

( ) ^{8}Many celebrities do not live normal lives. ^{9}They must

( )   hire housekeepers, secretaries, business managers, and

      others to shop for them and do many things that most of us

( )   normally do for ourselves. ^{10}Because they are easily

      recognized in public, they cannot do the normal, everyday

      things.

( ) ^{11}The famous have no privacy. ^{12}The public knows the

( )   celebrity's face, address, family members, and everything

( )   the famous one does. ^{13}The possibility of blackmail is

( )   often present. ^{14}No part of life can be protected from the

( )   meddling of news reporters. ^{15}The public is let in on every

      move, all the personal and financial affairs.

( ) ^{16}Yes, many more bad things than good things can

( )   happen to a celebrity. ^{17}Fame is often more dangerous and

      troublesome than it is rewarding.

Follow-up

You may have noticed that once a person has been assassinated, all other misfortunes seem unimportant. It would be wise, then, to order details of the essay so that they build from the merely annoying toward the finally disastrous consequences of fame. Even the final paragraph of the first draft has erred in putting the "dangerous" before the "troublesome."

Revising for

Economy

*In composing, as a general rule,
run your pen through every other
word you have written; you have no
idea what vigor it will give your
style.*
Sydney Smith (1771–1845)

Polonius, adviser to the king and queen in Shakespeare's *Hamlet,* declared, "Brevity is the soul of wit." Alas, Polonius himself was a tedious old busybody who could not put a plain tale briefly. The impatient queen urged him to say his piece using "more matter, with less art."

The "matter" of our writing is its substance—what it has to say; the "art" of it is style—how the matter is said. The two cannot really be parted, for the *how* invariably affects the *what,* and the *what* should determine the *how.*

As important as brevity is, it is an achievement, not a gift. From the time we say our first words, we tend to babble, fascinated by the sound of our own voices. As we learn to write, we carry the habit over to the page, as if more words, like porters on a safari, could bear more weight. But most of our meanings are not weighty, after all. What we have to say can be said in few words—if the words are well chosen. Tedious or irrelevant details can be trimmed away. We can try for the one right word to do the job of three near misses; we can shake the chaff from a wordy phrase to expose the grain. As we revise our work, we can cut the babble and the roundabout expressions. We can learn to be brief.

Concise Wording

Readable writing does not waste words. If readers must slosh through a swamp of words to get to a meaning, they'll soon turn to other things. What they want, and what they need, is more ideas in fewer words.

The first step is to recognize wasted words in our own writing. If we've written "pay a visit to," do we really mean no more than "visit"? Many verb-noun forms become habitual in our speech and writing; in revision we can use the economical verbs instead:

take a look	(look)	have an intention	(intend)
give a listen	(listen)	be in attendance at	(attend)
tried a taste of	(tasted)	make a speech	(speak)
had an experience of	(experienced)	have a conversation	(converse)
be in favor of	(favor)	make a study of	(study)

If we've written "in a spoiled condition," we probably mean nothing more than "spoiled." We can drop the useless noun (and the preposition too) and let the modifier do the work:

kindly by nature	(kindly)	in a hasty manner	(hastily)
optimistic in outlook	(optimistic)	in a strange way	(strangely)
of easygoing temperament	(easygoing)	in a gruff fashion	(gruffly)

When we write general words, such as *house* or *run*, we may have to tack on modifiers to give readers a clearer picture: *little rustic* house or run *hastily* or run *at top speed*. We can save words and create better pictures with nouns or verbs that need no modifiers: *cabin* or *shack, scamper* or *sprint*. The more specific words carry their own modifying ideas; they do more work for us than the general ones do. General words with modifiers give us a first draft like this:

> A *little animal* had *come unwanted* into our *temporary quarters* while we were *going out for a walk* in the *wooded area.*

Strong, specific words give us a clearer, briefer revision:

> A *mongoose* had *stolen* into our *tent* as we were *hiking* in the *woods.*

Redundancies use two or more words for a one-word idea. An occasional redundancy may be useful for emphasis, but most are simply word wasters:

adequate enough	fall down	short in length
a.m. in the morning	few in number	small in size
and etc.	gathered together	square in shape
blue in color	heavy in weight	still persists
circle around	necessary requirements	sum total
climb up	now at this time	very unique
completely destroyed	past history	wild savages
covered all over	return again	young baby
different varieties	round circle	youthful teenager

Haste makes—well, everybody knows what. In the rush of a first draft, when we're trying to get our ideas down before they're forgotten, we often write more than we need to. We may introduce examples with "such as . . ." and then follow them with "and so forth," not recognizing that the phrases are redundant. We may write "the surroundings of our environment proved to be exciting," unaware (for the moment) that our surroundings *are* our environment and that the "to be" is wasted. Revision, a less heated process, allows us to see the waste and trim the final version: "Our surroundings were exciting."

Guideline

Trim wasteful words. Make every word do all it can.

Revision Practice: Concise Wording

Revise this essay for economy.

ROMANTIC ABIDJAN

1   Since the summer season is on its way, I am about to

2   take you along on a one-day trip. It won't last very long,

3   and I'm sure you will find it worth thinking about and

4   considering as a place where you might enjoy taking a summer

5   vacation some summer.

6   The destination we are going to is Abidjan, the capital

7   of the Ivory Coast, along the coast of West Africa.

8   At the dawn of the morning our plane touches ground.

9 The tiny little airport is similar to many others, but you

10 will soon come to see that Abidjan, though small in size,

11 is a place unique and unlike any other. Young boys running

12 around barefooted in a hasty manner have an eagerness to

13 take our luggage to a car.

14   After ten minutes of driving we come to a stream of

15 running water, where folks wash their clothes and spread

16 them on the grass while they bathe themselves in the water.

17 Farther down the road we share a glimpse of typical African

18 lifestyle at a colorful market, Treshville. Here one can

19 find all of life's necessary requirements. We stop to buy

20 many different varieties of ivory jewels as well as colorful

21 African shirts, called bubu.

22   As the midday sun's heat gets hotter, we make our way

23 to the car, wiping the sweat off our faces and carrying our

24 purchases in the other hand. Our car stops in front of a

25 fourteen-story pointed building. The building is the

26 largest hotel in Africa, the Hotel Ivoire.

27   In a hotel restaurant we have lunch. We have Acheke

28 poisson, the national food. It is made of barley and rice

29 sided by a grilled fish. We take a sip of a cool glass of

30 pineapple juice to satisfy our thirst.

31   After an hour's rest, we drive the car past many

32 numerous tiny villages where people live in huts made out of

33 bamboo. When we come to the coconut trees full of ripe

34 coconuts, we get out of the car to walk barefoot on the

35 white burning sand. We smell the crisp sea air from the

36 ocean. As big five-foot waves come crushing on our feet, our

37 first impulse is to dive into the blue-colored salty water.

38 We break a coconut and drink the milk. We lie down on the

39 sand admiring the furious surf. Even the crabs move freely

40 and unimpeded on the deserted beach. As the sun is going

41 down we feel a peace of mind.

42   Without a word we drive back to the airport in silence.

43   As our flight number is called, we look at each other.   We

44   must be having the same thought, that one day is not

45   sufficient enough. As we step out into the starry night

46   toward the plane, deep down in our hearts we know we must

47   return again to Abidjan.

Follow-up

Brevity is courtesy. Once we've mentioned "summer," no reader needs to be told it's a season. And when we've said it's "a one-day trip," to say that "it won't last very long" is no compliment to a reader's intelligence. Your revision has probably reduced the first paragraph to about thirty words from the original forty-eight, trimming the redundancy of "thinking about and considering," the wasted "taking," and the repeated "summer" (three times in the paragraph). If you have trimmed the redundant "destination we are going to" and "along the coast" (lines 6 and 7), you've saved eight words and have lost no meaning. Remember that "dawn" is always "morning," what's "tiny" is always "little," and what's "small" is so "in size" unless said to be otherwise. Have you cut "and unlike any other" (line 11) and "around" and "in a hasty manner" (line 12)? Your final version should have cut more than a hundred words from the original 480.

Concise Phrasing

Word groups have a way of cutting grooves in our minds. When we have a thought, it's likely to use the old grooves, so much easier than to cut new ones. So we develop a vocabulary of well-worn phrases, and we may write like this:

> Many times in this modern world of today we come to the realization that we cannot find true fulfillment because of the fact that we are at the mercy of machines in the first place.

Some of the worn phrases can be replaced by single words: "many times" means *often,* "come to the realization that" means *realize,* "because of the fact that" means *because,* and "true fulfillment" means only *fulfillment.* Other phrases can be dropped entirely: "in this modern world of today," "come to the realization that," and "in the first place." Our revision looks like this:

> Often we cannot find fulfillment because we are at the mercy of machines.

The original had too much fat in its diet. With concise phrasing we have reduced the sentence from thirty-five words to thirteen, without the loss of anything but flab. Here are a few more of those overweight phrases:

all of a sudden	(suddenly)	in consideration of	(considering)
a number of	(many)	in order to	(to)
any one of the two	(either)	inside of	(inside)
as a matter of fact	(indeed)	in the event that	(if)
as of yet	(yet)	in the near future	(soon)
at the present time	(now)	in today's world	(today)
at which time	(when)	is at	(is)
be of the opinion that	(think)	later on	(later)
best of all	(best)	off of	(off)
by the name of	(named)	on the basis of	(by)
come in contact with	(meet)	on the part of	(by)
come to realize	(realize)	pay a visit to	(visit)
due to the fact that	(because)	plan on	(plan)
during the time that	(while)	prior to	(before)
first of all	(first)	put in an appearance	(appear)
for the purpose of	(for)	without a doubt	(surely)
for the reason that	(because)	with the result that	(so that)
in all sincerity	(sincerely)	with regard to	(regarding)

Although such a phrase may now and then lend rhythm or emphasis, the shorter forms are generally better.

Our phrase "true fulfillment" is from another category of deadwood: the empty modifier. Words like *true, real, total, definite, actual, genuine,* and their adverb forms (*truly, really, totally,* and so on) are often used for emphasis. But the emphasis is seldom needed and may even make readers suspect an attempt to strengthen a weak point. Suppose we've written a first draft with such phrases as these:

> The movie arouses *real excitement.* Its *actual story* combines with a *definitely skillful* direction and *genuinely competent* acting to make it a *true hit.*

The empty modifiers emphasize too insistently. Trimming them in revision may give the style both brevity and believability:

> The movie arouses excitement. Its story combines with skillful direction and competent acting to make it a hit.

Readable writing uses such modifiers only when they contribute wanted effect.

Guideline

11 Trim flabby phrasing and empty modifiers.

Revision Practice: Concise Phrasing

Revise this essay, giving special attention to economy of expression.

OF THE EGO AND HUMAN FRAILTY

1 We human beings often have a tendency toward being very

2 self-centered and egotistical. We feel that the only way to

3 get ahead and progress in life is to struggle alone by

4 ourselves instead of cooperating together with others. But,

5 however, any event of the tragic sort that occurs in our

6 lives usually brings us to a greater closeness with our

7 fellow beings.

8 A few years ago, during the time that I was living with

9 my parents, my mother and father constantly quarreled all

10 the time between themselves. They practically disagreed

11 about almost everything. But one of the main problems they

12 had that my parents quarreled about was my grandmother, my

13 father's mother. My mother never liked my grandmother, and

14 my grandmother never liked my mother. Their aversion for

15 one another caused a lot of fights and disagreements between

16 my two parents.

17 One day my parents were having a really intense

18 argument about my grandmother. The whole situation was

19 extremely unpleasant and upsetting. It was so bad that my

20 father, being in a terrible rage, made some really violent

21 comment, and he slammed the door and left the house.

22   My mother stewed around for hours, continuing to mumble

23 and saying she hoped my father never came back again. But

24 all of a sudden that evening she got a phone call that came

25 from a doctor working at the emergency hospital. My father

26 had been struck by a car on the street. My mother then went

27 into a frenzy of concern. She forgot all about wishing my

28 father would never come home. She hurried quickly down to

29 the hospital to see whether my father was all right.

30 Luckily, my father was, except that he had only a broken

31 leg.

32   It must have been at that time that my parents came to

33 the realization that bickering makes people unhappy and

34 edgy, and thus makes us vulnerable to all sorts of

35 accidental happenings that can be injurious or even fatal.

36 Life is too short to waste on unhappiness. People are

37 basically what we have to give us a sense of worth and the

38 comfort of love, and life is too fragile and too precious to

39 jeopardize by making ourselves nervous and also accident

40 prone.

41   From that day on into the future my mother and father

42 always worked out any problems that arose in their lives by

43 discussing them calmly and serenely.

44   I am of the opinion that we human beings often

45 definitely need some disaster or tragedy to bring us to an

46 awareness of our frailty and of how easy it is for us to

47 lose our lives.   It is at the time of crisis that we come to

48 realize how much we need each other to survive in this world

49 and create an environment of happiness.

Follow-up

Recheck our list of wasteful phrases to make sure you have cut the deadwood from the essay. Have you trimmed away empty modifiers such as *true, real, actual, definitely*? Since "self-centered" and "egotistical" (line 2) mean the same, are both needed? And what of "get ahead" and "progress" (line 3), "but, however" (lines 4–5)? Redundancies like "constantly . . . all the time" (lines 9–10) and "practically . . . almost" (lines 10–11) should have been cut. Problems aren't problems unless we have them, so "they had" (lines 11–12) should have been dropped. You should have cut the original essay of 463 words to not more than three hundred words—not leaving out any of its essentials.

Lesson 12

Concise
Statement

Repetition is a powerful device. It engages the mind, and it sticks in the memory. Had Abraham Lincoln avoided repetition, we would not have the memorable line about our democracy: "of the people, by the people, and for the people." But like any other powerful device, repetition is not to be misused. If we repeat words or ideas without purpose, if we restate the trivial or the merely obvious, we annoy our readers and risk losing them to less boring pursuits. Consider this paragraph from the first draft of an essay:

Getting a traffic ticket can put you in a lot of trouble. First of all the traffic ticket can raise your insurance. It is not worth fighting city hall for the ticket, even if you think that you were not at fault. It just does not pay to fight the ticket. But when you get a ticket and you decide to fight the ticket, there are certain things you have to do before you go to fight it in court.

Readers are annoyed before they finish that much and probably will read no more. We have to trim the repetitions, find other ways of naming "the ticket," and get to the point fast. A revision may go like this:

> Getting a traffic ticket can put you in trouble and raise your insurance rates. To avoid that possibility, you may want to fight city hall. But even if you're sure you were not at fault, it won't pay to contest the citation unless you do certain things before you go to court.

Now "the citation" keeps us from repeating "the ticket," and "go to court" avoids our having to say "fight" again. The paragraph is much more readable.

We waste words (and our readers' time) when we write in circles. Consider this from a hasty first draft:

> A technological advancement in computer use is now in full progress. Because of new innovations and ideas, this can create great advancements in computer technology.

First we note the phrase "new innovations," wasteful because all innovations are new. Then we see that "this" must mean either the technological advancement or the innovations and ideas; if it means the advancement, then we're saying that "advancement can create great advancements"—a *tautology*, talking in a circle. We need to revise and trim:

> Because of recent innovations, a technological advancement in computer use is now in progress.

Consider two other first-draft tautologies:

> Adequate assistance could be of great help to people.

> Thought is a mental process that lies within the reasoning of the mind.

Sometimes, perhaps in these two cases, the best revision is omission, since the statements say virtually nothing.

Sentences can grow wasteful in other ways, too. One of them is the *passive voice*, a way of focusing on what receives an action rather than on what acts:

> Headache pills were taken by the billions in America last year.

The headache pills didn't act, the Americans did. If we revise using the *active voice*, we say who acted—and we save some words:

> Americans took billions of headache pills last year.

Sometimes, of course, we want the emphasis on the receiver and not on the doer, especially when the receiver is more important or more notable:

Howard Cosell was criticized by some fans recently.

Some fans criticized Howard Cosell recently.

Though shorter, the active voice is not better unless it puts the emphasis in the right place.

We may be able to trim overweight sentences by watching for "who," "that," "which," and the ever-present "there are":

People *who are* in love may neglect other interests.

Every event *that is* important is covered by the *Times*.

Florida, *which is* near Cuba, harbors many refugees.

There are a lot of people *who are* dependent on welfare.

Revisions save words:

People in love may neglect other interests.

Every important event is covered by the *Times*.

Florida, near Cuba, harbors many refugees.

A lot of people depend on welfare.

And, if we revise for active voice at the same time, we get still trimmer results:

The *Times* covers every important event.

Wasteful Signposting

Public speakers often find it helpful to guide their listeners along the path of ideas by using such devices as "Next, let me turn to . . ." or "Now, in conclusion, let me say. . . ." These signpost devices are less helpful in writing, since readers already have the help of titles, paragraphing, and sometimes subheadings. As readers approach the end of an essay, they can generally see that they are reading the last paragraph; they needn't be told that the end is coming.

Perhaps in a first draft of an essay we may use signposts to guide ourselves through our ideas, to keep ourselves on track. In revising we can save words and usually improve the whole effect by cutting them out. Signposts add words but do not add ideas.

Still less defensible in writing are such labels as "It is true to say . . ." and "in my opinion. . . ." If we write a statement, it will be assumed (unless we say otherwise) that we consider it true or that it is our opinion.

Sentence Length

Though there is no limit to the potential length of a good sentence, any over-loading of ideas into a single sentence may make it unwieldy. Readers need a chance to take in one thought before they are rushed headlong into another. See what can happen:

> Although experience can be considered valuable, it is not always positive, and unfortunately some people learn the hard way, as a friend of mine did when he wanted to experience drugs and overdosed one night, having to be saved by paramedics, and later admitted that his eagerness for "experience" was foolish, because, though the school of experience is not always fatal, negative experience can be harmful and too costly to be worth whatever it is one tries to gain from it.

A careful revision may sort the ideas into briefer sentences that can be read without a gasp for air:

> Although experience can be considered valuable, it is not always positive. Unfortunately some people learn the hard way. A friend of mine, who wanted to experience drugs, overdosed one night and had to be saved by paramedics. He later admitted that his eagerness for "experience" was foolish. The school of experience is not always fatal, but negative experience can be harmful and too costly to be worth whatever one tries to gain from it.

Here's another rambling rose:

> In reference to McCarthy's article in *Newsweek,* "Ousting the Stranger from the House," my opinion is, in light of the fact that I don't own a television, that if I have knowledge of, either by coincidence, allocated spare time, or otherwise, and I manage to plop myself in front of the TV to view a broadcast which I feel either is pertinent to a given situation, of aesthetic value, or entertaining in a pleasurable way, I will admit, I appreciate the TV for what it's worth.

This writer has asked readers to put several thoughts "on hold" while others are coming in. We don't find out what "have knowledge of" refers to until twenty-one words later—"a broadcast." The ornate and wordy paragraph has a pretentious tone and is far from readable writing.

Guideline

Cut useless repetition. Trim wasteful "there are," "who," "that," and "which" clauses. Watch for wordy passive voice and over-loaded sentences.

Revision Practice: Concise Statement

Revise this essay for economy.

LIBERTY AS SELF-CONTROL

1   <u>Liberty</u> is a word that is often misinterpreted and

2   hence, therefore, abused. If we are to use that term

3   meaningfully, it will be a necessary requirement for us to

4   take a look at what liberty implies and get in mind a clear

5   concept of the idea and what it implies.

6   Some people continue to persist in their thinking that

7   liberty means being entirely free of any control whatsoever,

8   that a free person is one who can do as he pleases. In that

9   view of the matter a free person is one who is not, like a

10   horse or an ox, under the control of another, but is one who

11   is not held back or pushed forward or turned this way or

12   that. But to be free of any control is to live outside the

13   social contract, and anyone, to be free of responsibilities

14   to others, must live quite entirely alone.

15   First of all, it is only in the imagination of our

16   minds that we can give our thought to considering a society

17   that has no laws, no police, no government, since nowhere

18   does total and complete absolute anarchy exist, and if we

19   do imagine a state of anarchy, then we must see that a

20   person who lives in that state is at liberty to come or go,

21   work or loaf, be truthful or lie, buy or steal, cause either

22   joy or pain, and cause either life or death--all without

23 having the responsibility to answer to others. But he must

24 live in uncertainty and fear, since the others need not

25 necessarily answer to him either. He may at any moment in

26 time be inconvenienced, pained, injured, robbed, or even

27 actually killed by others as they pursue their own

28 irresponsible living of their lives.

29   Within the social contract among people, we live by a

30 mutual surrendering to one another of what we have called

31 liberty. Willingly we submit to restraints placed on our

32 behavior, accepting those limits in exchange for the

33 benefits we can gain from restraints upon the behavior of

34 others. In other words, laws and social agreements are set

35 up and established to control us, rules that we agree to

36 follow and we expect others to follow so that we can more

37 easily foretell and predict what will happen to have an

38 effect upon our lives.

39   By such social contract some of our freedoms are

40 relinquished and given up by us. But their loss is balanced

41 by some gains: Our probabilities of such desirables as

42 safety and happiness, long life and prosperity, and etc.,

43 are increased. Of course, these gains are not absolutely

44 guaranteed; they are only made more likely.

45   Liberty, then, is undesirable when it implies lack of

46 control of any kind. Only that liberty is desirable which

47 implies control, restraint, limits. Such control, of

48 course, is best when managed not by others, not by a state,

49 not by police, not by outside force, but by the self. The

50 greatest of liberty, then, is self-control of the individual

51 over himself. Unless we act with self-control, we give up

52 our liberty and submit to forces outside ourselves or to the

53 unbearable consequences that follow from anarchy.

Follow-up

When your revision is finished, read it with careful attention to economy of expression and to tone. The revised version is certainly briefer (the original has just over five hundred words; yours should be no more than four hundred). Is the revision more emphatic, easier to read? Have you cut "that is" (line 1)? Do "hence" and "therefore" (line 2) mean about the same thing? Did you write "must look" instead of "it will be a necessary requirement for us to take a look (lines 3–4) and "think" instead of "continue to persist in their thinking" (line 6)? Doesn't "responsibility" (line 23) imply answering to others? Did you use active voice instead of the passive in lines 34–35 and 39–40? Did you write "affect" instead of "happen to have an effect upon" (lines 37–38)? Since consequences are what follow (line 53), did you write "unbearable consequences of anarchy"? What did you do about the long, overloaded sentence in lines 15–23?

Summary
Revising for Economy

Guidelines 10–12

10. Trim wasteful words. Make every word do all it can.

11. Trim flabby phrasing and empty modifiers.

12. Cut useless repetition. Trim wasteful "there are," "who," "that," and "which" clauses. Watch for wordy, passive voice and overloaded sentences.

Writing and Revising

For detailed suggestions on getting started, writing a first draft, revising the draft, and preparing the essay for submission, refer to the Introduction. Choose one of the following topics.

Topics for Writing

1. What distinguishes a profession from a job? Cite as many as you can of the qualifications that distinguish a professional from a nonprofessional. Jot a list of your ideas and devise a thesis on the topic. Select a purpose (such as *definition* or *contrast*, or a combination); then number the ideas in an appropriate order and write a first draft.

2. We are not born with "common sense." How do we develop it? By what traits can we identify someone who appears to lack common sense? Jot a list of your ideas and devise a thesis on the topic. Select a purpose (such as *definition*); then number the ideas in an appropriate order and write a first draft.

3. What do you think can be done to reduce the blight of graffiti in your town? Jot a list of your ideas and devise a thesis on the topic. Select a purpose (such as *analyzing cause and effect* or *arguing to convince*). Number the ideas in an appropriate order and write a first draft.

4. Henry David Thoreau once wrote, "A man is rich in proportion to the number of things which he can afford to do without." Consider things often thought essential in everyday life (newspaper, television, mail, automobile, telephone, shoes, friends, books—you name it). Which do you think you (possibly all of us) could well do without? Jot a list of your ideas. The thesis is suggested. Select a purpose (such as *division* or *arguing to convince*). Number the ideas in an appropriate order and write a first draft.

Follow-up

Read your first draft with special attention to economy of style. Review the list of redundancies in Lesson 10 and the list of empty modifiers in Lesson 11 and make sure you have avoided them. If you have used any passive voice, try revising with active voice instead. Look for wasteful use of "who," "that," "which," or "there are." If any sentence is longer than about twenty-five words, make sure you haven't tried to load too many ideas into it.

Review Quiz

In this quiz you may find wasteful wording, flabby phrasing, empty modifiers, useless repetition, "there are" and "who-that-which" clauses, wordy passive voice, and overloaded sentences. In the first five the trouble spots have been italicized; later you must find them yourself. Revise to make every sentence briefer and more readable.

1. Racism, *which is* dangerous, is an emotional reaction *that may enter certain situations.*

2. The *play presentation* was *of a very short duration,* and all *who were in the audience* were *full of eagerness* to see *still more.*

3. Having childcare provided *for their children* gives mothers the time to *work at a job* and *be able to* support their families.

4. *In many employment situations* if an employer *who hires employees* doesn't hire a certain minority *based on the fact that* the employer doesn't like *that minority,* he is ignoring the rights of *minorities.*

5. *It was* then *that* we *came to understand* what the *person who was leading* the group wanted *in the way of action.*

6. In the last analysis being simply honest and aboveboard is best of all the ways of behaving if you plan on keeping a good friendship.

7. In final conclusion, the harmful habits that have been acquired can be broken if as an individual one exerts sufficient enough willpower on himself.

8. The church minister, who had an amiable quality about him, had the ability at last to draw the large multitude into a concerted action together.

9. Probably I must have had a very red-looking face just at that time, for the reason that I knew that my friends had been embarrassed by my remark.

10. Being the head of a large family, my mother came to the decision that in order to reduce transportation problems that were confronting us, we needed to buy another car.

11. If the patient in question is covered all over with a skin rash, the doctor may put on an application of cortisone and then see whether the condition still persists.

12. Inasmuch as the recruiting program to find new players has not at all been completely successful, the team may find it to be impossible to win the championship title this season.

13. There are some people among our number who are in fear of being anywhere on the streets for the reason that they may happen to get mugged.

14. Just then all of a sudden there was a noisy piercing scream that was apparently shouted by one of the girls who had left the camp and gone off on a short little hike.

15. I have never as of yet been able to understand why there are so many joggers who like to run around breathing in the smog in the air.

16. It was definitely a real blow to the team's hopes for the season when Sammy Urmston fell down on the court during a game and broke an ankle bone.

17. All kinds of various emotions were mixed together in me, and I had never had a feeling of such excitement prior to that.

18. One young person in her teens, who was obviously too much over-excited, kept getting animatedly in front of the camera.

19. Neither of the two twins, as a matter of fact, had any intention to cast a vote for the actual amendment.

20. At sometime in the near future there will without a doubt be in existence a situation in which some deranged person will probably push the panic button.

21. After making a study of the question of the need for one-way streets in this community, I am genuinely of the opinion that we should vote against them.

22. In the case of an emergency what is truly needed is thinking that is done on the basis of efficiency.

23. The really competent worker always respects the necessary tools that are required to do the job, whatever it may be.

24. What struck me with amazement was that the huge structure spanning the Golden Gate required such an enormous amount of maintenance to keep it up.

25. Our society around us holds the belief that money is an essential thing, but, however, I am not entirely convinced of that essential need, and I would like to suggest that if money were entirely eliminated from our societies, we would no doubt adapt to living without it, because barter and other forms of exchange would still be possible and less worrisome than money itself, the love of which, as the tradition tells us, is the root of all evil, and certainly the world would be better off without it.

Revising for

Emphasis

*The art of writing depends a good
deal on putting the strongest words in
the most important places.*
F. L. Lucas (1894–1967)

We tend to notice what stands out
from its surroundings. One white cloud in a blue sky will draw our attention.
So will a shout that breaks the silence. We are easily drawn to the unexpected.

But an essay cannot be one white cloud or a single shout. When we write,
we blend many ingredients: a topic, a purpose, a point, and many contributing
details. We need to make the important ones stand out.

Emphasis begins, of course, with having something worth saying. If our
point is dull, emphatic statement of it will only make its dullness obvious.
Emphasis builds as we put things in clear and proper order. And there are
still further ways of making ideas stand out: We can put them in noticeable
places, shine a spotlight on them, stress them by repetition.

The most noticeable places in an essay are the beginning and the end. The
same is true in paragraphs and sentences. We can, then, revise for emphasis
by giving careful attention to beginnings and endings. But the middle of an

essay, the "body" of it, will also present details worthy of an emphasis of their own. We can shine smaller spotlights as we go, making ideas or details stand out by contrast to one another or by carefully repeating, as a song repeats rhythms, melodies, and words.

Surely an emphatic style, if it makes a worthy point and contributes to understanding and enjoyment, helps to make an essay readable.

Lesson 13

Catching Attention: Titles and Beginnings

No matter how worthy our writing is, it cannot reach an audience without catching their attention. And the best place to engage that attention is at the beginning.

What will be read first, of course, is the title. By the title we advertise what is to come, so we want those few words to entice the reader. Our title should do four jobs: (1) catch attention, (2) introduce the topic, (3) suggest the thesis, and (4) establish the tone.

1. *Catch attention.* A title must be easy to read; if it's not, readers may assume that the whole essay will be tough going. A good title may ensure readability by using familiar phrasing, something people will recognize quickly. But it must also have something new, something to suggest that what's to come is not just old stuff.

   Familiar phrases from history, literature, politics, sports—almost anything people know about—are fair game for use in a title. When Carl Bernstein and Bob Woodward wrote their book about the Watergate scandal, they remembered a line about Humpty Dumpty and changed it to *All the President's Men.* One student wrote about a gift she received at Christmas and how it brought her an unwanted reputation when she wore it. She called the essay "The Scarlet Sweater," using a twist on the classic title by Nathaniel Hawthorne.

The unexpected catches attention. If a title can introduce a familiar thought and then offer a surprise, it will do that part of its job.

2. *Introduce the topic.* A good title suggests what the essay is about. A mere label such as "Essay" or "English Assignment" won't do. The title must not promise what the essay cannot or does not deliver. If the title is "Love" or "Life's Troubles," the reader has a right to expect much more than any brief essay could cover.

3. *Suggest the thesis.* A title should hint at our central point—what we want readers to remember most. The hint need not be too strong, but it must be there. When readers have finished the essay, they should be able to see that the title foretold the thesis. Consider some titles that don't do the job and a few that do:

Forecasting the Weather	The Weather Guessers
My Unforgettable Holiday	Thanks, Turkey!
The Death Penalty	Society's Killer Instinct
Being a Twin	Two's a Crowd
A Male Look at Sexual Equality	How Can Men Get Even?
How My Hometown Influenced Me	A Wallflower Grows in Brooklyn

Clearly the titles in the second column give the reader a hint of their essays' likely points.

4. *Establish the tone.* Our attitude toward the topic should be built into the title, however subtly. We certainly do not want to write a somber title for a funny essay or vice versa. All the titles in the second column above give the reader a strong hint of the writer's attitude toward the topic; those in the first column do not (even "My Unforgettable Holiday" doesn't suggest whether the holiday was a pleasant or a bad experience).

The opening paragraph of an essay must do more thoroughly what the title has done by suggestion. It won't catch attention by giving readers what they already know; nor can it focus that attention if it doesn't get directly to the topic. A strong, emphatic beginning suggests the thesis and sets the tone for the whole essay. Here are some essay titles and beginnings by professional writers whose works often appear in college reader-texts. Let's see how they catch attention, introduce the topic, suggest the thesis, and establish the tone.

The Trouble With Baseball

The trouble with baseball is that it grew up and became engineering. When the country loved it with a passion, baseball was boyhood eternal, all bluster, innocence and bravado flashing across green meadows in the sunlight. The whole game was suffused with a mythic sense so gross that only boyhood could entertain it.

Russell Baker

Why Can't Computers Be More Like Us?

Everyone must have had at least one personal experience with a computer error by this time. Bank balances are suddenly reported to have jumped from 379 dollars into the millions, appeals for charitable contributions are mailed over and over to people with crazy-sounding names at your address, utility companies write that they're turning everything off—that sort of thing.

Lewis Thomas

How Language Shapes Our Thoughts

Language, more than any other human trait, makes us human, distinguishes us from all other creatures.

Stuart Chase

How to Find Fault With a Dictionary

It is probably fair to say that most present-day Americans show rather more respect for the dictionary than they do for the Bible. It is significant that we speak of "the dictionary" rather than "a dictionary," as if there were only one. When we say, "The dictionary says so," we feel that we have settled the matter once and for all, that we have carried the appeal to the final authority.

Paul Roberts

Not all of us will respond equally to these titles and beginnings, but we will probably admit that they are not mere platitudes, do suggest a thesis, do set an engaging tone.

Let's turn now to a first-draft beginning for an essay on what it takes to pursue a hobby for fun and profit:

Hobbies

There are many different hobbies in the world. Many of them are interests begun early in our lives and continued through the years. Others are taken up only when we have gained the background of knowledge they require or the money to support them. Anyway, a hobby is a healthful thing to have.

The title is weak, does not suggest a thesis or establish any tone; it is scarcely more than a label. And the beginning paragraph obviously needs work. Its opening sentence is a *truism*, a statement nobody will argue with, but it is hardly worth saying. The paragraph does not get to the real topic (what a hobby requires of us) and does not suggest the point (which is that a satisfying hobby is not pursued halfheartedly). The opening needs to be revised so that it will catch attention. If possible, the title and first sentence should offer an engaging challenge:

Lifelong Love

A satisfying hobby is a love affair, not to be neglected. To pursue one with pleasure and gratifying profit calls for devotion—and a few other personal qualities—and what you give to your hobby is what you get back, almost without limit.

Now the reader is set up to hear about those other qualities in detail.
Tickle the reader's mind. Offer a challenge. Promise something to come. Those are the ways to catch attention at the beginning of an essay.

Guideline

 Make your title and first paragraph challenge your readers. Introduce your topic, suggest your thesis, and establish your tone.

Revision Practice: Catching Attention

These ten titles and first paragraphs are dull beginnings. Revise each to ensure catching attention.

1.
REGULAR EXERCISE

```
     There are many kinds of physical exercise, and a lot of
people are pursuing some kind of fitness program these days.
Most of them are good for health if suited to the individual's
needs, but it is possible to do the body harm if the exercise is
not wisely chosen or is overdone.
```

2.   LEARNING BY EXPERIENCE

     Experience can be a wonderful thing. We get it by opening
our senses to life. We use our eyes to see. We use our ears to
hear. We use our whole bodies to touch. Our minds remember
these experiences, and thus we learn. But we can do more. We
can also do things, move about in the world and see, hear, and
feel more. Naturally some of what we experience will be bad.
Experience can be a horrifying thing.

3.   WAX CASTING

     There are certain things that have to be known and learned in
order to master any skill. Making anything, such as jewelry,
dentures, or art works, can be a difficult task without learning
how. One of these skills is wax casting. It is used in all the
above processes and many more.

4.   GUIDING PRINCIPLES

     Many times a law, or principle, is useful in life. Having a
law to guide us provides us with the ability to predict certain
events. Surprises, often unhappy, are thus avoided. An example
is the Law of Gravity. Thanks to our knowledge of that law, no
object will fool us by crashing unexpectedly to the ground.
Another is Murphy's Law: "If anything can go wrong, it will."
That law keeps us humble, knowing that we must not be careless.

5.   THE MEANING OF LIFE

     A great deal about life is unknown. There will always be
something more to learn or discover. The human mind is capable
of comprehending only so much at a given time. For this reason
we will always be acquiring new scientific knowledge. I don't
think there can ever be a truthful conclusion about the meaning
of life for everyone. But I am sure we should not give up
looking.

6.   PRIVATE LIVES

     It is not easy to write about a topic like privacy, because
who can say how much privacy you should have? As long as you
are going to be a part of society, you will have to be around
people almost every day. Almost every job has to do with other

people. How much you can control your own privacy is a very
tough question. From the minute you are born, your name becomes
a number in somebody's file.

7.   WRONG IDEAS

    Most people believe that their first impression of others
very reliable. Some believe that they can tell at first sight
what a person's character is. This belief in first impressions
is not always reliable. Though they are sometimes accurate,
still more often those impressions have to be revised.

8.   DIFFERENCES

    It is incredible how vast life is. There are so many
creatures. Yet no two of the beings in life's garden are quite
alike. There are many forms that lend variety, color, and
dimension. I believe that unless all the life forms are equally
nourished, the garden will diminish in size and uniqueness. The
differences among things are important and to be cherished.

9.   GUILTY

    Lots of people feel guilty about lying. Guilt can be good
or bad, depending on the person, the situation, and the lie.
The heavy beating of your heart, the perspiration on your forehead and the slurring of your speech come along with guilt. You
are not alone, for many other people have this same problem.

10.   POVERTY

    To be poor is believed by many to be an unpleasant thing.
I have heard people say that poverty is cruel, but I'm not so
sure. Isn't wealth, with its continuing struggle to earn and
keep, still more cruel? The poor, choosing to be "have-nots,"
avoid the curse of ambition, which condemns the "haves" to
constant expectation and a driving need to be other than poor.
The rich therefore, must struggle. But the poor accept their
poverty and do not struggle. Wealth can be maintained only by
work and responsibility. By comparison, poverty is easy
street.

Follow-up

Titles are best written when the essay is finished, when we know what we've
said and how we've said it. Still, you may have written some arousing titles for
these opening paragraphs. To begin the paragraphs, you should have pounced

quickly upon the *truisms,* the vapid remarks that draw only a "We know, but so what?" response. Everybody knows "there are many kinds of physical exercise," that "experience can be a wonderful thing," and so on. We want to challenge readers, not just state the obvious. Your title and your beginning paragraph should make you an author they can't refuse. But take care not to attract attention just for its own sake. In number 10 you must decide whether the point is to be taken seriously or as irony; both the title and the opening paragraph must set a tone that makes a reader understand how to take it.

Direct Statement

Readable writing puts ideas directly, not timidly. As mature writers we must take responsibility for our ideas. If we are wavering and uncertain, readers will not take us seriously. We need an authoritative yet modest tone.

This matter of tone is central to the readability of our writing. We certainly don't want to seem opinionated or conceited, since nobody likes a know-it-all. But if we go out of our way to apologize for our opinions, readers will sense that we have not given solid thought to the topic, and our style will lack vigor.

When we express an opinion, it should be well founded; then we won't have to be apologetic. Careful researching of our topics is a first step; clear thinking is another. If we have taken both steps, we need not fear being challenged—and should welcome it. Modesty is to be valued, and a genial *maybe* can keep us from seeming egotistical about ideas; still, we should set our ideas down firmly without having to hedge.

Hedging means setting up a cautious defense in case our ideas don't stand on their merits. We hedge with words and phrases like these:

In my opinion our national defense system is in trouble.

Of course, *I may be wrong*, but the courts *seem* too lenient.

It is possible that violence is due to inner rage or fear.

Traumatic experience *may be said to have* an effect on later behavior.

This last example avoids responsibility. Who says traumatic experience affects later behavior? In effect, nobody says it; it just "may be said."

This kind of indirection, the grammatical *passive voice*, occurs when the subject of a sentence is not the doer of the action. "I know this fact" is active, since *I* do the knowing. "This fact is well known" is passive, since those who know it remain unnamed—and possibly nonexistent. Indeed, the fact we speak of may not be a fact at all. Thus the passive voice lends itself to the uses of deception.

It *is widely believed* that our defense system is in trouble.

The criminal courts *are considered* too lenient.

Violence *is thought* to be due to inner rage or fear.

Just *who* believes or considers or thinks those things? If we don't hold the opinion, who does? We need to say who—or take the responsibility ourselves—with direct, active-voice statements:

Our national defense system is in trouble.

The author of *Victims Unite* says the criminal courts are too lenient.

Psychologist Tom Benton thinks violence is due to inner rage or fear.

That kind of direct, unhedged statement requires, of course, that we do our homework, that we know the facts and their sources and report them directly.

Euphemism is another sort of indirect statement. We hesitate to tread on sensitive toes, so we hide harsh thoughts behind soft words:

Lack of appropriate sanitary conditions makes *the inner city* an *unhealthful* place to live.

Direct statement would "tell it like it is":

Uncollected garbage, unrepaired plumbing, open sewage, and infestation by rats expose slum residents to disease.

Not all euphemism is bad. We'd be foolish as well as crude to insist on calling the handicapped person a *cripple* or the dead body a *corpse*. Pleasant words make the harsh world livable. But to use euphemism for deliberate deception is to avoid responsibility.

So we face a difficult problem of readability: how to establish a tone of justified authority without seeming arrogant. One way to solve that problem is to cut all hedging, passive statement, and euphemism out of an essay as we revise, and then judge our effect. If any statement seems unjustified without those devices, then we should consider cutting the statement entirely; it may be untrue or ill considered.

Readers have a right to our honest judgment and forthright presentation of ideas. A modest *perhaps* or *possibly* can help us avoid seeming overpositive, but obvious hedging, evasive use of the passive, or deceptive euphemism will dilute emphasis and weaken our style.

Guideline

 Be sparing in your use of hedging, apology, passive voice, and euphemism—and never use any of these to hide important truth.

Revision Practice: Direct Statement

Read this essay carefully with special attention to hedging, passive voice, and deceptive euphemism. Revise the essay to eliminate such indirections and give the writing more vitality and emphasis.

MISTAKES

1   Technological civilization perhaps has reached its

2   present "advanced" state by the trial-and-error behavior of

3   those who lived before us. Many of the most useful

4   discoveries and inventions were the result of mistakes when

5   people were looking for something else. The New World was

6   found by Columbus, who was really looking for India. The

7   discovery of penicillin was speeded by somebody who left a

8   loaf of bread out to get moldy. Think how far behind

9   ourselves we'd be now if mistakes were impossible for us to

10   make.

11   Our knowledge is also increased by our mistakes, if

12 only because once a mistake has been made, a way of

13 correcting it must be found. If the mistake had not been

14 made by us in the first place, we might have had no reason

15 to learn how things are done. As I wrote the first version

16 of this essay, I made a few minor errors. As a result of my

17 mistakes, since I did discover them, I learned the

18 difference between <u>continuous</u> and <u>continual</u>; I learned that

19 <u>useful</u> has only one <u>l</u> (and that the rule goes for hundreds

20 of other words, like <u>wasteful</u>, <u>harmful</u>, <u>spoonful</u>); and I

21 learned how to use a semicolon when a comma won't do. In my

22 opinion, had I made no mistakes in the first place, I might

23 have had a pretty good essay, but I would still not have

24 known why.

25   Of course, mistakes have to be recognized for what they

26 are. If Columbus had thought San Salvador <u>was</u> India and let

27 things go at that, the world would be smaller today. Had

28 the moldy bread been tossed to the birds, the birds might

29 have become healthy while human life went on suffering from

30 raging diseases. (I realize these statements are somewhat

31 doubtful, but now I'm so curious about Columbus and

32 penicillin that I'm going to learn the real facts

33 tomorrow.)

34   Mistakes are made by computers, but only rarely by

35 comparison with the human brain's continual bumbling. Human

36 beings, one might say, have emotions and desires and

37 prejudices that mistakes are the result of. Those quirks,

38 I think, are not things that computers have. Distraction

39 and fatigue are suffered by human beings but not by

40 computers. So it is possible to say that we are in a bit of

41 danger. If the time should ever come when most of the

42 world's work is done by computers rather than by people,

43 fewer mistakes will be made. And fewer mistakes will mean

44 fewer of those useful discoveries and inventions brought

45 about by the stumblings of the human species.

Follow-up

If you have cut out such hedging as "perhaps" (line 1), "in my opinion" (lines 21–22), "might" (line 28), "one might say" (line 36), "I think" (line 38), "it is possible to say that" (line 40), you've made the essay more emphatic. Still, you may keep one or two of those if you think they contribute justifiably to the essay's tone. Have you used active voice to replace the passive in lines 5–6 and 7–8? (That is, "Columbus found the New World when . . ." and "Somebody left a loaf of bread out to get moldy and thus speeded the discovery of penicillin"). You should have found more passive voice in lines 11, 12, 13, 25, 34, 37, 39, and 42–43, but remember an occasional passive-voice sentence, if not awkward, may be appropriate. Are the phrases "somewhat doubtful" (lines 30–31) and "a bit of danger" (lines 40–41) euphemisms? Is "should ever come" (line 41) a sort of hedging? When your revision is finished, read it over again to judge what the essay has gained in vitality and emphasis.

Effective Repetition

The human mind is fascinated by repetition. The fascination begins in the womb, where the mother's heartbeat is constant reassurance. It continues as long as our own pulse pounds, however silently, sustaining life. The beat of the drum, the rhythm of music, the cadence of language, and the recurrent patterns of sunrise, sunset, and the seasons—all are deep in our being.

Imagine life without repetition. All experience would be unfamiliar. We'd be always away from home, seeing only the new and strange, a continuous and bewildering novelty. We would certainly long for the familiar face, the recognizable voice, the recurrent sights and sounds. Home is comforting—and repetitious.

Yet we face a paradox. Familiarity, so the saying goes, breeds contempt. We soon find home too confining, too repetitious, and we chafe again for the new and different. So, though fascinated by repetition, we can also be bored by it. To discover the line between fascination and boredom and stay on the right side of that line is one of the challenges of life.

That discovery also challenges every writer.

Repetition is powerful. The repeated words and phrases of an Abraham Lincoln or a Martin Luther King resound in our minds. And we are charmed, hypnotized, by the jingle of nursery rhymes and singing commercials. Yes, there is every reason to hold repetition among the most useful of the writer's tools.

Simple Repetition

Now and then the simple repetition of a word or phrase can do wonders to increase the impact of an idea:

> Employers say "no experience necessary," but they don't hire the inexperienced. Their help-wanted ads are lies, lies.

> I want to retreat to simpler times, times when religion dictated belief, times of myths, times of karma.

Here's a sentence that balances several details yet remains unemphatic:

> Some say that aliens take away our jobs, misuse our public welfare, overload our Social Security system, and increase our crime rates; I say they are the convenient scapegoat.

By adding simple repetition of two words, we hammer home the point:

> Some say *that aliens* take away our jobs, *that aliens* misuse our public welfare, *that aliens* overload our Social Security system, *that aliens* increase our crime rates. I say *that aliens* are the convenient scapegoat.

Since it's a narrow line that separates fascination from boredom, repetition of words is at its best when spared for special occasion. We can so easily overdo it. Repetition without purpose is monotony, certainly no mark of readable writing.

Sound Effects

Sounds, too, the smaller components of spoken words, are tools of emphasis. We are all familiar with rhyme, the repetition of end sounds in words that are near together, as in *time* and *climb*, *measure* and *pleasure*, or *devilish* and *licorice*. (Since we speak of sound, the rhymes need not be alike in spelling.) Such rhymes draw attention and stick in the memory, and carefully handled they can bring much to the compressed language of poetry. But prose, the medium of the essay, avoids rhymes. Prose writers, including essayists like ourselves, are more likely to repeat sounds at the beginnings of words, as in *time* and *traffic*, *march* and *measure*, or *devilish* and *dangerous*. This kind of repetition of sounds is what we call *alliteration;* it can often help make a style more engaging, though (like anything else) it can be overdone.

Alliteration adds charm in this paragraph by William Zinsser, who advises us on how to find a variety of words:

> And don't scorn that bulging grab bag, *Roget's Thesaurus.* It's easy to regard the book as hilarious. Look up "villain," for example, and you will . . . find rogues and wretches, ruffians and riffraff, miscreants and malefactors, reprobates and rapscallions, hooligans and hoodlums, scamps and scapegraces, scoundrels and scalawags, jezebels and jades. You will find adjectives to fit them all (foul and fiendish, devilish and diabolical), . . . and cross-references leading to still other thickets of venality and vice. Still, there is no better friend to have around to nudge the memory than Roget.[1]

Repetition of sounds may occur in the middles of words, too, as in *time* and *pride, measure* and *rain,* or *devilish* and *irrelevant.* If the repeated sounds are vowels, it's assonance; if they are consonants, it's called consonance. Both are common in carefully crafted prose. We need not know their names; all we need is the good ear to use them as we write.

Symmetrical Arrangement

What we need is a sort of repetition that satisfies but never bores. Often we can find it in the symmetrical arrangement of ideas.

Balance displays ideas in repeated structures, presenting them as parallels, alternatives, or contrasts.

1. *Parallels.* Abraham Lincoln emphasized his ideas with this kind of balance in the Gettysburg Address:

> *We cannot dedicate—we cannot consecrate, we cannot hallow* this ground.

And he used the same device in his Second Inaugural with the well-remembered line,

> *With malice toward none, with charity for all. . . .*

We too, though brash to list our own in company with Lincoln's, can use parallels in everyday writing, as in the first paragraph of this lesson:

> the *beat of the drum,* the *rhythm of music,* the *cadence of language. . . .*

---

[1] William Zinsser, *On Writing Well* (New York: Harper & Row, 1976), pp. 32–33.

2. *Alternatives.* Another memorable American, Patrick Henry, is famed most of all for one sentence:

> *Give me liberty,* or *give me death!*

And Thomas Jefferson once wrote,

> I like *the dreams of the future* better than *the history of the past.*

3. *Contrasts.* Still another, John F. Kennedy, found balance of contrasts effective in his Inaugural:

> Ask not *what your country can do for you,* but ask *what you can do for your country.*

The German poet Goethe wrote,

> Everybody wants *to be somebody;* nobody wants *to grow.*

This balance of contrasts often goes by another name, *antithesis.*

Many writers use these symmetrical arrangements, making their writing emphatic, readable, memorable. Here's a paragraph from essayist E. B. White:

> There are roughly three New Yorks. There is, *first, the New York* of the man or woman who was born here, who takes the city for granted and accepts its size and its turbulence as natural and inevitable. *Second,* there is *the New York* of the commuter—the city that is devoured by locusts each day and spat out each night. *Third,* there is *the New York* of the person who was born somewhere else and came to New York in quest of something. Of these three trembling cities the greatest is the last—*the city* of final destination, *the city* that is a goal. It is this third city that accounts for New York's *high-strung disposition,* its *poetical deportment,* its *dedication to the arts,* and its *incomparable achievements.* Commuters *give* the city its tidal restlessness, natives *give* it solidity and continuity, but the settlers *give* it passion. And whether it is *a farmer arriving* from Italy to set up a small grocery store in a slum, or *a young girl arriving* from a small town in Mississippi to escape the indignity of being observed by her neighbors, or *a boy arriving* from the Corn Belt with a manuscript in his suitcase and a pain in his heart, it makes no difference: *each embraces* New York with the intense excitement of first love, *each absorbs* New York with the fresh eyes of an adventurer, *each generates* heat and light to dwarf the Consolidated Edison Company [emphasis added].[2]

---

[2] E. B. White, "Here Is New York," in *Essays of E. B. White,* p. 121. Copyright 1949 by E. B. White. Reprinted by permission of Harper & Row Publishers, Inc.

Antithesis often takes the form of a "this, not that" (or "this, rather than that") statement, as in this paragraph by political writer Michael Nelson in an essay on bureaucracy:

> People of all classes—the rich man dealing with the Internal Revenue Service as well as the poor woman struggling with the welfare department—felt that the treatment they had received had been *bungled, not efficient; unpredictable, not rational; discriminatory or idiosyncratic, rather than uniform;* and all too often, *insensitive, rather than courteous* [emphasis added].[3]

To see the effect of revising for balance and antithesis, let's consider a first-draft passage that lacks punch:

> Our streets and homes are no longer safe from burglars, muggers, rapists, and murderers. Our justice and prison systems are a joke. Criminals laugh at the law, the courts, the whole society. Crime is out of control, and the criminals are in charge.

If in revision we use balanced repetition, we get a different effect:

> Our homes are *no longer safe* from burglars, our streets *no longer safe* from muggers, rapists, murderers. Our justice *system is a joke;* our prison *system is a joke.* Criminals *laugh at* the law, *laugh at* the courts, *laugh at* the whole society. *We* do not *have control of crime,* but *crime has control of us.*

By using such careful symmetry of forms—the balance of parallels, alternatives, or contrasts—we can often enhance the impact of our ideas.

Guideline

15 To add emphasis to a passage, consider repetition of words, rhythms, and sounds, as well as symmetry of forms.

Revision Practice: Effective Repetition

Read this essay carefully with special attention to emphasis. Revise to enhance its impact by using devices of repetition. (Use the suggestions in the margin as a guide.)

---

[3]Michael Nelson, "The Desk," *Newsweek*, 16 October 1978, p. 17. Copyright 1978 by Newsweek, Inc. All rights reserved. Reprinted by permission.

1   BEING AWARE

2   I used to assist a high-school friend   *Change "assist" to*

3 deliver newspapers on Sunday mornings. I   *simpler word (alliteration)?*

4 drove as he would wrap papers and would   *Do "would wrap" and "would*

5 throw them onto lawns and porches.   *throw" balance "drove"? Keep tenses simple.*

7   Darkness was heavy at the beginning of

8 the route. Many houses remained dark, their

9 inhabitants sleeping late on Sunday. Few

10 people were on the streets, but now and then

11 I was startled by a passerby and felt   *Are "startled" and*

12 astonishment that he should be out in the   *"astonishment" in the same form?*

13 world so early.   *Can "felt" be cut?*

14   There is a time just as the sun's light

15 is seeping over the horizon when the world

16 takes on a strange and wondrous aspect.

17 Houses glow, as it were, for the light makes

18 them shiny, particularly the white houses.

19 Yards lose their shadowy aspect and suddenly

20 jump from the dark. The light comes rapidly,   *Change "jump" (alliteration with "lose")?*

21 changing the landscape from dark shadow to

22 make it glow softly within a few minutes.   *Does "glow softly" balance "dark shadow"? (Cut "make it")*

23   By then there would be more lights

24 in the houses as we passed, people rising.

25 They would be looking for their newspapers,   *Use balance for details in lines 25–27.*

26 their breakfasts would be under way, and

27 they would be in preparation for their new

28 day.

29   At such moments, I felt as if I were

30 seeing the world for the first time. Just

31 as the world was somewhere between dark and

32 light, I found myself between night and day,

Repetition of "between" may improve line 33.

33 sleeping and waking, the ritual of delivery

34 and the miracle of deliverance. I knew

35 myself different from the people we passed,

36 mere ordinary ones, for I had been up for

Repeat "people" (for "ones") in line 36?

37 hours, seeing a change come over the day

38 that they would miss. I was superior, awake

Repetition of "a change" may improve line 38.

39 when others were not.

40   To be awake is awareness. I have known

Repeat "to be" in line 40 to balance "awake" and "aware"?

41 those who indulged in self-hypnosis as a

42 means of improving their study habits, and

43 they were more awake in that state because

44 they were more aware than those of us who

45 merely wiped the sleep from our eyes and

46 faced a new day as if it were like any

47 other. I suppose it is possible for some to

48 have a certain awareness in their sleep.

49 Perhaps some night sleepers are as awake in

50 that state as the rest of us are at noon.

51   No day is like any other, and the more

52 aware we can become of the differences, so

53 we can call ourselves awake. Now as I go

54 about my midday affairs, the crowds about me

55 are bustling and seemingly awake. Yet since

56 I have known the world in the predawn light,

57 I feel more awake than any of them. I try

58 to see as I saw then, and at every hour

59 being more awake than ordinary people.

Repeat "the more" in lines 52–53?

Should "to be" replace "being" (line 59)?

Follow-up

Read your revision aloud. Does your version seem to have more impact than the original? Where have you made changes not suggested by the margin notes? Might you have added "slowly" in line 15 to further emphasize the rhythm and consonant sounds of "sun's light is seeping"? What word could you use to replace "shiny" (line 18) to achieve alliteration with "light"? How did you balance forms in lines 27–30 (possibly with words like *rising, looking, getting, preparing*)? Did you think of adding "now" in line 58? (Read that line aloud again to hear its consonance of *s* and *n* sounds.) Would you describe the tone of your revision as objective or subjective, arrogant or modest, ironic or straightforward, informative or suggestive, matter-of-fact or mysterious, honest or pretentious?

Writing and Revising

For suggestions on getting started, writing a first draft, revising the draft, and preparing the essay for submission, refer to the Introduction. Choose one of the following topics.

Topics for Writing

1. Time was when the college-educated person was set apart as special, almost assured of getting a good and rewarding position in life. Today that idea is often challenged. Taking the value of college education as your general subject, narrow the topic, devise a purpose (consider *arguing to convince* as a possibility), prepare a thesis, and write a first draft.

2. Nicholas Chauvin, a zealous French patriot and supporter of Napoleon I, gave his name to *chauvinism*. With that term and its contemporary applications ("male chauvinist," and so on) as general subject, narrow the topic, devise a purpose (consider *definition, classification,* and *arguing to convince* as possibilities), prepare a thesis, and write a first draft.

3. Most students find that college differs sharply from high school in almost every respect: curriculum, daily schedule, difficulty of studies, faculty-student relationship, social life, student politics. With that contrast as general subject matter, narrow the topic, devise a purpose (consider *contrast, description,* and *arguing to convince* as possibilities), prepare a thesis, and write a first draft.

4. It is often said that family life in America is "breaking down." With that idea as general subject matter, narrow the topic, devise a purpose (consider *comparison, contrast, example* or *illustration,* and *arguing to convince* as possibilities), prepare a thesis, and write a first draft.

Follow-up

As you read your first draft, look especially for hedging. How can you revise to make your views firmer without making them seem arrogant? If you have used any passive voice statements, try revising them to active voice. Have you resorted to euphemism? If so, make sure it is justified and not deceptive. What opportunities do you find for enhancing your effects by using *balance* (parallelism or antithesis)? Have you used (or can you now add) effective *repetition*? Is there opportunity for *alliteration* to help bring justified attention to any elements of your essay? When you have completed your revision, see Lesson 42 for a guide to preparing the manuscript for submission.

Lesson 16

Stress and Subordination

As we write a first draft, we are not sure of the relative importance of the ideas we are discovering. Ideas often come disarrayed, and we set them down as they come. It is later, in the critical revision stage, that we evaluate and determine which are the more important and which deserve less attention.

If we were lighting a scene for a movie, we'd highlight the most important things, what we most wanted people to see. When we write, we light the scene by emphasizing main points, subordinating the less important. We do it by careful placement and by careful choice of forms.

Subordination allows us to reduce the light on minor ideas, thus drawing attention to more important ones. A word or word group that by itself *cannot* form a full sentence is a minor form; a word group that *can* stand by itself is a major form. In a hasty first draft we may have put a major idea into a minor form:

They had been married six weeks when they had their first serious argument.

The serious argument, the important idea, has been expressed in a minor form, a "when" clause. We need to revise, subordinating when the argument happened and emphasizing the event itself:

REVISION: When they had been married six weeks, they had their first serious argument.

Another example:

The company had installed a new safety system just a week <u>before</u> three workers were killed in an explosion.

REVISION: Just a week <u>after</u> the company had installed a new safety system, *three workers were killed in an explosion.*

Combining Sentences

When two or more major forms (full simple sentences) appear in sequence, all the ideas seem equal in importance:

I decided to try the ministry. My father didn't like the idea.

If we determine that one of the ideas is more important than the other, we can use a minor form for the less important and make the main thought stand out:

REVISION: *I decided to try the ministry,* <u>although my father didn't like the idea.</u>

REVISION: *My father didn't like my decision* to try the ministry.

Ordinarily *what happens* is of greater importance than when, where, why, how, or under what condition it happens. We can subordinate the minor ideas by expressing them in word groups that begin with such subordinators as *when, where, while, as, before, after, since, until, because,* and *although:*

We live in the city. We must endure the sirens, the horns, the blaring telephones and screeching tires.

REVISION: *Because* we live in the city, we must endure the sirens. . . .

We may also subordinate by changing a verb to its *-ing* form:

REVISION: *Living* in the city, we must endure the sirens. . . .

Oscar drew 52 percent of the vote, and thus he won the election.

REVISION: Oscar won the election, *drawing* 52 percent of the vote.

We may put minor details into phrases that begin with such prepositions as *at, of, in, for, with,* and *from:*

A woman held a baby in her arms. She was running after a bus.

REVISION: A woman *with* a baby in her arms was running after a bus.

It was noon. The sun was high overhead and glaring. We stopped to rest.

REVISION: *At* noon, *with* the sun high overhead and glaring, we stopped to rest.

Now and then we can subordinate ideas by eliminating such verbs as *is, are, was,* and *were:*

Two miles beyond the ghetto are six ugly buildings. They are the basic industrial plants. They are producing little but dirt.

REVISION: Two miles beyond the ghetto, six ugly buildings, the basic industrial plants, produce little but dirt.

Alfred was my older brother. He was always my protector. He kept me out of trouble.

REVISION: Alfred, my older brother and always my protector, kept me out of trouble.

Brent was a computer technician. He was arrested for electronic theft of $2 million.

REVISION: Brent, a computer technician, was arrested for electronic theft of $2 million.

Active or Passive?

Another way of throwing more or less attention upon a detail lies in whether we treat it as performer or performed upon. If we write, "Sixty-five congressmen supported the bill," we stress the congressmen as active supporters of the bill. If we write, "The bill was supported by sixty-five congressmen," we stress the bill as a passive receiver of the support. When we stress the performer, we write *active voice;* when we stress the receiver, we write *passive voice*. Effective stress or subordination often depends on careful use of these two patterns. (See also Lesson 14 on the use of the active voice for direct and forceful statement.)

Reducing Fillers

Emphasis is lost when we use flabby fillers such as *begin, start,* or *become.* "I *trembled* at his words" is emphatic; "I *began to tremble* at his words" is weak. "Her eyes *danced*" is emphatic; "her eyes *started to dance*" is weak. "Today our world *mistrusts* kindness" is emphatic; "today our world *has become mistrustful* of kindness" is weak. In general, the one-word verb is more emphatic than the verb phrase.

Guideline

Stress important elements by form or position. Play down minor ideas, using minor forms.

Revision Practice: Stress and Subordination

Read this essay carefully with special attention to stress on important ideas and subordination of the less important. Revise the essay to improve its use of stress and subordination. Split or combine sentences as you think effective. Reduce the use of *is, are, was,* and *were* and flabby filler words like *began, started,* and *become.* Use the active voice except where the stress should be on what receives an action rather than on what does it. (In the first two paragraphs, the passive voice elements have been underlined.)

TO VOTE OR NOT TO VOTE: A MODEST PROPOSAL

1   Recent election statistics are available to show that we

2 Americans are staying away from the polls in droves. The

3 people by whom laws are made to govern us all are being

4 elected by fewer than half of our registered voters, and if

5 the trend continues, some say, we will not have a democracy,

6 not even a republic, but an oligarchy--a state governed by

7 an elite few.

8   Given the pitiful quality of representative government

9 as we have known it, I say the trend should be encouraged.

10 One of the troubles with government is that there are too

11 many fingers in the pie, so a government by an efficient

12 elite <u>is needed</u>, and that end <u>would be hastened</u> by reduction

13 of the number of voters.

14   Those who might vote but do not vote should be

15 encouraged by every means to continue their apathy and help

16 to spread it. The common excuses for not going to the polls

17 need to be publicized and praised.

18   Election day should be moved from November to early

19 October when it would coincide with the fourth game of the

20 World Series or with major hurricanes, snowstorms, and

21 floods. Polls should be opened only during prime time,

22 preferably during "Laverne and Shirley" and "The Johnny

23 Carson Show."

24   Taxes, of course, would then start to rise. National

25 deficits would be diminished, since the people would not

26 demand welfare or services in return for votes. The elite

27 could then begin to reign without the old annoying

28 interference by know-nothings. Those who complain could be

29 easily liquidated, all to the betterment of the country by

30 way of population control. There would be fewer people

31 driving cars, fewer polluting the land and air, and fewer

32 needing schools, fewer eating, and the numbers of voters

33 would be still further reduced. Old voting booths could be

34 turned on their sides and used as coffins.

35   It will be said that I have something personally to gain

36   by the adoption of this proposal, but that is not the case.

37   I have never been one of the elite, though I have always

38   wished them well.   It is they, indeed, who I hope will vote

39   for my proposal.   As for the rest of us, let's do the

40   sensible thing when this proposal comes to the polls and

41   stay away.

Follow-up

Revision from passive to active voice means turning an object (of a verb or preposition) into a subject (performer of an action). In other words, "by whom laws are made" becomes "who make laws"; and "The people . . . are being elected by fewer than half of the voters" becomes "Fewer than half of the voters are electing the people. . . ." Thus those who make laws and those who elect people—the doers—are emphasized. Have you eliminated "start" (line 24) and "begin" (line 27)? Did you split the long second sentence into two shorter ones? What about the long fourth sentence (beginning on line 10)? Did you emphasize the final "stay away" by giving it its own sentence: "Let's stay away"?

Lesson 17
Paragraphing

A readable paragraph is a group of sentences pulling together. Their purpose is to put forth, develop, and emphasize a single idea among the many ideas that make up an essay.

Although a sentence is a "complete thought," only rarely does one sentence make a complete idea. "One-liners" are often catchy, sometimes full of great truth, like these:

> Advertising is legalized lying.
> *H. G. Wells*

> Wagner's music is better than it sounds.
> *Mark Twain*

> I am not young enough to know everything.
> *James M. Barrie*

But such epigrams, complete as they are, are not paragraphs; they merely present an idea without developing it. A good paragraph expands on its topic, developing it by definition, description, example, illustration, reasoning, or other purposeful means.

Three qualities make a paragraph readable: (1) *unity* of topic, (2) *development* of idea, and (3) *coherence* of thought. Here, from Gilbert Highet, is a paragraph that displays those qualities:

> Too often, for too many of us, learning appears to be an imposition, a surrender of our own will power to external direction, indeed a sort of enslavement. This is a mistake. On the contrary, learning is a natural pleasure. It is a pleasure inborn and instinctive, one of the earliest pleasures and one of the essential pleasures of the human race.[1]

The paragraph's first sentence presents its topic, "learning." All sentences in the paragraph relate to and develop that topic, showing a contrast between what learning often appears to be and what it truly is. The paragraph not only has a topic but also presents a point about that topic. The paragraph has unity (one topic only), development (details), and coherence (all sentences in order, working together).

Now let's look at a less careful piece of writing. This, from the first draft of an essay on getting rich, appears on the page as a paragraph but doesn't have those three essential qualities:

> Getting rich is totally different from *being* rich. The process that most people use to get money is work. Working, no matter how hard, will not always make you rich in monetary terms. Other ways of getting rich are inheriting, investing, gambling, and stealing. There are those who try to "get rich quick." Dishonesty is some people's best policy. Getting that money gets to be a cycle sometimes. A bum can break into a millionaire's home and come out smiling with his pockets full. The millionaire might try to collect insurance to recover his money. This in a sense causes inflation and jacks up taxes. Taxes might not affect the poor but surely can affect others.

The writer has set down random thoughts on a general topic, "money and how we get it." But the thoughts have not become a paragraph. Indeed, there may be enough material here for several paragraphs.

To revise that "paragraph," we'll have to separate the ideas and develop them one at a time. And we'll have to cut whatever has nothing to do with the general topic (the thoughts on taxes seem irrelevant). We may develop several paragraphs, using these topics: (1) working, (2) inheriting, (3) investing, (4) gambling, and (5) stealing. Our first revised paragraph may go like this:

> Working, the most reputable way to get money, is slow, demanding, and not always successful. Seldom do you find a job that pays much more

---

[1] Gilbert Highet, *The Immortal Profession* (New York: Weybright & Talley, 1976), p. 3.

than it takes to live on, so getting rich by working is unlikely unless you save meticulously. Health often goes before wealth comes.

That paragraph has a single topic: "working" as a way to wealth. It will become a unit within an essay including our other paragraphs as well. The second paragraph, covering the "inheriting" topic, may develop like this:

Inheriting, acceptable but less reputable than working, is also slow, though all it demands is patience. It too is often unsuccessful. If you are to inherit, someone you know must have money, and you must be lucky enough to be chosen heir to it. And even if you are so chosen, you may put false hope in belief that the rich one can't take it with him. Don't forget that it may go before he does, especially if he is of sound mind.

All sentences in the paragraph are on the one topic, "inheriting money." The third subtopic, "investing," also gets a paragraph of its own:

Investing may be faster than working or inheriting. But it is also demanding, both of nerve and patience. You must have some money to start with, perhaps money you have worked for or inherited, and now you have to edge toward gambling to make it grow. If you are not extremely careful, you may end with less rather than more, especially since there are others in the investment field who have edged not only toward gambling but also toward stealing. Investment is an edgy game.

The string of paragraphs grows, with the topics of "gambling" and "stealing" still to be developed. Each will emphasize a subtopic of the whole essay.

Here is a "paragraph" from a first draft on another topic. As it stands, the paragraph lacks emphasis. Consider the instructor's suggestions in the margin:

There are many people who enjoy the modern way of living in the big city. However, I believe the	*Wordy ("There are," "who") ("the modern way of living in the big city")*
best way of living can only be gained by living in the country. The first reason is that people can	*Order (Save this thesis sentence for end of paragraph.)*
develop their own lifestyles. In the city, people have	*Word (Do we "gain" a way of living?)*
to adapt to crowded apartment living, where neighbors may be unfriendly. Homes are smaller and closer to each other than in the country. Away from the	*Order (Try to set up city things first, then country things, in each group.)*

city, people have more land to work with, and they

can build without any zone restrictions. In the city,

people tend to dress a certain way to feel accepted

in their society. In the country, people are accepted

for their own individuality rather than the way

they're dressed and their wealth. Another reason is

that the country is healthier to live in than the city.

There is less traffic, less air pollution, and less crime.

There is less competition and more chance for

relaxation. Finally, the country is more beautiful.

'People see more beauty surrounding them, and their

lives are more enjoyable.

Parallelism ("Neigh-bors" were not men-tioned for the country life.)

Parallelism ("the way they're dressed . . . wealth") ("Wealth" was not mentioned for city life.)

Parallelism ("Compe-tition," lack of "relaxa-tion," and lack of "beauty" were not men-tioned for city life.)

The instructor has suggested that the paragraph be reorganized. Details relating to the city and to the country may be developed each in turn: space, neighbors, dress, wealth, health, traffic, pollution, crime, competition, relaxation, and beauty. The thesis statement, now in the second sentence, may be saved for the end of the paragraph, where it will be emphasized. The revised paragraph may look like this:

1   Many people enjoy city life, but its contrast to country life is
2 sharp. Cities are jammed, and people must cram into apartments or
3 crowded houses, and neighbors may be unfriendly; but the country
4 is spacious and without any zoning restrictions, so neighbors have
5 more privacy and tend to be more friendly. The city's traffic, air
6 pollution, and crime contribute to ill health, to say nothing of intense
7 competition and small chance to relax; but the country has little
8 traffic, clean air, much less crime, small competition, and time and
9 space for relaxation. In the city, people cannot be themselves but
10 must dress to be accepted and will often be judged by their poverty
11 or wealth; but in the country, people dress as they please and are
12 accepted for their individuality. Cities are ugly, and city people have

13 little beauty in their lives; but the country surrounds its people with
14 the beauty of nature to make their lives more pleasant. Yes, the coun-
15 try offers the better way of living.

The paragraph is now more readable, its details in order. But there is still more to be done. The opening sentence is weak and unemphatic; proper subordination may help. The rhyme of "jammed" and "cram" in line 2 distracts. "Without any zoning restrictions" may be an inaccurate guess; the phrase can be left out. The rhyme of "tend" and "friendly" in line 5 is awkward; perhaps *neighborly* would be better. Attention to word choice, subordination, economy, and figurative language helps us to produce a final draft:

1   Although many enjoy city life, its contrast to country life is sharp.
2   Cities are push and shove, people crammed into apartments or
3   crowded houses, often with unfriendly neighbors; but the country
4   is spacious, and neighbors, having more privacy, tend to be more
5   neighborly. The city's traffic, air pollution, and crime bring ill health,
6   intense competition, and seldom a chance to relax; but the country
7   has little traffic, clear air, much less crime, small competition, and
8   time and space for relaxation. City dwellers, afraid to be themselves,
9   must dress to be accepted, for they are often judged by their poverty
10 or wealth; but country people dress as they please and are accepted
11 for their individuality, not for their finery or lack of it. Cities are ugly,
12 and city dwellers have little beauty in their lives; but the country
13 surrounds its people with the beauty of nature to make their lives
14 more pleasant. Yes, the country offers the better way of living.

The opening sentence from the second draft now subordinates the first clause, emphasizing the contrast to country life. "Cities are push and shove" (line 2) has given a figurative twist to the idea. Words have been cut (lines 6 and 8) for economy.

Guideline

Make every paragraph cover just one phase of the essay's topic.

Revision Practice: Paragraphing

This essay has been marked by an instructor, who has suggested how the paragraphs may be revised. Your job is to read the essay carefully, then revise each paragraph in turn and submit a new version of the entire essay.

VERSATILE VOLLEYBALL

1. With an increased emphasis on physical fitness, more and more people are engaging actively in sports. *Repetition?* Many people have come to realize that sports offer *Economy?* other benefits besides exercise. Through sports participation, people gain skills that are also *Does first paragraph introduce the real topic?* applicable to their everyday lives. Players learn how to develop and apply strategy. Players also learn to work in pressure situations. If it is a team sport, individuals learn how to work cooperatively in a group.

2. One especially rewarding team sport is volleyball. *Repetition?* Volleyball is played by an estimated 60 million players *Combine Sentences* throughout the world. In the United States volleyball is considered one of the most popular participant *Use active voice* sports. The game appeals to people of all ages and is highly adaptable to the various needs and skills of the *Economy?* players. For instance, when younger children play, the nets can be raised or lowered. When playing recreation *who's playing?* in coeducational ball, the rules can be easily modified.

3. Being such a diverse sport, the stress level in *Is "stress level" a diverse sport?* volleyball can range from not being strenuous to being extremely demanding physically. Basically volleyball can be divided into three levels of play: social level, *Repetition?* recreational level, and competitive level. Playing on

the social level is usually impromptu and takes place
at beaches and public parks. On the recreational
level, volleyball is played at schools and churches,
often led by a recreation director who determines the
required degree of skill, and participation is many
times planned in advance. The highest level, the
competitive, relies on skill and ability. There are
many plays and patterns employed, and the strategy
involves intricacy and imagination. Some coaches claim
that volleyball is 90 percent mental and only 10
percent physical. This theory becomes more apparent at
the competition level.

4.   Social level volleyball is spontaneous. When
large groups of people are at barbecues, beach parties, *Deadwood*
or picnics, volleyball games are often haphazardly   *Repetition*
organized. Instead of the game being based on skill,
the purpose of the volleyball match for everybody is to
have a good time. Often the number of players on each
team is considered trivial. Except for allowing up to *Active*
                                                        voice
three hits per side, no specific rules are followed.
What results is a game commonly known as "jungle" ball. *Repetition*
"Jungle" ball involves no level of skill and the sole
goal is for everybody to enjoy themselves.

5.   Seemingly enough, the attitudes of the players   *"Seemingly"?*
change at the recreational level. Individuals whom are *"whom"?*
                                                         (case)
athletically inclined pursue volleyball for a hobby.

Besides being a convenient study or work break, playing
ball is an excellent way to meet people. People if
they can <u>share common</u> interest can get together to play   *Redundant*
and get to know one another better. At the intramural
level players' skills are competent and they follow the
rules. The game is approached with a somewhat more
serious attitude than at the social level. Since gyms
are open at certain set times, many players become
regulars. Winning, at the recreational level, is   *Relevant?*
considered less important than receiving a good
workout.

6.   The third level, competitive, differs greatly   *(Has
from the other levels. Much of the match is mainly   purpose
thinking, this time also at an unconscious level.   of the essay
                                                        changed?
Participants concentrate and take the game seriously,   are you
                                                        really
and winning becomes the key to the game. Players at   discussing
                                                        the conscious
this level give their best effort and then some, even   and unconscious
                                                        levels? Omit
                                                        all materials
while tired.   except those
                                                        that help to
7.   Many of the unconscious elements concern the   distinguish
                                                        three levels
athlete not thinking about his or her body movements.   of play.)
After learning and practicing certain court fundamen-
tals, an experienced player instinctively moves to the   *Order?
                                                        (combine
correct position for offense or defense without   paragraphs
                                                        7 and 8.)*
thinking.

8.   Although there seem to be three levels of play,
social, recreational, and competitive, a player can

easily move back and forth <u>between two levels</u>.   ) *among all*
) *levels?*
Volleyball can be satisfying for all ages sizes, and   /

skills.

Follow-up

Have you eliminated all irrelevant details? Are remaining details in clear and reasonable order? What details have you subordinated to make more important ideas stand out?

Lesson 18

Summing Up: Endings

$\quad$ **E**ndings are the most emphatic parts of essays. The beginning must catch attention and establish topic, thesis, and tone. The middle must develop the central topic by giving adequate detail in support of the thesis. But the ending, like the climax or summation of a mystery, is where all elements are brought together, their point nailed emphatically into place. The ending must leave the reader understanding—and satisfied.

$\quad$ To be satisfying, an ending should not merely repeat what's been said. A good summary echoes *with variation,* giving the central point a firmer emphasis than it had in the beginning or middle.

$\quad$ Let's consider an essay whose ending is unsatisfactory:

Lie and Consequences

$\quad$ Trust builds slowly. It may take years of honesty to establish confidence between two people, and even then the belief may be fragile. Consider the effect of a hasty lie.

One summer I was working at Nautilus Spectrum, a health spa, where the director was typically tall, dark, and handsome. Because of his strong attraction, I found it extremely difficult to do my work. As the days went by, the attraction grew, despite my continuing three-year relationship with my boyfriend, Scott.

On an August day the director asked me to be his date at his best friend's wedding. My heart bounced, and I blurted "Yes." I was so excited about going to that wedding with that handsome man that Scott was, for the moment, far from my mind, and no thought of guilt had a chance.

But when the day of the wedding came around, reality struck. I spent the morning with Scott, and guilt was written all over my face. Scott had no idea what I was up to, but I was convinced he had me all figured out. I made an excuse for the afternoon and went to the wedding.

As bride and groom said their "I do's," I could think only of Scott and my guilty feelings. After the reception, my handsome date saw me home and we parted, with him probably thinking what a nervous ninny I was. I called Scott immediately, my voice quivering as my heart beat two hundred to the minute, and my hands shook as I held the phone.

I chattered incessantly about nothing, hoping Scott wouldn't ask about that afternoon. Half an hour of rambling went by, and just when I had begun to think I had pulled it off, the question came: "What did you do this afternoon?" Frantic, I told him I had taken my dog to the veterinarian.

Scott believed. Not only that, he said he was very sorry my dog was ill. I felt more guilty than before.

Scott has never brought up that day again. My rational mind tells me he has never thought of it. But I can never be sure. I quake now and then to think he may have an idea where I actually was and know that I lied to him.

The essay comes to a climax, but not to a finish. The final paragraph does not remind us of the central point of the incident. The reader is left without a firm understanding of what it all means.

One way to bring an essay to a satisfying finish is to present an echo of some idea that has appeared in the beginning, perhaps using some of the same words but in a more emphatic statement. A "full-circle" ending satisfies because it brings the reader "home" again to the point of departure after a journey through ideas. The ending, with its echo of a thought from the beginning, makes the journey understandable. An emphatic ending should also cinch the central point and remind the reader of some of the essay's supporting details. The ending of "Lie and Consequences," in its present draft, does not come full circle and does not review. Let's offer a revision:

Scott has never brought up that day again. My rational mind tells me he has never thought of it. But I can never be sure. I quake now and then to think he may have an idea where I actually was and know that I lied to him. Whether he ever does know . . . or he never does, I have seen first-hand how fragile trust can be. What years have built can be destroyed in a minute by a hasty lie.

The echo of words and phrases from the essay's beginning ("fragile," "trust," "years," "a hasty lie") brings the thought full circle, and the final sentence emphatically states (in slightly different words than before) the essay's central point.

Guideline

Bring your essay to a full-circle ending that echoes (but does not merely repeat) the essay's central point.

Revision Practice: Summing Up

The essay "Offspring" was written by a student from the point of view of his own father. As it stands in first draft, the essay has an unsatisfactory ending: It quits but does not finish. Revise its final paragraph to give it an emphatic ending, bringing the essay full circle with a return to the wording or details of its beginning.

OFFSPRING

The old saw "Like father, like son" has a haunting truth to it. I often look at him and ask myself how I could have raised such a rotten kid. Yet I see more of me in him than I would like to see. We share an uncanny number of traits.

I stand six feet even, though at his age I was five foot ten, as he is now. My skin went through the same stages as his, starting baby soft, going through the adolescent years looking like a pizza. Mine eventually cleared. He has bigger muscles than I ever had, and a clear athletic superiority. I swat the ball at tennis; he strokes it. Our eyes are the same color, our hair nearly so. His hair, once too long, shows less and less now. The biggest fight in our household was over a haircut. Today he is meticulous about what he calls his "GQ" appearance.

He has one hell of a heart. Too often he thinks with his emotions; here we differ, for I tend to feel with my mind. I've seen him cry harder than anyone I've known, and I've felt sorry for a kid of eighteen who has had such traumatic experiences, many of them caused by me. When he was younger, he'd come into my room late at night, his tail between his legs, and we'd make up and hug. Now the problems seem more complicated.

From early age he has had an interest in girls, yet he avoids commitment. He has seen the problems between his mother and me; I don't think he wants to follow in his father's footsteps. I also think he can't hold a girl for long; he's so ambitious, rarely content. I wish he'd turn some of his ambition toward his schoolwork; my father no doubt wished the same of me.

He knows that although I make a good living, I can't give him everything. I try to give him what I can, yet he never seems satisfied. He can be pleased for the moment, but in the long run his wants extend beyond reality. He has big dreams that one day he'll make it rich and be able to give his kid a Porsche. Now and then we have run little experiments to see what he can do without, and he usually fares pretty well.

He's jealous of everything. I'm jealous of everything. We are jealous of each other. I want his youth; he wants my wisdom. I want his vitality; he wants my security. If we were

to change places, we'd both still be jealous.

The greatest thing he has is the ability to love. For most

people love is intangible; my son can touch it. I've seen him

show love--toward others--with more feeling than you could

imagine. I wish he'd express that love more often toward me.

No doubt he wishes I would do likewise toward him. In this,

neither of us is quite grown up.

Follow-up

If your revision can reasonably echo words and phrases from the essay's beginning, the ending will probably be more satisfying. But remember that you
should not merely repeat whole sentences or ideas from the beginning; instead,
you should vary them somewhat, make them more emphatic than they were
before.

Summary
Revising for Emphasis

Guidelines 13–18

13. Make your title and first paragraph challenge your readers. Intro-
    duce your topic, suggest your thesis, and establish your tone.

14. Be sparing in your use of hedging, apology, passive voice, and euphe-
    mism—and never use any of these to hide important truth.

15. To add emphasis to a passage, consider repetition of words, rhythms,
    and sounds, as well as symmetry of forms.

16. Stress important elements by form or position. Play down minor
    ideas, using minor forms.

17. Make every paragraph cover just one phase of the essay's topic.

18. Bring your essay to a full-circle ending that echoes (but does not
    merely repeat) the essay's central point.

Writing and Revising

For detailed suggestions on getting started, writing a first draft, revising the draft, and preparing the essay for submission, refer to the Introduction. Choose one of the following topics.

Topics for Writing

1. "Buyer beware!" To what extent are people you know really careful about their shopping for and buying of consumer products? What part does advertising play in their decisions? Do they seem to look for quality—or for price? Does "consumer education" help? Consider these and other aspects, narrow the topic, select an appropriate purpose, order the details, and write a first draft.

2. What are the values of discipline? Does it have possible drawbacks? With discipline as general subject matter, narrow the topic, devise a thesis, select an appropriate purpose (such as *definition* or *arguing to convince*). Order the details, and write a first draft.

3. What is your favorite holiday? (Choose one from any culture you know, not necessarily American.) What makes it special for you? How do you defend it as meaningful for society? Consider these and other aspects, narrow the topic, select an appropriate purpose, order the details, and write a first draft.

4. Henry Clay said, "I'd rather be right than be president." But we often think we're right when we're not. When we have argued strongly on a point and later discover we've been wrong about it, what are some strategies for "saving face"? Consider these and other aspects, narrow the topic, select an appropriate purpose, order the details, and write a first draft.

Follow-up

Consider each sentence. Have you thrown the spotlight on main ideas with appropriate *emphasis*, reducing the less important by *subordination*? Can you eliminate filler words like *begin, start,* and *become*? Consider *paragraphs:* Does each cover a single phase of your topic? Is the order of ideas within each paragraph reasonable? Does your final paragraph bring the essay full circle by presenting an echo (not merely repetition) of thoughts from the beginning? When you have completed your revision, see Lesson 42 for a guide to preparing your manuscript for submission.

Review Quiz

These passages (including some titles) are first drafts that lack emphasis for several reasons. Revise each according to suggestions offered in the margin. Refer to p. 143 for a refresher on guidelines.

1. A CAREER IN COURT

During my brief lifetime so far my ambitions have changed often. Yet I feel I have finally decided what I want to do. Ambition can be *Active voice? (guide-*
line 14)
defined as having a strong desire for power or a high position in life. All people have to work in order to reach their goal. Whether one opens *Paragraph unity?*
(guideline 17)
up a new business or inherits a business from parents, it takes hard work. I am willing to *Suggest thesis: what*
ambition? (guideline
work hard to build a successful career in a very *13)*
important profession.

2. BEST MEDICINE?

This essay may not seem like one about laugh- *Hedging? Apologiz-*
ing? (guideline 14)
ter, but I will do my best. Laughter is often a way of covering pain. We laugh to keep from crying. I've been known to laugh and kid along, but if the joke is carried on forever, it grows stale and dies, and I don't want to hear it again. Anticipation is another cause of laughter, as when we laugh at Chevy Chase's pratfall that we know is sure to come. We also laugh at the unexpected,

as when someone trips over his own feet. I have
a friend named Dave. He likes to get me started
laughing so he can watch my face change colors.

Irrelevant? (Unity: Save these details for later: guideline 17)

3. GOING BACK

Many of us are disillusioned with modern
times. This attitude shows in a social frustration,
and in my opinion shows that people want to reduce
the role of technology in society. Social values
have lagged behind technology. Personal adapta-
tion to rapid changes is difficult, so our technology has acquired a bad name.

Does title suggest thesis? Does beginning suggest thesis? (guideline 13)

Hedging? (guideline 14)

Emphasize. (guideline 16)

Is repetition of "technology" awkward?

4. DRIVERS

One of the types of driver may be referred to
as the "sadistic" driver, who enjoys torturing
other drivers to feed his ego and and find satisfaction. He ranges from the egocentric millionaire
driving a new candy-apple red Lamborghini to the
tramp driving a '59 Plymouth junker. Since he
thrives on cutting drivers off, giving the finger,
and running red lights, he is in constant search
of fulfillment.

Put main idea in main clause and subordinate minor ones. (guideline 16)

Again. (guideline 16)

5. WEIGHTWATCHING

Weightwatching was once the fat lady's
necessity. Today almost everybody does it as a

Try balance and repetition to improve the emphasis. (guideline 15) pastime. The exercise has swept the nation. We are also caught up in dieting. Many take pills to help them lose weight. We are determined to die thin, even if it means dying early.

6. NOISE

Our city has become polluted by sound. We endure the telephone bell and the typewriter clatter. We hear the rumble and screech of traffic. The sirens of ambulance, fire engine, and police car are everywhere. At home it is radio and the blaring television commercial. Perhaps the most annoying discord of all is that of the patrol helicopter circling tumultuously above.

Would "is" be more emphatic than "has become"? Or would active voice be better? (guideline 14)

Try balance to emphasize these details. (guideline 15)

7. CRIME

I have a modest proposal, like Jonathan Swift. Today's problem is crime, so let's return to "frontier justice." Already neighborhood watch groups, "guardian angels," and vigilantes are appearing nationwide. Let's carry that idea forward. Possibly the hands of thieves should be cut off. Public torture would be a cure for rapists. All murderers should be hanged. Dope pushers could be liquidated by injection. Society might

Is order of ideas emphatic in first sentence? (guideline 16)

Revise passive voice and hedging. (guideline 14)

Avoid euphemism ("liquidated") that hides the essential truth. (guideline 14)

soon win the war on crime and have such a lot of
fun doing it. And we can set this plan in motion
now, starting with those who object.

8. THE ECONOMY

Inflation continues, and poverty and starva-
tion rise. As a member of the middle class, I see
myself beginning to drift downward. Many of us
see the rich getting richer as the rest of us lose
what we have. Many businesses are on the edge of
collapse. Factories have been closed, and many
millions are jobless.

*Emphasize the main
idea by subordinating
the less important.
(guideline 16)
Why "beginning"?*

*Try balance here.
(guideline 15)*

*Put important idea at
end for emphasis.*

9. PRIVACY

People need privacy in order to get ideas and
situations clear in their minds without interference from others. For some, privacy is a very
deep and emotional need. As I look around, I find
that most people do not have enough privacy. I
fall into that category. There should be some
limits to privacy, but I am not really sure what
situations these limits should pertain to. The
public should have the right to know the private
affairs and involvements of officials and others
whose conduct bears on the public interest.
When I have private moments, I value them greatly.

*Is paragraph unified?
Is it about the need for
privacy, the limits to
privacy, or the proper
use of privacy? (guide-
line 17)*

*Try making three brief
paragraphs of this one,
adding details as
needed from
imagination.*

People need to learn how to use their private
moments constructively and recreatively.

10. SUNRISE

I was not a morning person, and it always
took forever for me to get my mind into gear.   No
alarm had rung, and the clock said 5:18.   What was
I doing up at that hour?   When I got up to use the
restroom upstairs, on the way I looked through a
window, where I saw a breathtaking sunrise.
Hazily I thought of my camera and went down to get
it, but I lay down again instead and went to
sleep, so I missed the picture.   I am still
not sure that I really saw that sunrise, because I
have begun to wonder whether I saw God.   I am no
longer the same.

Put main ideas in emphatic positions and forms. (guideline 16)

Make ending emphatic by full-circle method. (guideline 18)

Is "begun to" emphatic? Try "I now wonder. . . ."

Revising for

Variety

Repetition has useful effects, as we have seen in revising for emphasis, but it also has limitations. Even a pleasing image or sound may put the mind to sleep, and repetition, if carelessly handled, loses its charm. To make writing readable, we need the full range of appeals to the mind, including the spice of variety.

The readable essay has a definable purpose and a central point; it does not wander. And it pursues both purpose and point with a dominant tone. These qualities give the essay a unity, a oneness, that leaves no doubt. But its substance is made of a variety of elements—what dominates is made continually appealing by the surprises of thought and style that set it off.

Variety thus begins with the substance itself. An idea undeveloped is a stone unpolished. We cannot appeal to readers by stating a point and offering no support to bring it to life. Good readers, the kind we hope for, will ask questions and want them answered: How do we know our point is true? What evidence can we offer? Who says so? Are there examples to prove it? What can we bring from real life in illustration of the point? Are there other ways of looking at it? Why is this way best? Are we offering a real and relevant variety, or are we just repeating the point? An essay without variety of substance may be a waste of time.

What we have to say must also be made delightful by how we say it. If our sentences are all of a kind, even our best ideas may seem lifeless. If our sentences all have about the same length, like the swing of a pendulum, and put the same horse before the same old cart without an occasional cart coming first, they may leave no idea standing out—and no readers awake.

The words and idioms of our language need variety too. A procession of *there*'s and *person*'s and fuzzy *was*'s bring no sparkle to the style. If we pick our words from a narrow range, either the formal or the informal, the new or the old, the long or the short, they will spark no lightning. For lightning, a mixed selection is best. And if our thoughts run in the old familiar patterns ("in this day and age," "all of a sudden," "believe it or not," "a rude awakening," "a sneaking suspicion"), there will be no thunder either.

Lesson 19

Original
Expression

Until we get our minds warmed up to our writing, we tend to think without imagination. What come to us are old ways of saying things, overused phrases that nearly everyone has heard—like some of these:

> Then *all of a sudden* there was *a dull thud* that *scared the wits out* of us. We stopped *dead in our tracks*. Our hearts were *pounding like jackhammers*. We imagined every kind of threat *in the book—you name it*.

Such stale phrasing deadens the mind. We need to revive it with fresh ways of saying things—if not markedly original, at least not worn out:

> Just then an awesome thump startled us. We stood still, our hearts hammering to get out of our ribs. We imagined every appalling threat that fantasy allows.

The trouble with clichés is that they don't challenge the mind. Our thoughts fall into the old patterns so easily that our ideas take on no sparkle of their own; they are merely clones of other people's thoughts. And our readers, once we've started one of those musty phrases, can finish it for themselves: quick as a . . . , dead as a . . . , no sooner said . . . , a fate worse than . . . , beyond the shadow of a . . . , by the same . . . .

If we want a more readable style, we'll have to "bend over backwards" to keep clichés "few and far between." The first step, of course, is to recognize the stale phrase when we've written it. Let's complete our own checklist of such phrases, just as a reminder:

better late than _____	on the spur of _____
a bolt out of _____	our pride and _____
a sneaking _____	quick as a _____
burning the midnight _____	sadder but _____
by the skin of _____	sharp as a _____
down in the _____	sink or _____
fine and _____	the bottom _____ is
get in there and _____	the facts of _____
green with _____	the more the _____
in dire _____	the _____ straw
in one fell _____	the straight and _____
in the nick of _____	to all intents and _____
in the twinkling of _____	tried and _____
it goes without _____	truth is stranger _____
it stands to _____	up in _____ about it
off the beaten _____	with malice _____

Completing the list has "quickened our awareness" of clichés so that others will "ring a bell" for us whenever they "rear their ugly heads."

But readable writing doesn't avoid clichés entirely; now and then a familiar phrase may be useful. And now and then we can turn an old pattern to a new use by giving it an imaginative twist:

This hamburger joint is a frying shame.

These days getting an education goes without praying.

The professor likes to strike while the irony is hot.

Truer words were never plagiarized.

But these twists have limited uses; they are *epigrams*, bright sayings in brief form. Such lines will only occasionally be useful in college essays.

Deliberately playing with clichés, this brief essay has charm despite—or perhaps because of—them:

Breaking the Ice

Hitting it off with a new friend is easier said than done. Believe it or not, it's entirely possible that the new person couldn't care less about making your acquaintance. It goes without saying that you may not be jumping with joy to meet him, either. Some relationships are doomed from the word *go.*

Let's face it: When you open up to a perfect stranger, you put yourself at his tender mercies. And chances are he is not all that experienced at providing tender loving care. Besides, likely as not the two of you will not be into the same things. It stands to reason he will want to go on doing his own thing, and heaven knows you won't change your habits until hell freezes over.

If there's going to be any kind of lasting relationship at all, something's got to give. And that something may, alas and alack, be you. As a matter of fact, if you learn to give (yes, to give, when all is said and done, is better than to receive), you may find that the new acquaintance will come around too. In the final analysis, you may by some odd chance discover that, in spite of everything, lo and behold, a good time is had by all.

Unless you use a worn phrase intentionally and do something purposeful with it, you should find a fresh expression to replace the cliché. Using the familiar phrases may also lead to mixing of metaphors (see Lesson 36).

Guideline

If you've often heard an expression, don't use it unless for some special purpose.

Revision Practice: Original Expression

Read this essay with special attention to its use of familiar phrases. Revise the essay, trying to avoid the clichés.

WHY I ATTEND COLLEGE

1   When I came to college, to all intents and purposes

2 I had no more idea than the man in the moon what my career

3 intentions were. It goes without saying that I was not sure

4 college was for me. Since I was no budding genius, and

5 since I had no career in mind, I had no way of beginning to

6 prepare for one. Let's face it, I even had a sneaking

7 suspicion that I should stay out of college and get some

8 kind of job or other.

9   Before I knew it, though, I had begun to see a higher

10 usefulness in college. Beyond a shadow of a doubt, there is

11 more to life than earning a living. I began to see college

12 as a growth experience, one that would first and foremost

13 help me to discover myself and my interests. My path became

14 crystal clear: I would continue in college for the simple

15 reason that I wanted to find me.

16   College, I have at long last decided, is the best

17 possible experience for personal growth that can be had in

18 such a short time. It's a rare bird who will finish four

19 years of college without filling in the void of his abysmal

20 ignorance to some appreciable degree. College holds forth

21 an opportunity that should not be taken lightly. It serves

22 as a useful transitional device from adolescence to

23 adulthood.

24   It would be difficult at best to fully utilize college

25 as an aid to ripening the intellect, but I am fully aware

26 that I can make substantial progress toward self-discovery

27 by exploring my interests, discovering my aptitudes, and

28 developing my talents to the fullest possible extent.

29 Meanwhile college is furnishing me with insight into how

30 other people think, and that insight helps me to establish

31 my own identity.

32   So far in college I have noticed that if I look beyond

33 the course titles and leave no stone unturned in seeking

34 knowledge of the subjects I pursue, what I learn will become

35 part of the great and incomprehensible puzzle that I call,

36 for want of a better name, "All Knowledge." I don't want to

37 turn my back on any subject just for the simple reason that

38 it brings me no immediate advantage. It may, when all is

39 said and done, fit in with all the other pieces that form

40 the structure of the puzzle.

41   I don't want to specialize too much or get all tied up

42 in the piddling details of a narrow field of knowledge. I

43 want to keep my eye on the big picture and now and then go

44 off the beaten track. It's as certain as the day is long

45 that I'll never complete the puzzle; no one does, since it

46 includes all man's present knowledge and all knowledge yet

47 to be discovered. But I want to collect my share of the

48 pieces and maybe understand the puzzle a little better every

49 day. The process of seeking the solution, rather than the

50 solving, is in the last analysis the real value of going to

51 college.

52   With the personal growth I achieve at college, I should

53 come to appreciate the finer things in life as well as to

54 master a few skills. When my four years are done, I may not

55 have found all of myself or completed my share of the

56 puzzle, but I will be ready to pull my own weight. In the

57 modern world of today, the person who can't shoulder

58 reponsibility is totally out of it. I know there is no free

59 lunch, and when the dust settles, I don't want to be left

60 high and dry or at the tender mercies of the power

61 structure.

62   Something tells me I have made a wise decision in going

63 to college. Suffice it to say that I am bound and determined

64 to do my utmost to make the most of it.

Follow-up

Did you find as many as thirty clichés in this essay? In its twenty-eight sentences the essay actually uses forty-seven familiar and overworked phrases. Many such expressions can be simply left out: "to all intents and purposes," "it goes without saying," "let's face it," "beyond a shadow of a doubt," and many others are seldom of any use. Others can be simplified: "for the simple reason that" becomes *because;* "to the fullest possible extent" becomes *to the fullest*; "in the modern world of today" becomes just *today.* Remember, however, that an occasional cliché may be useful and not offensive; it's better to use a cliché than to strain to replace it.

Lesson 20

Variety
of Words

Readable writing uses plain, exact, and specific words. But if we use the same words again and again, no matter how easy they are to read and how precisely they fit, monotony will deaden our writing. If variety spices life, it will surely spice our writing too. So we need to uncover a variety of words to fit our thoughts, words that charge our writing with delight.

"Fit our thoughts" is central here. The words we choose for our final drafts must be just right for what we want to say. An artificial use of words just for variety's sake will not do. It is better to repeat the simple *said* than to stretch for showy synonyms like *stated, declared, exclaimed, shouted, screamed,* or *articulated,* especially if the word we choose is simply wrong for the situation, as in Leo Rosten's famous parody, " 'Shut up!' he *explained.*"

Where do we find that variety of words to fit what we want to say? One useful source is *Roget's Thesaurus,* a kind of reverse dictionary where we look up meanings to find words. Suppose we've written, "Later I was sorry for my decision, which was too quickly made." We want a word to help us say "too quickly made," a word that will be just right. *Roget's* helps by showing us a host of words:

agile, brief, brisk, cursory, fast, feverish, fleet, flying, furious, hasty, head-long, hotheaded, hurried, impetuous, nimble, pressing, rapid, speedy, swift, urgent

They don't all fit, of course; we choose the few that come near our meaning: hasty, headlong, hotheaded, hurried, impetuous, swift. We let *Roget's* help us also with "sorry," where we find:

apologetic, chagrined, concerned, heartbroken, horrified, regretful, remorseful, sorrowful

Then we try a few revisions of our sentence:

Later I *regretted* my *headlong* decision.

Later I was *remorseful* for my *impetuous* decision.

I was later *chagrined* for my *swift* decision.

Later I was *heartbroken* over my *hotheaded* decision.

Later I was *sorrowful* for my *hasty* decision.

Some of the words are too fancy, or they suggest more emotion than is called for by the occasion. Plain words are often best, so we go with them for our final draft:

I later *regretted* my *hasty* decision.

The search in *Roget's* produced no lightning, but it gave us something more readable than our first draft, and only half as long.

To make sure we are choosing our words carefully, we may refer to a good dictionary, since *Roget's* does not define the words for us.

The Right Tone

Tone is the result of our attitudes: how we feel, whether consciously or not, about ourselves, our topic, and our readers. If we are cheerful and optimistic at the moment of writing, we'll probably choose words that reflect that attitude. We reveal, largely through the connotations of words, whether we take the topic seriously, whether we are angry about it or pleased, whether we admire or make fun. And our words will show what we assume about our readers: Do we think they are intelligent, informed, sophisticated—or do we assume they are not? Do we feel superior to the readers, or inferior, or equal?

If we choose words that reveal our knowledge but not how we feel about it, we write an "objective" tone. Consider the tone of this paragraph about new antisexist terms such as *salesperson, mail carrier,* and *firefighter,* used to avoid saying sales*man,* mail*man,* or fire*man:*

> Most such terms used to replace sexist words are longer than the original or require more words. The problem can be resolved by the feminists, but whether it is wise to encourage roundabout expressions in these times when most Americans already are too prolix remains in question.

The paragraph expresses opinion, but it is nevertheless objective in tone; the writer doesn't seem personally involved. See how the tone changes when the writer chooses different words—as does columnist Russell Baker:

> In almost every case the alternative for the "sexist" word to be purged is either a longer word or a combination of words. Instead of "sexism," we have verbosity. It is a dilemma that feminists will have no trouble resolving, but whether it is a good idea to encourage more windiness in an age when most of us already talk like politicians on television is arguable.[1]

Baker's attitude is clear. He writes "purged" rather than "replaced"; he writes that "feminists will have no trouble resolving" rather than the passive "can be resolved." He writes "whether it is *a good idea,*" not "whether it is *wise.*" He writes "windiness," not "roundabout expressions"; and instead of "too prolix," it's "talk like politicians on television." His choice of words brings forth an entirely different tone, one with a real person behind it.

In revising a first draft, we do well to consider tone. Does the essay have too little warmth—or too much? Does it seem too angry? Does it seem arrogant—or too timid? Is it too formal—or too slangy? We can change our choice of words to make the tone more appropriate to the topic, more suited to the readers we have in mind, more like "us."

Guideline

Use your own vocabulary with imagination and let *Roget's Thesaurus* lead you to words that suit your intended tone.

Revision Practice: Variety of Words

Read this essay with special attention to the tone established by its author's choice of words. Using your own vocabulary (and the help of *Roget's Thesaurus*), revise the essay, starting with the title. Find more suitable words to replace those underscored.

---

[1] Russell Baker, "Purging Stag Words," *New York Times,* 22 October 1974, p. 41. Copyright © 1974 by The New York Times Company. Reprinted by permission.

AN INTERESTING PASTIME

2   It is thought that a Belgian schoolmaster in 1850

3   introduced the hobby of collecting stamps. To attract his

4   pupils to an interest in geography, he told them to decorate

5   their atlases with as many fitting postage stamps as were

6   then to be had. His little suggestion added fun to the

7   classroom exercises, and now stamp collecting has become one

8   of the world's most interesting and educational hobbies.

9   Postage stamps are a continual reminder of the variety

10   of interesting facts and important occasions relating to

11   every country in the world. That function alone makes stamp

12   collecting a first-rate hobby. The attraction of unusual

13   places and their ways brings valuable rewards.

14   As a stamp collection increases, the collector becomes

15   more and more captured by its pleasures. The book becomes a

16   collection of pictures of charming faces, strange animals,

17   and foreign landscapes. It is a kaleidoscope of colors, a

18   purseful of centimes and lire and rubles. Going through the

19   pages from Azores to Ethiopia, from Ghana to Jamaica, from

20   Nippon to Zambia, the mind is affected by the utter variety

21   of details of history, literature, science, and the arts

22   that stamps uncover. The thrill of it all arouses, but

23   fortunately can never satisfy, the curiosity.

24   And though a stamp collection builds up to great value,

25   the expense is but little at a time and seldom of notice in

26   the budget.   <u>Really,</u> a stamp collection is a <u>cheap</u> and

27   <u>unequaled</u> source of <u>happiness.</u>

Follow-up

For "thought," of course it is easy to think of *believed, assumed,* or *supposed;* you must decide which is most appropriate for the context. For "introduced," perhaps *began, started, launched,* or *initiated* will do—but which? What does *Roget's* help you find for "attract" (line 3), and for "decorate" (line 4) and "fitting" (line 5)? Even before finishing your revision, you may have begun to see (and hear) the difference in tone. You should, of course, try to maintain a consistent tone throughout the essay.

Lesson 21

Pronouns
and
Synonyms

Imagine having to read a book or a long essay written like this sample paragraph:

> Then the man told the woman that the man's job depended on the woman's not reporting the man's mistake to the man's superiors. The superiors had threatened to fire the man if the man caused another complaint.

Tough going. The ideas would be easier to follow, more readable, if the writer used some pronouns such as *she, he, her, him, his, they, them:*

> Then the man told the woman that *his* job depended on *her* not reporting *his* mistake to *his* superiors. *They* had threatened to fire *him* if *he* caused another complaint.

But pronouns, handy as they are, can present problems. If the reader doesn't know at first glance what a pronoun stands for—what *this* means or who *they* are—the writing is certainly not clear. What can readers make of something like this?

The mother with the baby, who seemed confused, said she had been awake all night because of the crying. When she got to the hospital, she said it was terrible. She couldn't stand another one like that.

Who was confused, the baby or the mother? Which had been awake? What was terrible—the hospital, the baby, the night? Which of those could "she" not stand? Readers are asked to make wild guesses about the information, since it is unclear what "who," "she," "it," "one," and "that" stand for.

The mother seemed confused. She had been awake all night because of her baby's crying. At the hospital she said the experience had been terrible and she couldn't stand another night like that.

By eliminating the phrase "with the baby," the revision avoids our mistaking "she" to mean the baby. The unclear "it" has been replaced by "experience," and "one" has been clarified as "night." The pronoun "she" is clear enough, since no reader is likely to assume that the baby talks.

Synonyms help us avoid repetition, and they risk less misunderstanding than do pronouns. Consider this from a first draft:

Politics is a rigorous pursuit, and seeking public office takes a lot of work. Going into *it* means giving up most of *his* leisure time and family life, and *they* must be willing to support *it*.

The passage is almost unreadable. We assume that "it" means politics. "His" must refer to the person who goes into politics, but that person was not mentioned earlier. "They" is also unclear: "leisure time and family life," or "members of the family"? And does the final "it" refer to politics, to the candidacy, or to the whole career? If we use synonyms, nouns rather than pronouns, we can make the passage easier to read:

Politics is a rigorous pursuit. A *candidate* must give up most leisure time and family life, and the *spouse and children* will have to support *the career.*

Our "candidate" is a synonym for "politician"; "the spouse and children" is a synonym for "family." "Career" specifies what's meant by the unclear "it."

When we do use a pronoun, we must first name what it stands for. Otherwise, we ask the reader to delay understanding:

Although *they* are tasty and filling, most of us can get little satisfaction from *junk foods.*

What "they" means isn't clear until we get to "junk foods" at the end of the sentence. For easier reading, the noun should appear earlier than its pronoun:

Although *junk foods* are tasty and filling, most of us can get little satisfaction from *them*.

Especially handy, and especially troublesome, are the pronouns *this* and *that*. A common temptation is to use *this* or *that* to refer to a whole idea:

> The scales of justice are usually tipped in favor of the experienced criminal, so the big-time mobster gets by with stealing while the petty thief goes to prison. *This* makes it seem that crime does sometimes pay.

We can't be quite sure what "this" stands for: the tipping of the scales of justice, the mobster getting by with stealing, or the thief going to prison. The passage can be readable only if the reader knows at first glance what "this" means. This writer should use a synonym (or even a repetition) to remind the reader that

> ... *This imbalance* shows that crime does sometimes pay.

Pronouns, used clearly, help us avoid awkward repetition. Nouns used as synonyms can do the same thing—and can help us make things clear.

Guideline

 Avoid awkward repetition by using clear pronouns and synonyms.

Revision Practice: Pronouns and Synonyms

As you read this essay, look for awkward repetition and unclear pronouns. Revise the essay, using synonyms and clear pronouns for variety.

TIMID TIM

1   My cousin Tim was the most timid person in my family

2 and possibly the most timid person on the whole world's

3 stage. He afforded us many laughs, and our laughs must have

4 caused Tim untold anguish. This is one of them.

5   Timidity did not come to Tim through heredity, since my

6 aunt and uncle were notoriously fearless and faced life with

7 uncommon daring. It was well known in the family. Tim was

8 also terrified by both his parents, as he was by almost

9 everyone and by most animals. They would often insist that

10 Tim go along on some unthinkable adventure.

11   He was not afraid of cats. Cats were his constant

12 companions. He cared more for cats than he cared for any

13 other thing. There always seemed to be a cat slinking along

14 at his heels or, more often, leading the way, for Tim would

15 have backed away with hair on end at the sight of a mouse.

16   Tim was quite unable to assert himself in public.

17 Even in private, as far as I knew, Tim took no chances.

18 Surely Tim trembled as he faced each new day, and he was

19 rendered absolutely rigid by the thought of night.

20   Perhaps because of that Tim came through dating age

21 without dating. Tim was hopelessly incapable of talking to a

22 girl. But he was interested, and he actually developed a

23 silent crush on one girl who lived along the circuitous

24 route from school. Tim got so he would stop near her house

25 and watch the house, even if he could not see Irene. He was

26 often late for dinner.

27   One day after school he stopped to watch Irene's house.

28 As the hours passed and lights came on inside, Irene herself

29 was visible through a window. Fascinated, Tim stayed to

30 watch until it was quite dark. Suddenly he remembered that

31 the dark was filled with horrors. But he also feared my

32 uncle's rage, and that hastened his steps toward home.

33   Tim knew it was possible to save twenty minutes by

34 walking through the graveyard rather than around it--and

35 that must have stirred some unsuspected courage, for he took

36 off through it. As he told me later, it was a moonless

37 night, and the graveyard was very dark. With his every

38 step, he was certain, uncounted ghosts kept pace. Suddenly

39 something grabbed Tim's pantleg. A howl of terror split the

40 night, and Tim arrived home ten minutes before the cat did--

41 in time for dinner but in no condition to eat it.

Follow-up

Sometimes simple omission will avoid an awkward repetition. Have you replaced "person" in line 2? In the second sentence (lines 3–4) would it be clearer to put "Tim" first and "he" later? What is meant by "this" and "them" in line 4? What is meant by "it" in line 7? Who are "they" in line 9—animals? How can the annoying repetition of "cats" (lines 11–12) be avoided? What does "that" in line 20 refer to? Does "it" in line 30 mean the house? What does "that" in line 32 refer to? Might "it" in line 41 be taken to mean the cat? Reread your revision to consider its variety of expression.

Writing and Revising

For detailed suggestions on getting started, writing a first draft, revising the draft, and preparing the essay for submission, refer to the Introduction. Choose one of the following topics.

Topics for Writing

1. English statesman Benjamin Disraeli once said that one trouble with money is that the wrong people have it. Was he right? Who *should* have money? The topic is narrowed. Jot a list of your ideas and devise a thesis on the topic. Select a purpose; then number the ideas in an appropriate order and write a first draft.

2. One way to hold on to childhood is to learn nothing about history—or to learn nothing from it. What value have you found in the study of the past? Jot a list of your ideas and devise a thesis on the topic. Select a purpose; then number the ideas in an appropriate order and write a first draft.

3. Consider work as drudgery and work as self-fulfillment. If you could live your whole life without working, would you? Explain why. Jot a list of your ideas and devise a thesis on the topic. Select a purpose; then number the ideas in an appropriate order and write a first draft.

4. Some people face the knowledge that they have but a few months to live, not because of old age but because of some incurable malady. What attitudes toward life may be of use and comfort to such people? Jot a list of your ideas and devise a thesis on the topic. Select a purpose; then number the ideas in an appropriate order and write a first draft.

Follow-up

Read your first draft carefully, considering its substance. Is its topic sufficiently developed with a variety of material? What of the essay's originality of expression? Have you permitted any clichés to deaden your effects? If so, can they be revised in fresher terms? Is the tone appropriate to your topic and suited to your attitude toward it and toward your readers? Can you improve the tone by using *Roget's Thesaurus* to find more suitable words? Consider your use of pronouns: Is every pronoun understandable? Can you use synonyms for variety? When you have completed your revision, see Lesson 42 for a guide to preparing the manuscript for submission.

Lesson 22

Variety of Sentence Forms

When we put words together in sense-making patterns, we form three kinds of word groups: phrase, clause, and sentence. It will help to know how they differ.

- *A phrase* includes two or more words working as a unit, but it does not include a subject-verb combination.

- *A clause* includes a subject-verb combination. An *independent* clause makes a full statement or question, but a *subordinate* clause does not.

- *A sentence* includes a subject-verb combination and does complete a full statement or question.

Now let's take a sentence apart and find those three forms. We'll use a sentence by the late French entertainer Maurice Chevalier:

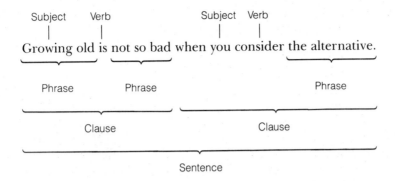

About Phrases

A phrase is always more than one word: The three phrases in the example above are "growing old," "not so bad," and "the alternative." Also, a phrase works as a unit of meaning; its words affect one another. *Growing* is not quite the same as "growing old." The two words now have a meaning together that neither of them had when apart. Third, a phrase may be (or include) a subject *or* a verb, but it may not include *both* subject and verb.

About Clauses

A clause includes both subject and verb, and it may include other words and phrases as well. By itself, a clause does not always form a complete sentence. The first clause, "Growing old is not so bad," *could be* a sentence; the second clause, "when you consider the alternative," could not.

If a clause could be a sentence by itself, we call it a "main" or "independent" clause. If a clause could not form a sentence by itself, we call it a "subordinate" clause.

A subordinate clause works as a unit of meaning; it either names an idea or modifies one. The subordinate clause, "when you consider the alternative," tells us under what conditions the main idea, "Growing old is not so bad," is true. The subordinate clause, in other words, works as a modifier.

About Sentences

A full sentence always includes at least one independent clause; it *may* also include other clauses of either kind. We can form four types of sentence:

1. A sentence with just one clause (independent) is a *simple* sentence: "Growing old is not so bad."

2. A sentence with more than one independent clause is *compound:* "Growing old is bad, but not growing old is worse."

3. A sentence that includes a subordinate clause is *complex:* "Growing old is not so bad when you consider the alternative."

4. A sentence that combines types 2 and 3 is *compound-complex:* "Growing old is bad, but, when you think about it, not growing old is worse."

Part of the work of revising for style is determining the most readable forms for our many "bits" of information. Maurice Chevalier, instead of putting his idea into the sentence we have seen, might have used some different forms. The phrase "growing old" might have been put into a single word: *aging.* Instead of saying "not so bad," he might have used a single word: *pleasant.* And instead of his subordinate clause "when you consider the alternative," he might have used a phrase: *considering the alternative.* If we make these changes, we get quite a different way of writing the idea:

Aging is pleasant, considering the alternative.

But form is never a thing apart from substance. Now that we've changed the form, we have also subtly changed the impact of the idea. If we were writing an essay, we'd have to consider which form would do most justice to the intended idea, be most clear and emphatic, and affect our readers as we want it to.

Now let's try using these forms (phrases, clauses, and sentences) to revise a brief idea in a variety of ways:

We rowed toward shore. Two sharks swam nearby. They looked hungry.

Our "idea" has three parts, each now written as a simple sentence. We may combine any two of them, or all three:

We rowed toward shore as two sharks swam nearby. They looked hungry.

We rowed toward shore. Two sharks swam nearby, and they looked hungry.

We rowed toward shore as two sharks, looking hungry, swam nearby.

We rowed toward shore with two sharks swimming nearby and looking hungry.

As we rowed toward shore, two sharks swam nearby, and they looked hungry.

Two sharks swimming nearby looked hungry as we rowed toward shore.

As we rowed toward shore, two hungry-looking sharks swam nearby.

Rowing toward shore, we saw two hungry-looking sharks swimming nearby.

In a sense we have been "tinkering" with our idea, trying to improve it. When we find the version that is just right for our purpose, we have the satisfaction of craftsmanship, the pleasure of full self-expression.

Of course, we would probably not do that much tinkering with every idea in an essay. But this exercise, like most of the revision exercises in this book, may help us get the habit of revising for readable variety.

The one-idea simple sentence of few words can be a direct, clear, readable way of putting an idea. Using only that kind of sentence, Herman Melville might have written the beginning of *Moby Dick* like this:

> Call me Ishmael. My story took place some years ago. I had little or no money in my purse. There was nothing particular to interest me on shore. I decided to sail about a little. I wanted to see the watery part of the world.

Each sentence is clear enough; the first one, "Call me Ishmael," would be hard to improve. But the passage trudges along, offering no variety; all are simple sentences of about the same length. Had Melville written it that way, readers might have found it monotonous. We can add variety by using *and, or, but, so, yet,* and other such words to form compound sentences:

> Call me Ishmael. My story took place some years ago, *and* I had little or no money in my purse. There was nothing particular to interest me on shore, *so* I decided to sail about a little, *for* I wanted to see the watery part of the world.

Now the passage is more varied but still rough. We can try for still more variety by using such connecting words as *when, since, because,* and *so that* to combine the ideas, making complex sentences:

> My story took place some years ago, *when* I had little or no money in my purse. *Because* there was nothing particular to interest me on shore, I decided to sail about a little, *since* I wanted to see the watery part of the world.

If we use both kinds of connecting word (both the *and* sort and the *when* sort) to link ideas, we write a compound-complex sentence:

> My story took place some years ago *when* I had little or no money in my purse, *and, since* there was nothing particular to interest me on shore, I decided to sail about a little, *so that* I could see the watery part of the world.

But now the passage is wordy, a bit too complicated, and its one sentence is overloaded, asking the reader to take in too many ideas without pause. We can use phrases to replace clauses and perhaps cut some words and phrases entirely. We then put the whole passage into one simple sentence:

Some years ago, with little or no money in my purse and nothing particular to interest me on shore, I decided to sail about a little to see the watery part of the world.

By experimenting with sentence form, we have brought a variety of possibilities to the passage. Here's how Melville, perhaps after several revisions, finally wrote it:

Call me Ishmael. Some years ago—never mind how long precisely—having little or no money in my purse, and nothing particular to interest me on shore, I thought I would sail about a little and see the watery part of the world.

Melville puts variety of sentence form to work for an important purpose: to help reveal character. Ishmael is shown as a person whose mind can range from the simple, blunt, and forceful (in the brief first sentence) to the analytical and complex (in the long second sentence).

Guideline

22 Vary sentence length and form.

Revision Practice: Variety of Sentence Forms

Read this essay carefully with special attention to its sentences. Revise the essay, combining or separating ideas for more effective coherence, greater emphasis, and economy. Wherever in doubt about effects, try revising the passage in several different sentence forms before deciding which is best. Take care to avoid running two sentences together without proper connective or punctuation.

TILL TEMPTATION DO US PART

[1]Adulterers are no longer publicly stoned or burned at the stake. [2]It is not necessary today for anyone to feel stigmatized after having an affair outside of marriage.

Combine first two sentences?

[3]Those who practice monogamy because they have religious convictions may recall the stories of

Is 3 really two sentences? Can they be made into one?

Abraham, Solomon, and David, all had extramarital love affairs. [4]Did God favor them any less because of what they had done?

[5]Yet many of us still hold to some very old ideas about marriage. [6]Such ideas are old but not necessarily "quaint," not yet without validity. [7]The time-honored (by long lip service, at least) concept of marriage "till death do us part" has not perished from the earth. [8]But our reasons for holding to monogamy are sometimes less than pure. [9]Could monogamy be a wall that we build around our marriages to protect ourselves from the pains of jealousy?

Can 5 and 6 be combined?

Can ideas in 9 be combined in one simple *sentence?*

[10]If we marry with the expectation that our mate will be absolutely faithful, chances are that we are set up for disappointment, because we have not fully understood what faithfulness is, and we may not really know how we or our mate will respond to temptation, or what shortcomings within our relationship may make temptations the more tempting. [11]The once assumed solution was to enter into marriage "for good," recognizing that what later occurred might be "for better or for worse." [12]In such a marriage it was assumed that even if a partner should succumb to temptation,

Is sentence 10 overloaded with ideas? Can it be separated into two sentences?

the marriage would survive. [13]It would be held together by sheer determination, by fear of public or family opinion, by concern for children, or by angry and stubborn unwillingness to let the wavering spouse off the hook. [14]Sometimes even by tolerant winking at the situation.

[15]Today there are fewer such guarantees of continued matrimony, and the divorce rate climbs and would perhaps climb faster if it were not for the fact that many separating couples have never married in the first place but merely live together in what used to be called sin and is now called "openness."

[16]Open arrangements, whether "living together" or "open marriage," are not licenses for orgy but are insurance against moments of weakness in the face of temptation as well as against disillusionment. [17]Knowledge of a lover's infidelity can hurt, even in an open marriage, so partners do not have an absolute right to free love outside the partnership. [18]The degree of commitment is open to negotiation. [19]It is, of course, also subject to surprise.

[20]Some still hold that love conquers all, but again, love varies in degree, and some lovers are more devoted, more constant than others. [21]The

How can 12 and 13 be combined?

Link fragment 14 to its sentence.

Is sentence 15 overloaded? Can its ideas be put into two or three sentences?

Break 16 into two sentences for greater emphasis?

Combine 18 and 19 in one simple sentence?

Break 20 into two sentences?

question is whether two people are enough in love

so that their relationship will not be destroyed by   *Cut wordiness*
                                                        and simplify
a sexual affair outside it if that affair is but of   *sentence 21?*

a moment and is not accompanied by real devotion.

²²Even if love does not conquer all, love may

endure all.

Follow-up

Read your revision with attention to how well its sentences present the ideas emphatically, economically. What words did you cut? What did you add? Did you find that the keys to sentence combining lie in connective words such as *and, so, but, or, yet* (making compound sentences) and *which, although,* and *when* (making sentences complex)?

Lesson 23

Ellipticals

Much of our everyday conversation goes on without full sentences. We "shorthand" some sentences when we're sure their meanings will be clear anyway:

"Feeling all right?"	"Are you feeling all right?"
"Just tired."	"I'm just tired."
"Up late?"	"Were you up late?"
"Right."	"Yes, I was up late."
"Big date, huh?"	"You had a big date; is that right?"
"No. Studying."	"I didn't have a big date. I was studying."
"Finals coming up?"	"Are your finals coming up?"
"Naturally."	"Naturally, my finals are coming up."
"Good luck."	"I wish you good luck."
"Same to you."	"I wish the same to you."

Not one sentence in the whole conversation. Only pieces of sentences. All understandable, though.

Such shorthand sentences can sometimes—though not often—be used in writing. They can pack a lot of punch when carefully handled by capable writers. We call them *ellipticals,* a fancy word for expressions that lack one or more elements essential to grammar but not needed for understanding. They add to the variety we can give our sentences.

But ellipticals should be distinguished from annoying *fragments,* pieces of sentences that really should be attached where they belong. Except in our informal conversations, we're not likely to be understood easily if we use a word, phrase, or subordinate clause as if it were a sentence. When we write, we have to make very sure that the partial sentence, the elliptical, is easily readable and will be fully understood.

Look again at the top of this page. When you first read those three "sentences," were you aware that they were not really full sentences? If not, then they did their job; they were effective ellipticals.

Most readers, though, and certainly most teachers of writing, will not accept awkward fragments like these:

> My home town is a special place. *Because of its industries.* Many new residents have come here. *In the last few years.* It has developed a new community spirit. *As if it had had a transfusion of ideas.*

The fragments make the passage hard to read. For one thing, we can't tell whether "because of its industries" belongs with the sentence before it or with the one after it. And the same goes for the phrase "in the last few years." And the final "as if it had had a transfusion of ideas" should be attached to the sentence before it. A careful revision of the awkward fragments gives us a more readable passage:

> My home town is a special place. Because of its industries, many new residents have come here in the last few years. It has developed a new community spirit, as if it had had a transfusion of ideas.

The sentence parts are now all attached to their sentences in meaningful, readable order.

Unwanted fragments often appear when we present a list of things as examples:

> Everyone has two sides to his personality. *A public side and a private side.*

That kind of fragment easily attaches to its sentence, after a comma, dash, or colon:

Everyone has two sides to his personality: a public side and a private side.

How can we tell an effective elliptical from an unacceptable fragment? As a general rule, a partial "sentence" written unintentionally is likely to be a bad one. To write effective ellipticals, we must be aware of what we are doing. Clearly Charles Dickens knew what he was doing in the opening chapter of *Bleak House:*

> Fog everywhere. Fog up the river, where it flows among green aits and meadows; fog down the river, where it rolls defiled among the tiers of shipping, and the waterside pollutions of a great (and dirty) city. Fog on the Essex marshes, fog on the Kentish heights.

None of the "sentences" has a complete independent clause, yet readers easily understand what's meant and need no more. The ellipticals create a feeling, a tone, appropriate to Dickens's subject: After all, fog keeps us from seeing more than glimpses of things, and from the foggy glimpse of meadow or marsh, river or dock, we are able to "see" the whole meadow, whole marsh, whole riverside scene. Here are some ground rules for using effective ellipticals and avoiding awkward fragments:

1. Never use a partial sentence unless you have some clear purpose for it, such as dramatic emphasis.

2. Make sure all other sentences have at least one subject-verb combination.

3. Remember that a clause beginning with such words as *if, because, while,* or *although* cannot be a sentence by itself.

4. Remember that verbals ending in *-ing* (like *singing, watching, delaying*) are not verbs.

5. Remember that a preposition usually begins a phrase; the noun that ends that phrase cannot be the subject of a verb.

Guideline

Use ellipticals ("shorthand" sentences) sparingly for special effects. Never allow an awkward fragment.

Revision Practice: Ellipticals

Revise this essay, using no fragments. Use ellipticals only where you find them suitable to the essay's subject matter and tone.

AS THE TWIG IS BENT

[1]Words have enormous power, and many of the attitudes that guide us through a long life are acquired in childhood. [2]In the form of words. [3]Sayings that are heard again and again while our ways of thinking are being formed. [4]My early family life was full of words to give backbone to character. [5]To free (or to shackle) a spirit forever.

[6]In my home we often heard "Early to bed and early to rise." [7]My parents intoned the phrase repeatedly. [8]And lived by it. [9]It made them healthy and, I think, wise. [10]It might have made them wealthy had it not been for its inevitable result.

[11]My parents brought into this world an enormous family. [12]Six brothers and four sisters. [13]All living together. [14]Until two of the boys left home. [15]To join the navy. [16]We were never quite sure whether Eddie and Walter went sailing to get away from the crowd.

[17]My mother and father always got up early, particularly on Sunday. [18]To go to church. [19]Responding to "Rise and shine!" we were all up within a quarter hour after Dad's own arising. [20]At the sound of his voice, we arose perforce. [21]Though we did not always shine. [22]Now and then I tried to point out that the Lord Himself rested on Sunday, but Dad countered with an amused, "And what did you create this week?" [23]So I got up.

[24]Before I was six I had learned from both parents and four older siblings that procrastination is the thief of time. [25]Of

course, I was nine before I knew just what procrastination was.
[26]By that time I had heard the saying hundreds of times and,
although I was never allowed to put off homework or household
chores, I was secretly in love. [27]With procrastination.

[28]I sometimes tried to introduce a saying or two of my own,
such as "Better late than never." [29]Not exactly a wise saying.
[30]More of an excuse, as I knew. [31]Hopeless. [32]Trying another
tack, I once arrived at the table purposely early. [33]Announcing,
"First come, first served!" [34]Again, my saying did not catch on.

[35]Now and then I suffered some hurt at a brother's hand and
spent many hours planning ways of getting even. [36]Mother would
usually interrupt such brooding. [37]Advising, "Don't let the sun
go down on your wrath." [38]I didn't know what wrath was either.
[39]Although I knew it had something to do with grapes. [40]And the
Lord, Whom I clearly saw trampling those grapes. [41]It didn't
matter. [42]Mother had spoken, and I seldom went to bed remembering what I had been angry about.

[43]As we grew, we all came to know that money did not grow
on trees. [44]At a rare moment Dad would give a child a few
pennies. [45]Always with the advice that a penny saved is a penny
earned. [46]By the age of eight I had saved sixty-seven pennies.
[47]In a glass jar. [48]I believed that I had earned them all;
actually I had found fourteen of them and had been given twenty-
six. [49]The others came in mysterious ways. [50]Ten from the tooth
fairy. [51]But I knew they had not grown on trees.

^{52}I kept careful count, knowing by rote that if I took care of my pennies, my dollars would take care of themselves. ^{53}I had never had a dollar, so I assumed mine were taking care of themselves. ^{54}Probably somewhere in a bank. ^{55}I knew they would someday come to me. ^{56}After all, I was to be made wealthy. ^{57}By going early to bed.

^{58}Often, as I counted my pennies, I was reminded by a jealous sister that money is the root of all evil. ^{59}I had no idea what evil was, but I knew I was in love with its roots.

^{60}To this day my ways of life are those that came from the oft-repeated sayings of my childhood. ^{61}I have never counted unhatched chickens, and I have never put all of anything into one basket. ^{62}I am still in love with procrastination, money, and trampled grapes of good vintage. ^{63}But most of all, I think, I love to laugh. ^{64}It's a love encouraged by my mother. ^{65}Who said--so many times--"Smile, and the world smiles with you; weep, and you weep alone." ^{66}I have never wept alone.

Follow-up

You should have found twenty-three incomplete "sentences" in the first draft. Most of them you probably absorbed into their appropriate sentences by attaching them directly or by using a comma, a colon, or a dash: ^{11}"My parents brought into this world an enormous family: ^{12}six brothers and four sisters, ^{13}all living together ^{14}until two of the boys left home ^{15}to join the navy." Did you find any groups suitable to stand as ellipticals? You may have considered using 29–30 as elliptical: "Not exactly a wise saying; more of an excuse, as I knew." And 31 might stand by itself: "Hopeless." Are there others? Make sure that ellipticals are entirely clear in meaning and suitable in tone.

Lesson 24

Figurative Language

When we use words to mean what the dictionary says they mean or what most people assume them to mean, we are using *literal* language. The words *nail* and *boot* are used literally in "he had a painful nail in his boot."

But we may use words to mean something they don't ordinarily mean. If we write, "Hennessy was nailed deep in his own territory and had to boot the ball out of there," we are using *figurative* language. Now *nailed* means *tackled* and *boot* means *kick.*

Figurative language opens the door to imaginative variety, allowing us to say things in new, sometimes delightful ways. We can use figurative language in any of three ways: (1) association, (2) comparison, or (3) contrast.

Association. Our minds are constantly seeing connections among things, so that we can name one for the other, as we do in writing *boot* for *kick, brains* for *intelligence, diamond* for *field,* or *the blue* for *the sky.* We also associate a thing with what it's made of, calling a golf *club* a *wood.* We associate a thing and its parts, using *wheels* for *car.* The trouble with most of these figures is that they are heard everywhere; the associations are common and not imaginative.

Associating the sounds of words offers a bit more room for originality. We can bring some sparkle to our writing by using *puns* when they are appropriate to what we are saying. Twists on the sounds and meanings of words often make good titles, like the one written by a student for an essay about the time she was "let off" instead of being ticketed for not seeing a traffic light. She titled the essay "Near Cited."

Possibilities also arise from *epithets*, names that express associated qualities. We might call a professor "Old Red Ink" or our decade of serious matters "The Weighty Eighties." Such figures must be appropriate, not merely cute.

Comparison. When we call something what it isn't, we may be comparing it to something else: "He's a snail" compares the person to the snail, suggesting slow movement; "she's lightning quick" compares her quickness to that of lightning. The first one is a *metaphor,* saying he *is* the snail; the second is a *simile,* saying she is *similar* to lightning. Find the metaphors and similes here:

He has an umbilical attachment to the welfare department.

The speaker made hash of the issues.

She tried to preserve her secrets in the baggie of her mind.

A pickle floated in the leftover salad oil, a lonely alligator in a swamp.

All his hopes collapsed, like walnuts in a vise.

Metaphors and similes have a way of turning into clichés. For interest and readability we need to revise the old ones and find originals.

Another sort of figurative comparison occurs in *analogy.* To make clear a point, we compare it to something in which we see similar qualities: "His mind was like a desert island." But the thought may not be fully understood; to clarify it, we expand by mentioning several ways in which the two things are alike:

His mind was like a desert island, insulated from the larger world, his ideas arising without outside influence. But it was subject to occasional storms.

And another:

Individuality is important for mental growth and well-being. If we didn't recognize individuality, it would be as if our eyesight were limited to seeing only in shades of gray.

Analogies are useful when they really clarify a thought. But they are subject to error if not carefully thought out. The two things compared should have clear points of similarity. If readers may think of ways in which the two things are quite unlike, the analogy is weak.

We use *personification* when we compare abstract ideas (like time, beauty, success) or inanimate objects (trees, waves, clocks) to human beings. Thus we say that "Time smiled at her" or "success beckoned with an index finger" or "the wave curled its arms about him." We also personify when we give animals human characteristics: "The cat winked knowingly" or "the penguin bride wore white under her tuxedo."

When we personify abstractions, we ordinarily capitalize: "My grandmother was a matchmaker, introducing Beauty to Age and suggesting they live together."

Contrast. If our words contrast with our meanings, we write *irony:* "We looked forward to meeting the dean and to a draught of poison with the same joyful anticipation." When our words mean less than they say, we use *hyperbole:* "My brainy friend checked out four tons of books for his weekend reading." And when our words mean more than they say, we use *understatement:* "The offer of a million-dollar salary was of some interest to me." We may also understate with *litotes,* a way of denying the opposite of what we intend: "Two weeks of mononucleosis is not a Caribbean cruise."

Whichever sort of figurative language we use, we must revise critically. If a figure is one we've heard often, it's unlikely to bring variety to our work. And if the figures in any one passage clash with one another, we have to revise for consistency (see Lesson 36).

Guideline

Try for variety and color through figurative language.

Revision Practice: Figurative Language

Read this essay carefully to absorb its present tone. It offers many opportunities for the variety of figurative language. A few such opportunities are indicated by the underscored words. Revise the essay, trying to create metaphor, simile, personification, epithet, hyperbole, or other figures to enhance its tone.

STOP THE WORLD

¹As I awaken, my looming <u>math test comes</u> back into my still <u>unclear</u> mind. ²I <u>drink</u> coffee and eat cereal as the mind clears a little, and I

¹Can the math test be personified? Mind as unclear as what?
²Is the mind a bit like a computer?

think through the day's agenda. ³School, math, work; I'm afraid I'll never get through it. ⁴I feel <u>half dead</u>. ⁵But the coffee has its effect, and I am away and about my day.

⁶At school I <u>don't hear much</u> of a history lecture as the math test <u>goes through my head</u>. ⁷In math class, <u>confused by everything</u>, I finally get through the test, submit the papers, and <u>find the way back</u> to my car. ⁸I punch the clock at work and go back to the making of PaperMate pens. ⁹The <u>clock moves slowly</u>. ¹⁰The pens assemble automatically on a moving bench before me until quitting time at last.

¹¹When weeks of such workdays end, I'm shouting inside. ¹²My nervous tension and stored aggression have me screaming, "Stop the world--I want to get off!"

¹³What can restore the soul at such times? ¹⁴My best device is bodily exertion. ¹⁵I go to the karate studio, and there I punch, kick, chop, and yell my way out of the tension. ¹⁶Muscles I haven't been using are put back to work. ¹⁷My lungs fill with air. ¹⁸My pores exude the poisons, and my skin once again feels the scintillation of sweat. ¹⁹The movements of the kata, gracefully

³*Can that computer talk?*
⁴*Half dead like a . . . what?*

⁶*How much of the lecture is heard? Is the math test still personified?*
⁷*"Everything?" Name one thing. In terms of math what's the short way back to the car?*
⁹*What slow thing moves the clock?*

¹³*Is the soul sick? What cures illness?*

¹⁶*Can muscles,* ¹⁷*lungs,* ¹⁸*pores, and skin be personified?*

rounded and precisely timed, take the aggression

out of me and give me a new look at things.

[20]Physical exertion turns my fatigue into new

[20]Is the change performed as by magic?

vigor. [21]When the karate session is over, my world

has slowed to an easy pace. [22]When the next day

[22]Return to an image from the beginning of the essay.

comes, I'm ready for math and work again--this time

with less fear of not getting through.

Follow-up

If you were able to personify the math test as an intimidating enemy (threatening, grinning), the revision must have more life than the original. And the talking computer-mind has possibilities. Consider the figurative effects of a beginning such as this:

[1]As I awaken, my coming <u>math test grins</u>

Personification

at me, sufficiently alarming, through a <u>foggy</u>

Simile

<u>mind</u>. [2]I inhale coffee and cereal as <u>the fog</u>

<u>lifts</u> a little and the day's <u>agenda prints out</u>

Metaphor

<u>on my mental screen</u>. [3]School, it says; math

it says; work, it says; you'll never get

through it, it says; you're a zombie, it says.

[4]The <u>fog yellows into smog</u>, and I am away

Metaphor

and about my normal day."

Compare your revision with the original. Has the figurative language made the essay more interesting, more readable?

Summary
Revising for Variety

Guidelines 19–24

19. If you've often heard an expression, don't use it unless for some special purpose.

20. Use your own vocabulary with imagination and let *Roget's Thesaurus* lead you to words that suit your intended tone.

21. Avoid awkward repetition by using clear pronouns and synonyms.

22. Vary sentence length and form.

23. Use ellipticals ("shorthand" sentences) sparingly for special effects. Never allow an awkward fragment.

24. Try for variety and color through figurative language.

Writing and Revising

For detailed suggestions on getting started, writing a first draft, revising the draft, and preparing the essay for submission, refer to the Introduction. Choose one of the following topics.

Topics for Writing

1. Can anyone really predict the future? To what extent is it desirable to do so? Can prediction be dangerous? Jot a list of your ideas and devise a thesis on the topic. Select a purpose; then number the ideas in an appropriate order and write a first draft.

2. What makes a person pessimistic? Discuss the effects of pessimism on the personality and on one's social life. Consider whether there is any real connection between pessimism and seeing life "as it is." Jot a list of your ideas and devise a thesis on the topic. Your purpose is to *analyze cause and effect.* Number the ideas in an appropriate order and write a first draft.

3. What is a "victimless crime"? Does such a crime actually have a victim after all—the one who commits it? Should such acts be decriminalized? Jot a list of your ideas and devise a thesis on the topic. Your purpose

is *definition* and *arguing to convince.* Number the ideas in an appropriate order and write a first draft.

4. Ishmael, the narrator of Herman Melville's *Moby Dick,* says that whenever he finds himself "growing grim about the mouth," he tries to get to sea as soon as he can. Where do you like to go (or what do you like to do) to escape the doldrums? Jot a list of your ideas and devise a thesis on the topic. Select a purpose; then number the ideas in an appropriate order and write a first draft.

Follow-up

Read your first draft with a listening ear. Consider the length of sentences. If you've written three or four long sentences in a row, you need to use an occasional short sentence for variety. Try separating or combining sentences in patterns other than their present ones. Is every sentence complete? If you have used any incomplete sentence, try attaching it to one of your complete ones. Leave an *elliptical* expression only when you think it is just right for the occasion. Where have you used (or can you use) *metaphor* or *simile* for variety and emphasis? Is there any detail you can express appropriately with *irony, hyperbole,* or *understatement?* Try these in your revision if you think they will fit your tone.

Review Quiz

In this quiz you may find monotony or repetition of words (rep), unclear pronouns (ref), clichés (cliché), choppy or monotonous sentence patterns (sent), fragments (frag), or dull use of literal language (lit). In the first five items the problems are italicized and labeled; later you must find them yourself. Revise to make every sentence more readable.

1. Tami was healthy, happy, and well adjusted to life. *The kind of daughter*

    every parent would like to have as a *daughter.*
                     frag   rep

2. Carla didn't want to give up that job until she had another *job. It* was
                                                                  rep ref
    her *security blanket.*
         cliché

3. A person can have too much humility. *Which can keep a person from*
                                                                  rep
    realizing the person's own worth.
              rep   frag

4. Beth influenced me. I was nineteen. *A very susceptible age.* She was
   _{frag}
   the same age. She was different from any other nineteen-year-old.

   That difference was the reason for her influence.
   _{sent}

5. The supervisor was angry *as she could be.* She *came* into the office. She
   _{lit} _{lit}
   put a notice on the bulletin board. *She went* out. *Slamming the door.*
   _{rep lit}   _{frag}

6. We always enjoyed holidays with the family. They were really something else.

7. One advantage of population control is that there is a better chance
   to live in a thinly populated area than in a thickly populated area.

8. Istanbul, my home city, creates many moods. You can approach it
   from inland. You can see its thousands of lights from miles away. You
   can smell the sea.

9. The school I attended was an Innovative Program school. It was a
   school within a school. One of the school's purposes was to expose
   students to self-awareness. It offered a different kind of education
   from that of the regular school.

10. My sister and I were staying with our aunt. One afternoon I was
    alone and was bored, and I was curious, so I decided to investigate
    the contents of a chest of drawers that had two small drawers on each
    side of a mirror, and with one of these drawers my trouble started,
    because it got stuck before I got it all the way out.

11. I do not like being dominated. I relish being pursued, however. I
    enjoy having a door opened for me. Not out of pity, but respect. I
    love compliments and consideration from the opposite sex.

12. It was a small farm by today's standards, but to us kids it was a place
    of mystic possibilities. Full of surprises that took our breath away.

13. Mildred Avenue is a typical shortcut for the typical person who is
    "running late." Neither stop signs nor traffic lights are a hindrance.
    Most cars build up a breakneck speed as they race down Mildred
    Avenue. Drivers don't notice that they are barreling down an avenue
    that cuts right through "the war zone" of which my neighborhood is
    a part.

14. I don't remember the first stories that were read to me. Only the
    thrill of them. Fairy tales and Greek myths probably came later. I
    still remember many of them. Medusa's head haunted me for many
    nights. By the time I entered high school, I was addicted to books.

15. At about midnight we were attacked. It was like nothing I had known

before. Bullets were flying everywhere. Flames were all over the place. Explosions! Frightening. I found myself hugging the ground and wetting my pants.

16. Rock music came from two other types of sounds. They were the rhythm-and-blues and the down-home country sound. By the middle of the fifties it had grown like wildfire. It was something young people could identify with. Something they could call their own.

17. Jack Sterns always looked a little sloppy. He had a beard and a mustache. Usually not trimmed. Also he always wore his hat tilted in a funny way. His uniform was usually dirty. Ring around the collar. And there were always food stains on it. Jack didn't think of himself a lot. Only of other people and what he could do for them.

18. Many people go through their lives committing small acts of crime. Most of these crimes seem petty. Such as stealing from a store. Taking the easy way out and getting something for nothing. This keeps building until you're stealing money from your job and your friends, always taking the path of least resistance until there's nothing you won't do for a fast buck.

19. In Israel the whole attitude toward hitchhiking is different from the attitude toward it in the United States. In Israel if a person doesn't have a ride, he hitchhikes. It is a normal thing to do. No one thinks too much about it. But hitchhiking in the United States is feared. Hitchhiking is not a normal thing to do here.

20. To me all my friends are just as important to me when I am not in need. Need is an unhappy time. I know what sympathy is like, and I don't want it.

Revising for

Clarity

The chief virtue that
language can have is
clearness, and nothing
detracts from it so much as
the use of unfamiliar words.
Hippocrates
(460?–370? B.C.)

Writing so that we can
be understood is not the end of the job. To make our work readable, we should
make it so clear that it *cannot be misunderstood.*

Seldom do we write that well in first draft. But in the revision stage we can
go for that level of clarity. Now we become half writer, half reader. We have
put a lot of words down on paper; our next job is to get them off the paper
again and into the reader's mind.

Jonathan Swift, who wrote *Gulliver's Travels,* said that style is "proper words
in proper places." Now, as we revise what we have written, we look with a
critical eye at our words, sentences, and paragraphs. Are those words just the
right ones? Are they in just the right places? Do the sentences say what they
mean? Are the paragraphs clear units of developed thought?

Words, at their readable best, spark immediate and fitting ideas and images
in the reader's mind. To make them do that, we need a lot of respect—and a
certain amount of love—for words. We need to know what words can do,
including which ones can do what. And we need to have acquaintance with a
fairly broad range of words: little ones and big ones, plain ones and fancy

ones, polite ones and gruff ones, words from the temple and the concert hall, from the playground and the construction site, from the physics lab and the latest news.

Even the most familiar words say little if they aren't put together right, so we need to understand what can go wrong. What noun does our pronoun stand for? Where does that modifier belong? What are we comparing with what? To make it all clear, we'll need those "proper words in proper places."

Lesson 25

Plain
Words

Words more than two inches long are not likely to fit in your reader's eye. Not that readers don't know many words; they probably do. But big words aren't the ones they find readable. Try this sentence for word size:

> It is oftentimes incomprehensible that numerous individuals desire to participate in recreational activities that produce such a minimum of beneficial effects.

Tough reading, isn't it? The words are big ones, stuffy ones, and they get between the reader and the idea. Let's try it again, this time with smaller, more familiar words:

> It is often hard to realize that so many people want to take part in games that do them so little good.

The trouble with our original sentence is that the words are bigger than they need to be, so they sound stuffy. We know what those words mean, all right, and one at a time they wouldn't seem so bad. But when big words deploy in full platoons, they camouflage meaning. As readers, we don't want to be slowed down by needless difficulty in figuring things out. We want clarity without a hassle.

We usually talk in plain words. Why, then, do so many of us *write* such big words? Maybe we're afraid that our ideas aren't very important, so we try to inflate them. We think our work will be more impressive if we write "often-times" instead of "often." We think "numerous" sounds like more than "many." And impressed by our own style, we write "desire," looking down our noses at a plain word like "want." After we've written "participate," plain "games" won't do; we must have "recreational activities."

The words we feel easiest about are the ones we learned in childhood and grew up with in our first dozen years. Many of the words we've learned since then are likely to be bookish, some of them real "two-dollar" words that we seldom use in a friendly conversation—and sparingly in readable writing:

Stuffy	Readable	Stuffy	Readable
accordingly	so	nonessential	not needed
additionally	and	numerous	many
approximately	about, nearly	paraphernalia	gear, equipment
assistance	help	participate	take part
contemplate	intend, think of	previously	earlier
encounter	meet	proceeded	went
endeavor	try	proficiency	skill
indicated	said	purchase	buy
initially	first, at first	respectively	in turn
likewise	and	terminate	end, stop
nevertheless	still	uncoordinated	awkward, clumsy

If we write the big words habitually, we write with a stuffy style; our tone tells readers that we are formal, pretentious, rather unfriendly, perhaps even afraid to be ourselves. Such stuffiness has often marred the writing of those who hope to impress business clients or executives. George Orwell once showed the poverty of such writing, imitating it by turning a passage from the Bible into modern "officialese" or "gobbledygook":

Objective consideration of contemporary phenomena compels the conclusion that success or failure in competitive activities exhibits no tendency to be commensurate with innate capacity, but that a considerable element of the unpredictable must invariably be taken into account.[1]

Almost unreadable, isn't it? Orwell called it "modern English of the worst sort." Would readers suffer through it willingly? Not if they knew they could get the message from Ecclesiastes:

> I returned and saw under the sun, that the race is not to the swift, nor the battle to the strong, neither yet bread to the wise, nor yet riches to men of understanding, nor yet favor to men of skill; but time and chance happeneth to them all.

And the race goes not to big words, but to the small. Writer Joseph Ecclesine, in a little essay on "Words of One Syllable," puts it this way:

> Small words move with ease where big words stand still—or, worse, bog down and get in the way of what you want to say. There is not much, in all truth, that small words will not say—and say quite well.[2]

Guideline

25

Keep long words few and don't crowd them.

Revision Practice: Plain Words

Revise this essay, changing its stuffy style to one less pretentious.

```
1              WHAT MOTIVATES HUMAN EFFORT?

2       Infrequently do we expend our efforts without expecting

3    remuneration.  Behind all our endeavors lies a motivating

4    vitality.  However, though we recognize and concede that

5    vitality, what can we conclude initiates it?  What makes us

6    perform as we do?
```

---

[1] George Orwell, "Politics and the English Language," in *A Collection of Essays* (New York: Doubleday, 1954), p. 169.

[2] Joseph A. Ecclesine, "Words of One Syllable," *Reader's Digest*, July 1961, p. 45. Reprinted by permission of the author.

7   As children we are recipients of rewards extended as
8 positive reinforcement of our desirable behavior. As we
9 learn to dress and feed ourselves, first under the guidance
10 and assistance of our parents, we are encouraged by their
11 congratulatory comments. We are thereby led to understand
12 that our learning behavior is considered satisfactory, and
13 to acquire more such approval we aspire to continue the
14 behavior that has inspired it. Thus achievement and self-
15 esteem are cultivated.

16   As we mature to adulthood, verbal reinforcement of our
17 acceptable behavior recedes into the background. What we
18 receive as reward for conduct deserving of approbation now
19 becomes tangible, and we are remunerated financially for our
20 developing skills and for our willingness to perform to the
21 benefit of our associates. Money, then, becomes the visible
22 evidence of our worthy behavior in society. Though we do not
23 forego our desire for verbal approbation, we cannot survive
24 on words alone, and we develop an expectation of being paid
25 a monetary stipend for our expenditure of energies and
26 display of skills. Indeed, we often gauge our degree of
27 success in business and in society by the amount of money we
28 can demand for our services.

29   Whether our efforts be recognized and rewarded by
30 verbal acclamation, financial compensation, or personal
31 fulfillment, we must see ourselves remunerated for efforts

32 exerted. These rewards remain essential to our continuation

33 of exertions. If there were no such recognition, surely we

34 would soon find it less troublesome to eschew indulgence of

35 our mental or physical potentials. We would, in brief,

36 cease performing to the expectations of society.

37   We must conclude, then, that what motivates humankind

38 is recognition, remuneration, and self-realization. Lacking

39 these, we remain unproductive and accomplish only to an

40 insignificant degree.

Follow-up

Beginning with the title, you have probably improved the tone of the essay by using everyday words to take the place of many of the long ones. Remember, however, that a big word is now and then just right for its job, so you need not have avoided every one. The readable style uses words of many kinds, both plain and fancy—but no one sort in excess.

Exact
Words

Words have a way of flitting about like butterflies. If we put our finger on one, as if to hold it in place, we diminish its life. Only when a word is dead, no longer much used, can we pin it down with certainty. Yet our words must carry our meanings, and if we allow them to flutter too much, we can't be sure of saying what we mean.

We can't have a word for every separate thing in the universe; there are just too many things. So, many words have two meanings, or dozens of meanings, and we're left to read them in context to tell what they mean at the moment: We may use *trip* to mean "a journey," "to step with agility," or "to fall over something." And when we write, we can't expect readers to understand us unless we provide the right clues to the meanings of words.

Careless use of words can create a quagmire of meaning:

Neighborhood kids use to aggravate Grandpa. I remember a time where they were teasing him unmercilessly. They grabbed for his cane, and he left them have it.

Is "use" supposed to mean "used," past tense? Was Grandpa really "aggravated" (made worse) or was he "irritated" (annoyed)? Is a "time" really a "where," or should it be "when"? Can "unmercilessly" mean "without lack of mercy"? Did he "leave" them have it or "let" them have it? And does letting them have it mean he "allowed them to take" the cane or that he "struck them" with it?

If we fumble our way through the language, our writing is sure to lead readers astray or to make their reading just too much trouble.

Some inexact words are just misspellings, often caused by similarity in the sounds of words; others are confused because of mispronunciation or because of mistaken meanings. Use a dictionary where you need it to distinguish these words commonly confused:

Misspelled Sound-Alikes

affect	effect	lead	led
capital	capitol	passed	past
cite	sight, site	there	their, they're
complement	compliment	to	too, two
coarse	course	who's	whose
for	four	your	you're
its	it's		

Mispronunciations

accept	except	precede	proceed
advice	advise	quiet	quite
allusion	illusion	stationary	stationery
censor	censure	than	then
formally	formerly	use	used
loose	lose	weather	whether
have	of		

Mistaken Meanings

amount	number	imply	infer
because of	due to	incredible	incredulous
between	among	less	fewer
conscience	conscious	persecute	prosecute
convince	persuade	principal	principle
detract	distract	respectfully	respectively
famous	notorious		

Now and then, in the haste of writing a first draft, we put down a word in a confused form—adding a syllable or omitting one, grafting a wrong ending, leaving out letters, or making other unconscious bloopers, perhaps like some of these:

Sometimes we *rationize* our *shotcomings*.

My friend glanced at me *sarcasmically*.

Knowbody goes through life without some *tramatic* experiences.

The cause of the mistakes lies in the haste of the first draft: At the time of the writing, we are thinking of what we want to say, not of how we're saying it. In revising we get a second chance, this time with our minds less hurried.

Sometimes we confuse words when we aren't quite sure what they mean and they sound like something else. Columnist Jack Smith of the *Los Angeles Times* has a collection of such "pullet surprises"[1] that were first published by high-school teacher Amsel Greene:

The Rocky Mountain road was the most cynic of our trip.

Space flight may be affected by comic rays.

Moses went up on Mount Cyanide to get the Ten Commandments.

The banker's money was well infested.

Ted was good at multiplication and derision.

Columnist Smith declares that he finds such bloopers "accelerating." But we don't want to get caught using words that way—unless we do it on purpose. Pullet surprises do not win Pulitzer Prizes.

Guideline

Challenge words. If a word may be wrong, it probably is. "The difference between the right word and the almost right word is the difference between lightning and a lightning bug." (*Mark Twain*)

Revision Practice: Exact Words

Read this essay carefully with special attention to accuracy and appropriateness of words. Revise the essay, replacing mistaken words. If you need help, refer to the earlier guidelist of often confused words.

---

[1] Jack Smith, *How to Win a Pullet Surprise* (New York: Franklin Watts, 1982), pp. 50–51.

SMILES TO GO

1   Who nose were or how the human being began to smile?

2 What we do know is that everybody likes a smile, and that a

3 smile and a cheery deposition are both contiguous.

4   History tells us little about cave men and women. We

5 easily get the impression that they seldomly smiled, for

6 life in the Stone Aged must of been hard. Its hard to image

7 a cave person braking into a grin or laughing historically

8 over something said during the day shift down at the locale

9 query. Daily living in that age being grim, perhaps a

10 grimace or two were as close as cave men could come to a

11 smile.

12   However it was, the humane race did learn to smile,

13 weather the smile was a gift from God or a skill learned to

14 make life more easily. It was in either case a wondrous

15 requisition, and today we have turned smiling into an art

16 that can be practiced by everyone with a friend to smile

17 at--or an axe to grind.

18   We all know the "hello smile." We use it when we meet

19 in the market or in an elevator or when we stare from car to

20 car in heavy traffic. This kind of smile often makes words

21 superfluent, working as a silent but cheerful "hello."

22   Everybody needs an "aha smile." That's the one we use

23 when we don't believe a word our friend is saying and want

24 him to know we don't but don't want to tell him we don't.

25 The trick is to put on an effected smile (its often call a

26 smirk) and say, "Aha."

27   Early in life we come to know the "mother smile." This

28 one comes not from within but from years of Mother's saying,

29 "Don't forget to smile!" There are deviant versions of this

30 one for the social worker, for the photographer, for the

31 minister, and for Aunt Millie, whose very rich.

32   This study of smiles wouldn't hardly be completed with

33 omittance of the all-purpose "student smile." This one,

34 accompanied by little nods of the head and a sparkling

35 (sometimes glassy) eye, is intentioned to persuade the

36 professor to believe we are hanging on every word. It works

37 until exam time, when the professor realizes that few of

38 the words are hanging on us.

39   Life would be too monogamous without the flirtatious

40 "maybe smile." It goes from man to woman as a worldless

41 question, meaning "How'd you like to smuggle up with me?"

42 And it goes from woman to man as a silent respond. Of

43 course, in these days of sexual libation, it may be the

44 other way around. The "maybe smile" is a risk, for what

45 comes back may be a "buzz off" sneer. But we often try it

46 anyway, having little to loose but our pride.

47   Later in life comes the "Honest John" smile of the use-

48 car dealer and the politician. This one goes with a right

49   hand slipped into yours and a left hand slipped into your

50   pocket.

51   There's also the "smug smile" that we enjoy when, due

52   to finding a soft drink that has less calories, suddenly

53   we've loss eight pounds.

54   But there is one smile we all love to feel sprawling

55   across our faces. It's the "accomplishment smile," the one

56   we no when we've finely done something right. We feel it

57   when we except the reward we've worked so hardly to obtain.

58   And the best smile of this kind is the one that breaks out,

59   quiet spontaneitly, when the essay comes back graded "A."

60   Smile, your on candied camera!

Follow-up

If you found thirty mistaken words, you've developed a fairly sharp proof-reader's eye. Actually there are forty-four such bloopers in the essay. What words did you decide to use instead of "deposition" and "contiguous" (line 3), "historically" (line 7), "query" (line 9), "requisition" (line 15), "superfluent" (line 21), "effected" (line 25), "deviant" (line 29), "omittance" (line 33), "intentioned" and "persuade" (line 35), "worldless" (line 40), "libation" (line 43), "except" (line 57), "spontaneitly" (line 59)? Did you catch the little bloopers on "Aged" and "Its" (line 6), "locale" (line 8), "humane" (line 12), "weather" (line 13), "whose" (line 31), "smuggle" (line 41), "loose" (line 46), "use-car" (lines 47–48), "loss" (line 53), "no" and "finely" (line 56)? Is "wouldn't hardly" (line 32) right? If you decided not to change "monogamous" (line 39), you may have seen that its play on ideas does fit its context. Your own bloopers may be harder to find than those made by others.

Lesson 27

Specific Words

How would you draw a picture of "an animal," "a vehicle," or "some furniture"? Wouldn't it be easier to draw a dog, a motorcycle, or a table and chair? Specific things are easier to draw than general ones because they are easier to *picture* in the imagination. And when we read, specific words arouse clearer pictures than do general words.

When we write, then, we can help readers call up clear pictures in their minds. As we revise our work, we can look for specific words to replace general ones that leave only fuzzy ideas:

The building was damaged in a disaster a few years ago.

Can you imagine the building? What kind of building? Damaged how? What sort of disaster? Just how long ago? Specific words will give us more information and call up clearer pictures:

The log cabin was destroyed in a fire in 1979.

Writing about action, we sometimes use flat, colorless verbs or verbals:

> After the exam Tom *went* across the campus. *Putting* his books on the lawn, he *sat* down to wait for Judy.

In revision we can replace the flat, colorless verbs "went," "put," and "sat"; we can pick verbs that suggest Tom's attitude, maybe how he felt about that exam:

> After the math exam Tom *shuffled* across the campus. *Flinging* his books on the lawn, he *slumped* beside them to wait for Judy.

The more specific verbs arouse clearer pictures and make the writing more readable.

Of course, a search for colorful verbs can be overdone. The verbs must be suited to the situation, not forced. If we try too hard, the effect may seem ridiculous:

> Judy *clutched* the knife and *hacked* the sandwich in half before she *munched* it.

Maybe the clutching, hacking, and munching are just taking, cutting, and eating after all. Make verbs colorful but not outlandish.

Guideline

 Use specific words, not merely general ones, as often as you can.

Revision Practice: Specific Words

The underscored words in this brief essay are general. Revise each, providing specific words to give the essay more life and interest.

FIRST IMPRESSION WELL LOST

1   Upon my first meeting Sonny I was ready to go to blows

2 with him. He was an <u>employee</u> at a <u>motorcycle</u> shop where I

3 had my <u>machine</u> serviced. It was <u>nearly the weekend</u>, and I

4 was going to <u>take part</u> in <u>an event</u> early next morning. <u>Part</u>

5 <u>of my bike</u> was <u>damaged</u> and needed to be <u>fixed</u>. He said that

6 it would not stay together, even if repaired, without some

7 extensive modification. I told him I just wanted to get

8 through the race.

9   There was the cause of our disagreement. I just wanted

10 something "mickey moused" together, and that wasn't Sonny's

11 style. He didn't want to do something incorrectly just to

12 get by. What was worse, you could not have found two more

13 inflexible people.

14   Eventually I said that I just wanted to have the thing

15 repaired sufficiently to last the race, because after that

16 it was going to be replaced. When at last Sonny agreed

17 reluctantly, the moment of emergency ended. I left, sure

18 that Sonny was no good. But he did the job (even better

19 than I expected it done), and I won that event.

20   After that Sonny began helping me get more out of my

21 machine. I learned to value what he said. I came to see

22 him as a perfectionist and a man of great ability and high

23 standards of conduct. He learned that I too had some good

24 ideas. Our mutual respect grew. Finally I went to him with

25 another night-before-the-race problem, and in his calm,

26 analytical way he took care of my problem with ease.

27   By then Sonny and I had become friends. We began going

28 to each other's home for dinner, and we began discussing

29 things. We took our families doing things together.

30   Now, long after that first bad feeling, Sonny and I

31 are inseparable. Now and then I look back and <u>see</u> that had

32 I <u>listened to</u> my first impression, I would have missed my

33 most valued friendship.

Follow-up

The more specific a noun is, the fewer things it names. There are many more machines than vehicles, many more vehicles than motorcycles, many more motorcycles than racing bikes. We thus step down the ladder from general to specific. To find a more specific word, ask yourself "What sort?" or "Which?" or "In what manner?" What sort of "an employee" (line 2)—a manager, a foreman? What kind of "motorcycle" (line 2)? What specific kind of "machine" (line 3)—a three-wheeler, a racing bike? What day is "nearly the weekend" (line 3)? What sort of "event" (line 4)—a rally, a race, a motocross? "Damaged" in what way (line 5)—bent, chipped, cracked, smashed? "Fixed" how (line 5)—straightened, welded? What "thing," specifically (line 14)? And what "things," for example (line 29)—politics, philosophy, four-wheeling, skiing, camping? What sort of "feeling" (line 30)? Is there a more forceful word for "inflexible" (line 13)?

The more specific a verb is, the more it reveals the manner or quality of an action, the attitude behind it. "Said" in what manner (line 14)—complained, explained? "Value" in what way (line 21)—respect, regard? Use *Roget's Thesaurus,* perhaps, to help you find specific words for brevity and clearer pictures. In lines 16–17 "agreed reluctantly" may mean yielded, conceded, or condescended. Does "ability" (line 22) mean talent, skill? And can "high standards of conduct" (lines 22–23) be called principles?

Writing and Revising

For detailed suggestions on getting started, writing a first draft, revising the draft, and preparing the essay for submission, refer to the Introduction. Choose one of the following topics.

Topics for Writing

1. The word *fan* is short for *fanatic.* But in common usage, a baseball fan or movie fan is not quite a fanatic. When does an enthusiast become a fanatic, and what attitudes and behaviors are truly "fanatical"? Jot a list of your ideas and devise a thesis on the topic. Select a purpose

(such as *definition* or *arguing to convince*—or a combination); then number the ideas in an appropriate order and write a first draft.

2. How important is the opinion of friends and neighbors—or public opinion—in guiding our ways of behaving (our dress, our recreation, our choice of career, our religious or political affiliations)? How important should the opinions of others be? Jot a list of your ideas and devise a thesis on the topic. Select a purpose (such as *arguing to convince*); then number the ideas in an appropriate order and write a first draft.

3. "Whatever is worth doing is worth doing well." Is that axiom open to challenge? Is it still respected? To what extent do you find it guiding the work, study, and recreation of people around you? Jot a list of your ideas and devise a thesis on the topic. Select a purpose (such as *definition* or *arguing to convince*); then number the ideas in an appropriate order and write a first draft.

4. Are you a "dreamer" or a "practical person"? Consider your own attitudes and behavior and those of a friend whose traits seem opposite to your own. Jot a list of your ideas and devise a thesis on the topic. Select a purpose (such as *description* or *contrast*—or a combination); then number the ideas in an appropriate order and write a first draft.

Follow-up

Read your first draft with special attention to your choice of words. Have you used many words of four or five syllables? If so, do they produce a rather formal, perhaps even stuffy, tone? Is the tone appropriate to your intention? Try to replace long words with short synonyms; consider the change in connotation and tone. Check your first draft for any of the confusable words shown earlier. Check also for general words and revise with more specific ones.

Clear
Reference

In revising for variety we found that pronouns, handy for avoiding repetition, can also be tricky. What can a reader get from sentences like these?

> Pete told Frank that his father had called about the car keys. Had they been in the car? It was really inconvenient.

Whose father called? Had Pete and Frank—or the keys—been in the car? What was inconvenient? The "his," "they," and "it" are not clear in reference.

Of course, readers may guess what the pronouns mean. But suppose the guess goes wrong? The infamous Murphy's Law applies: If anything can go wrong, it probably will. And writing that makes readers guess at meanings is sure to be hard to read.

Especially tricky are the pronouns *this, that,* and *which.* In the heat of writing a first draft we may use such words loosely:

> Emerson said beauty is in the eye of the beholder; we all know *this.*

My parents told me to go out on my own, and *that* took a lot of courage.

Weirdos and kooks now threaten to spoil Halloween, *which* is a shame.

Do we all know that what Emerson said is true—or only that he said it? What took courage: to go out on my own—or telling me to? What's a shame—Halloween? Readers are left guessing, and Murphy's Law applies again.

Let's try revising the three sentences to eliminate unclear pronouns. We do it by saying what we mean by *this, that,* and *which:*

Emerson said beauty is in the eye of the beholder; we all know *he was right.*

My parents told me to go out on my own, and *telling me to do so* took a lot of courage.

Weirdos and kooks now threaten to spoil Halloween, and *the loss of its delights* would be a shame.

As we read our own first drafts, we can sharpen our eyes for pronouns, especially *he, she, it, they, this,* and *that.* And it's useful to be a "which-hunter," making sure that every *which* has a clear meaning. It's best to make each pronoun refer to a stated noun rather than to a whole idea.

Guideline

When you use a pronoun, make sure what it stands for will be clear at first glance.

Revision Practice: Clear Reference

Many pronouns in this essay do not clearly refer to what they are intended to stand for. In the first three paragraphs the problem words are underscored. Revise the essay, making every pronoun reference clear.

SECOND-CLASS

```
1     When someone says the Boy Scout movement makes them

2  more conscious of the realities of life, I know they are

3  right. My own awareness of realities began one summer while

4  I was a scout.
```

5   I had joined <u>them</u> several months earlier and had passed

6 my second-class requirements, <u>which</u> had taken me out of the

7 tenderfoot class. I had a merit badge in fire building and

8 another in swimming, and <u>that</u> gave me remarkable confidence

9 in my abilities. That summer when we went to camp, <u>it</u> made

10 me think of myself as a pretty smart scout.

11   One day a friend and I went on a special hike. We

12 intended to bring back some rock specimens; <u>it</u> was required

13 for another merit badge. We had been told where the most

14 interesting rocks were to be found, but <u>they</u> had forgotten

15 to tell us that <u>those</u> were heavily wooded areas.

16   We had gone about two miles when my friend sat down to

17 rest. A moment later he pulled out a cigarette pack and

18 asked whether I wanted a smoke. Nobody in the troop, as far

19 as I knew then, smoked them, so I was shocked. I knew that

20 smoking leads to many diseases, which everybody knows, but

21 they keep on smoking. This was dumb, as far as I could see,

22 and I said I didn't want a smoke.

23   Well, he fished in his pockets for a match but didn't

24 have any. I remember taunting him about being a Boy Scout

25 and not being prepared, but he said he must have used the

26 last of them to light the campfire the night before.

27   This was my chance to show off my skills. I told him I

28 would give him a light. I got out my flint and steel and

29 gathered a bit of tinder from the brush. In a moment I had

30 a small flame going. I was fascinated as he knelt down over

31 the flame with the cigarette in his mouth and puffed. He

32 started holding it in fancy ways, like a movie star, and

33 putting it in his mouth and choking every time he inhaled

34 some. It was funny. In a few minutes he couldn't stand

35 that anymore, so he snuffed it out on a rock. We got up

36 and went back to our hiking.

37   The path narrowed and seemed to disappear in the woods,

38 which led us to think we had been deceived about the rock

39 site. We had gone maybe two hundred feet when we smelled

40 smoke. We looked back toward our resting place, and we saw

41 flames. "Hey," he yelled at me, "you forgot to put out that

42 tinder!"

44   A ranger at a station about a half mile away saw the

44 flames, and in only a few minutes a fire truck came and put

45 it out before it spread very far. They asked us how it

46 started, but we said we didn't know anything; we were just

47 out looking for rocks.

48   One officer said we were lucky to be alive. The whole

49 camp could have been wiped out, so they were lucky too. He

50 said he suspected our story about the fire wasn't true,

51 which it wasn't. I felt lousy, not at all like a smart

52 scout. I finally confessed that I had started it with my

53 flint and steel, but I didn't mention my friend's

54 cigarettes. He never brought that up again. I understood

55 then that one of life's realities is that you can show off

56 too much, and I began to wonder whether I'd ever be first

57 class.

Follow-up

What's meant by "them" (line 1)? Certainly it can't be the Boy Scout movement; it must be the "boys." Can "they" (line 2) refer properly to "someone" (line 1)? And "them" (line 5) surely doesn't refer to "a scout" or "movement"; it must refer to "the scouts." If you've become a "which-hunter," you probably decided that "which" (line 6) couldn't refer to "requirements" but would have to mean the boy's passing them; revision is called for: ". . . and, having passed my second-class requirements, I was no longer a tenderfoot." In line 8, what is "that"?—"my skills"? In line 24, should "any" be changed to "one"? As you read your revision, make sure that every *it, this, that, he, they, them, which, one, some,* or other pronoun has a meaning that will be clear at first reading.

Lesson 29

Clear
Modifiers

When we *modify* a word, we add words that narrow its meaning in some way. And the narrower the meaning, the clearer it is.

Readers can't be sure what a *bird* looks like. When we tell them it's a *red bird*, they know more. And when we add that it's a *red* bird *with a yellow beak*, they know still more. The word *red* and the phrase *with a yellow beak* are modifiers; they help us describe and clarify the meaning of *bird*.

Modifiers don't help much, though, unless the reader is sure what they modify. If a description isn't clearly connected to what it is intended to describe, the reader may be mystified—or amused by what appears ridiculous:

Red on the wings, the beak was yellow.

What? Did the beak have wings? The description "red on the wings," intended to refer to the bird, now illogically describes the beak.

Here are some more misapplied modifiers:

Lean and muscular, his clothing always fit well.

Being the youngest, her family spoiled her.

Dependent on a part-time job, my studies have suffered.

Football is more fascinating after *learning the rules.*

By *doing an equal share* of the housework, many unhappy situations can be avoided.

Was the "clothing" lean and muscular? Was the "family" the youngest? Were the "studies" dependent on the part-time job? Had "football" learned the rules? Who is supposedly doing an equal share of the housework?

In each of these examples, the writer forgot to make clear who the modifying phrase applied to. In revisions we can show the proper connections and make the sentences more readable:

Because *he* was lean and muscular, his clothing always fit well.

Being the youngest, *she* was spoiled by her family.

Since *I* am dependent on a part-time job, my studies have suffered.

Football is more fascinating after *we* learn the rules.

When each *spouse* does an equal share of the housework, many unhappy situations are avoided.

Revisions make clear who (or what) the ideas apply to.

There's more to this modifier business. Sometimes, in the haste of a first draft, we may not realize that we're putting a modifier where it doesn't belong. The thing we want to describe is in the sentence, but the modifier is closer to something else:

It is easy for an observer to interpret what he sees *incorrectly.*

People have to plan for later years *when they are young.*

The painting showed a nude girl sitting on a bicycle *with long, tangled hair.*

Does the observer "see" incorrectly—or "interpret" incorrectly? Are people "young" in later years? Does the "bicycle" have long, tangled hair? To make sense of such sentences, a reader must solve a puzzle or make a wild guess. Anticipating the reader's problem, we must put the modifiers where we really intend them:

It is easy for an observer to interpret *incorrectly* whatever he sees.

When they are young, people have to plan for their later years.

But we have to be careful. A quick revision may produce still another misplacement:

> The painting showed a nude girl with long, tangled hair *sitting on a bicycle*.

We're left with "hair" sitting on a bicycle. The revision will have to be more thorough:

> The painting showed a nude girl sitting on a bicycle. *She* had long, tangled hair.

Now and then, in the haste of writing a first draft, we may produce a thicket of modifier problems:

> I had many dreams of becoming famous as I grew up like many other youngsters.

If we solve one of the problems, we may be left with another:

> As I grew up, I had many dreams of becoming famous like many other youngsters.

The solution lies in careful placement of both of the modifying phrases:

> As I grew up, I had—like many other youngsters—many dreams of becoming famous.

As we write a first draft, we are properly thinking of what we want to say rather than how we are saying it. Later, we have to take the reader's point of view and look at our work as if someone else had written it. If we're able to do that, our misplaced modifiers may shout for revision.

Guideline

 Put modifiers near what you want them to apply to, making sure they can't be misapplied.

Revision Practice: Clear Modifiers

Read this essay carefully with special attention to clarity of modifiers. Revise the essay, avoiding misapplied modifiers.

LOOK BACK--OR ELSE

"History is bunk."--Henry Ford

1   History, that unending procession of dates, names, and

2   events, lets us see our civilization in a rear-view mirror.

3   It gives us some understanding of our own daily lives and

4   gives us a foretaste of the future that is of great value.

5   As we look back, we see what as we move ahead to avoid.

6   Ignorant of history, the past would not reveal its

7   fascinations to us. We would not enjoy the wonders of the

8   strange beasts that roamed the areas we live in millions of

9   years ago. The great pyramids of Egypt would tell us

10 nothing, and the ancient Romans with their roads and

11 aqueducts and Colosseum that ruled most of the world for so

12 many centuries would not warn us of the potential fall of

13 civilizations.

14   When growing up, all the stories of romance of the

15 Middle Ages would be but a blank with no exposure to

16 history. The medieval knights in shining armor for us would

17 rescue no fair maidens and kill no dragons. The wondrous

18 events would be forgotten of all times, and all the great

19 masters would be unknown in the arts and sciences. Indeed,

20 there would be little science, since much depends on the

21 buildup over the centuries of knowledge. Little would stir

22 our imagination. Every day we would have to start to learn

23 everything fresh.

24   Our religions would have no lasting basis and would

25   change at every whim, which depend so much on tradition.

26   Lost in forgotten times, we would have no traditions, in

27   fact. There would be no established churches. Since we

28   would have no remembrance of creation, we would know no

29   God perhaps.

30   Boring as it may be to us in school, our world of today

31   only would have little that we could call civilization

32   without history. Our governments would be all not based on

33   anything lasting, and we would absolutely have no dependable

34   institutions. None would have remembered roots among us, so

35   we would not know which ways to grow. And our children

36   would remember us not long.

37   So if you think history is bunk like Henry Ford,

38   reconsider. Revealing all the wonders and useful guides

39   that the past has known, we would live blind lives without

40   history. To move into the future, our past must give us

41   direction. We would almost have nothing if we lost our

42   sense of the past. We need to keep certainly one eye on

43   that rear-view mirror.

Follow-up

If you have found and revised twenty-five badly placed words and phrases in the essay, your version is surely clearer than the original. Is it the future (line 4) that is "of great value"? Did you write, ". . . a valuable foretaste of the future"? The placement of "as we move ahead" (line 5) is disturbing; did you write "what to avoid as we move ahead"? Is the past (line 6) "ignorant of history"? What should "millions of years ago" (lines 8–9) apply to? Was it the

Colosseum "that ruled most of the world" (line 11)? Who was "growing up" (line 14)? What's the intended meaning of "everything fresh" (line 23)? Should the sentence read, "Every day we would have to start *afresh* to learn everything"? Is the phrase "bunk like Henry Ford" (line 37) misleading? When your revision is finished, read it again; does it seem noticeably clearer and more emphatic than the original?

Lesson 30

Clear
Comparisons

When we use the words *more* or *less*, we are probably comparing one thing to another thing:

Americans drink more coffee than the British do.

Arizona has less rainfall than Utah has.

But we sometimes neglect to name *both* of the things we want to compare:

People in the West Indies tend to be more relaxed.

When we shop at Gimbel's, we spend less.

Readers may ask, "More relaxed than what?" or "Spend less than what?" Revision can make the thoughts clear by providing the other half of the comparison:

People in the West Indies tend to be more relaxed *than we are on the mainland.*

When we shop at Gimbel's, we spend less *than when we shop at Tiffany's.*

When the comparison is complete, readers don't have to guess what we may have meant.

The clearly comparative *more* and *less* are not the only words we must watch. Often the words *as, so, such,* and *that* imply comparison, and if we use them to express vague emphasis, we may overlook an incomplete idea:

Even on weekends he is just *as busy.* (As busy as what—or as when?)

The Arizona climate is not *so humid.* (Not so humid as what?)

My father was a man of *such character.* (Of character such as what?)

I didn't think the movie was *that exciting.* (How exciting?)

Careful revision can make the comparisons clearer and thus more readable:

He is just as busy on weekends as he is on workdays.

The Arizona climate is not so humid as Missouri's.

My father was a man of decisive character.

I didn't think the movie was as exciting as the book.

Now and then a comparison is misleading because we use a false term; that is, one we don't really intend:

A shark has teeth sharper than a whale.

Swimming in fresh water is more fun than the ocean.

The Hawaiian skies are bluer than New York.

Readers may understand what we mean, but they may interrupt their reading to laugh at such illogic. We draw attention not to what we're saying but to how we've said it. The misleading comparison needs to be revised:

A shark has teeth sharper than a *whale's.*

Swimming in fresh water is more fun than *swimming* in the ocean.

The Hawaiian skies are bluer than *those* of New York.

To revise a misleading comparison, make sure that you express both things you intend to compare—and that each is what you really mean.

Guideline

30 Make every comparison complete and accurate.

Revision Practice: Clear Comparison

Read this essay with special attention to words or phrases of comparison. Revise the essay to make every comparison complete and accurate.

MY PLYMOUTH ROCK

1   For eighteen years my family owned an older oceanside

2 cottage in a superb campground near Plymouth, Massachusetts.

3 Every summer, when my last day of school was over, we left

4 hot and sticky Boston and headed for the cottage. There I

5 had a group of friends who were much more fun.

6   Since the outdoors was more exciting, my friends and I

7 pitched tents and slept out every night. We spent most of

8 the warm nights chattering and listening to the pounding

9 waves.

10   Every morning I woke up earlier, so I always took a

11 walk to start my day. I'd start alone toward the woodland

12 in that most beautiful park. The park was filled with pines,

13 and the needles on the ground were damp with the morning

14 dew. The cool morning breezes were always so much fresher

15 than Boston.

16   I would walk to my favorite rock and perch there to

17 enjoy the scenery. Brown and white rabbits would bounce past

18 me, and a chorus of birds converse as cheerily. Sitting on

19 my rock, I had such beautiful thoughts.

20   Then I'd walk to the still deserted beach and dig my

21 toes into the wet sand. The sound and smell of the ocean

22 made me feel more awake. Gulls would soar above me, so

23 beautiful and free. I would walk along the beach until the

24 sun rose higher.

25   On my way back to the cottage I would stop to watch the

26 deer and peacocks and chickens. The animals seemed so much

27 freer than the zoo, and they added a broader sense of

28 communion with the wilder creatures.

29   Back at the cottage as I ended my stroll, the others

30 were just getting up. It seemed to me the late risers

31 didn't look all that filled with joy. I was sure they had

32 much less awareness of the beauties around them. I'd say to

33 myself, "They've missed half the day already."

34   To me, those summers at Plymouth were the most exciting

35 and satisfying. And early morning, so much more fresh and

36 peaceful, never failed to stir in me a greater eagerness for

37 life.

Follow-up

Have you supplied full comparisons wherever *more* or *less* appears? "More fun"
than what (line 5); "More exciting" than what (line 6)? "More awake" than who
(line 22)? "Less awareness" than whose (line 32)? "More fresh and peaceful"
than what (lines 35–36)? How have you handled the faulty comparison of the
morning breezes and Boston (lines 14–15)? Birds sang "as cheerily" as what

(line 18)? "Such beautiful thoughts" as what (line 19)? How free is "the zoo" (line 27)? What is meant by "all that filled with joy" (line 31)?—how much filled? And have you given the reader a full comparison for each *-er* word: "older" (line 1), "earlier" (line 10), "higher" (line 24), "broader" and "wilder" (lines 27–28), "greater" (line 36)?

Summary
Revising for Clarity

Guidelines 25–30

25. Keep long words few and don't crowd them.

26. Challenge words. If a word may be wrong, it probably is.

27. Use specific words, not merely general ones, as often as you can.

28. When you use a pronoun, make sure what it stands for will be clear at first glance.

29. Put modifiers near what you want them to apply to, making sure they can't be misapplied.

30. Make every comparison complete and accurate.

Writing and Revising

For detailed suggestions on getting started, writing a first draft, revising the draft, and preparing the essay for submission, refer to the Introduction. Choose one of the following topics.

Topics for Writing

1. Imagine that you are another person (your mother, father, brother, sister, or close friend). Describe your own personality (not merely your appearance) as that other person probably sees you. Jot a list of impressions of yourself as they might occur to that person. Consider a dominant impression; then number the ideas in an appropriate order and write a first draft. (Remember that you are writing as if you were that other person.)

2. "Memory," said Ernest Hemingway, "is never true." To what extent was he right about memory's fallibility? What can explain our remembering things as different from what they were? Jot a list of your ideas and devise a thesis on the topic. Select a purpose (such as *definition, analyzing a process,* or *arguing to convince*); then number the ideas in an appropriate order and write a first draft.

3. From childhood on, life is full of games. The games we play can be placed in categories according to their characteristics: who plays them (childhood games, adolescent games, adult games), what devices are used (cards, balls, boards, movable pieces), number of players (individual games, team games), and others. Narrow the topic; then jot a list of your ideas and devise a thesis. Select a purpose (such as *classification, comparison, contrast,* or *description*); then number the ideas in an appropriate order and write a first draft.

4. The Bible (in 1 Corinthians 13:13) discourses on faith, hope, and charity, saying, "But the greatest of these is charity." If charity means more than giving to the poor, what are its larger meanings? Do you find charity in many people around you? Do you find it in the society at large? Jot a list of your ideas and devise a thesis on the topic. Select a purpose (such as *definition* or *arguing to convince*); then number the ideas in an appropriate order and write a first draft.

Follow-up

Read your first draft with special attention to pronouns. Whenever you have used *this, that, these, those, which, it,* or *they,* make sure the meaning is clear: Can the reader be sure what is referred to? Search your draft for modifiers: Are all of them near what you intend them to modify? If you have written comparisons, make sure that your reader can easily see what is being compared to what.

Review Quiz

In this quiz you'll find big words (bw), wrong words (ww), general words (gen), unclear reference of pronouns (ref), dangling modifiers (dm), misplaced modifiers (mm), and careless comparisons (comp). In the first five items the problems have been italicized and labeled; later you must find the troubles yourself. Revise to make every sentence more readable.

1. The *notification* from the court *indicated* that I had *run* into a city
   bw   bw   gen

   lamppost *driving my car,* but I didn't know what *they* were *inferring.*
              mm   ref   ww

2. If *overweight, going* a few blocks every morning may *assist* in losing a
       dm   gen   bw
   few pounds, so we should all do *this.*
                              ref

3. My mother likes music *more than my dad, which* he is *cognizant* of.
                           comp   ref   bw

4. When *growing up,* his *relatives* had never really seemed happy, but he
         dm   gen
   didn't know the *causation* of *it.*
               bw   ref

5. Tokyo, Japan, is the *place* of Mieko's *nativity. Their* traditions are dif-
                    gen   bw   ref
   ferent from *other countries.*
             comp

6. After gaining some skill in sports, watching it becomes more fascinating.

7. King Lear's senility affected his judgment, which seemed more obvious to his daughters; accordingly, they would not obey him.

8. If a person loves truly, their love will not be selfish. That will make them less malcontented.

9. Lying outdoors on her patio furniture, a bird was singing in a nearby tree.

10. The sales clerk counted out my change peering through thick glasses.

11. When a teacher in his youth asked Alexander how he could help him, Alexander said that he should stand out of his light.

12. The doctor proscribed some pills to relieve my dad's high-pretension.

13. Spreading for miles down the coast, the visitor will observe sandy beaches arriving by air.

14. No one likes to be laughed at in his heart.

15. When pregnant, a doctor will usually suggest precautions against diseases that one can observe.

16. The author should have expressed his ideas on how to make a tree house more clearly.

17. Depending on their situation, the smallest chore can be more burdensome to a handicapped person.

18. Reading a good book has been my escape long enough to forget when I first got interested in them.

19. Margery had a masculine acquaintance who went into a tree in his van and severely sustained numerous lacerations and abrasions.

20. One person put out his hand to take the rope and put it across the water, which operated like a bridge for the others.

21. The old photo was remnant of the days long ago when the admirable had been stationed at the San Diego navel base.

22. After studying Russian and traveling there, Parsons got a position of employment as an interloper for the United Nations.

23. Everyone hushed as they heard footprints in the hall.

24. The star witness had purged hisself while giving testament in the case.

25. So we deported, each looking forward to a rejoinder at the next summer camp.

Revising for

Consistency

Change is not made without inconvenience.
Richard Hooker (1554?–1600)

Earlier in these pages we pointed out that variety is one of the virtues of readable writing. Here we make the same claim for coherence, for *consistency*. What's going on here? Aren't variety and consistency opposites?

Actually, they're not. To explain, let's distinguish two separate levels of what goes into writing. We'll call one level essential and the other important. What is *essential* cannot be done without, but it is not what really matters to us. What is *important* is what deserves our time and attention, what brings quality and interest to our lives, what we really want to be thinking about.

In our everyday living, breathing is one of the essentials. We could not live without doing it, but it is not what really matters; we wouldn't want to have to give our time and attention to it. Breathing is best when it goes on automatically without our thinking about it. If we *had* to think about it, we'd have time for nothing else. What we do want to think about are the important matters: love, friends, music, beauty, work, ideas, faith, hope, knowledge.

In readable writing, some elements are *essential:* good spelling, helpful punctuation, customary grammar. They are to writing what breathing is to life: essential but not important. If we have to think about them, we don't have time for the important. Like breathing, these elements should be done well without our having to think about them; they should be made automatic.

What is *important* in our writing is what we are saying—our message. Of course, some messages are more important than others, but without substance our writing wouldn't be worth the time to read it. It is what love, friends, music, beauty, work, ideas, faith, hope, and knowledge are to life.

Now back to that matter of variety and consistency. We need variety to keep the reader's mind from wandering off. An unexpected but relevant thought, a twist of words, a new way of looking at ideas—all these keep the reader's attention on our message. But variety in spelling, punctuation, or grammar would be disastrous. In those essential (but not important) things, the reader expects consistency. A new way of spelling, a purposeless comma, a strange twist of grammar—any of these might make our work unreadable, throwing the reader's attention off the important thing, our message.

In revising, we make sure those essentials are handled consistently. We want a consistent point of view, an orderly handling of tenses, a careful treatment of singulars and plurals, and a reasonable harmony among the images we use to bring our ideas to life.

Lesson 31

Point
of View

Perhaps you have heard the expression "Look Out for Number One!" It refers to the self, of course: "Take care of yourself first." In your world, you are number one. When you speak or write, you refer to number one as *I* or *me* or *myself*, and you refer to your own group as *we* or *us* or *ourselves;* those are the *first-person* pronouns.

First person, then, is the writer or the group the writer belongs to. The first person is referred to with *I, me, my, myself, mine.* The second person is the reader, always referred to with *you, your, yourself, yours.* The third person is whoever or whatever is being written about, referred to as *it, she, he, they, Frank, Erica, the sunset, carrots, economics*—any person, thing, or idea other than the writer or the reader.

When we write, we assume a *point of view.* If it's a first-person point of view, we write about our own thoughts, attitudes, and experiences:

> When *I* was younger, *I* thought *my* opinions were worthless. *My* parents and brothers always seemed to *me* to know about things. But *I* never knew; *I* only wondered, and mostly to *myself.*

233

If we take a second-person point of view, we write to readers as if they were the ones with thoughts, attitudes, and experiences:

> If *you* are a romanticist, *you* ache for adventure. *You* want to get away from *your* surroundings, from *your* humdrum life (*you* call it an "existence"), and find *yourself* doing exciting things in exotic places.

If we take a third-person point of view, we write not about ourselves or about the reader but about other people, other things:

> *One* of the wonderful *things* about *trout-fishing* is that *it* always takes place in beautiful *surroundings*. When a *fisherman* has a *fly* in the *stream*, *he's* in a perfect *world*.

These three separate points of view allow us to approach ideas with a variety of attitudes, some inward (subjective) and some outward (objective). But readers expect the point of view in any one essay to be consistent. To begin with a first-person approach and then wander to second or third may make a reader lose track of our point. Note the effect of the shift of person in this passage:

> The sea, in its power and majesty, really affects *one's* mind. It fills *you* with a sense of being part of the grand scheme. The sea is, to *me*, inspiring.

Are we talking about the third-person "one," the second-person "you," or the first-person "me"? The sudden shifts, having no purpose, are disturbing. A revision of the passage makes the point of view consistent and more effective:

> The sea, in its power and majesty, really affects *my* mind. It fills *me* with a sense of being a part of the grand scheme. The sea is, to *me*, inspiring.

Or, if we want to try a more objective tone, we may use a consistent third-person point of view:

> The sea, in its power and majesty, really affects the mind. It fills the soul with a sense of being a part of the grand scheme. The sea, to almost anyone, is inspiring.

To revise for point of view, we may try out one or two of the approaches in order to determine which best fits the message and tone we have in mind. Then we make nouns and pronouns fit that approach (first, second, or third person) consistently.

Guideline

Keep to a single point of view.

Revision Practice: Point of View

The writer of this essay has handled point of view inconsistently, shifting person almost randomly. Revise the essay, adopting a consistent point of view.

READING FOR THE PIANO

1   All of us have probably dreamed, at least once, of

2   playing the piano. The trouble is that if one is to play

3   that instrument well we must read music with some skill,

4   since often many notes must be struck at one time while the

5   player keeps the proper beat, the right key, and the

6   appropriate tempo. So it is good for the piano student to

7   begin early to master three areas of musical theory--timing,

8   key, and tempo.

9   Before you play one note, you must interpret what

10   timing is indicated. On the musical staff the timing is

11   indicated in the form of a fraction. The upper number tells

12   us the number of beats per measure; the lower number

13   dictates which type of note will equal one beat. The music

14   student will have to master twenty-eight different time

15   signatures.

16   Further, we have seven distinct "notes" to be learned,

17   from the whole note down to the sixty-fourth. You must come

18   to recognize the symbols that represent them.

19   The musical key signatures are in the form of sharps

20   (like little number signs) and flats (like little <u>b</u>'s). On

21   the surface one might think that there are only seven notes

22   from "do" to "si," but actually there are twelve--and forty-

23   eight different ways to represent them in print. And the

24   pianist must know sixteen keys, or scales, indicated by the

25   number of sharps and flats arranged on the staff at the

26   beginning of the music.

27   And you have to learn some terms in Italian, since many

28   of the directions on how to play the music are in Italian

29   words. If it says "largo," we play slow; if "larghissimo,"

30   very slow. "Moderato" is fairly obvious to most beginners,

31   but "presto" doesn't mean magic; it means you play fast;

32   "prestissimo," very fast. We must also learn many other

33   terms for inflection.

34   Once able to understand and apply these three aspects

35   of musical notation, the player must work on making the

36   music sound natural and effortless. It takes time,

37   sometimes years. But if we stick to it, "presto!" Well,

38   maybe "larghissimo," but at last your dream comes true.

Follow-up

Before starting your revision, you had to decide which point of view to use: first person ("we"), second person ("you"), or third person ("the player," "the piano student," "one"). Have you held to that one point of view consistently?

Time
Frame

Verbs tell what happened, happens now, or will happen: past, present, future. The variations of a verb that show differences of time are called *tenses.*

Our language does not limit us to simple past, present, and future. Since we can hold in the mind some complications about time—such as two things that happened in the past but one of them earlier than the other, or possibly one thing that happened before now but continues—well, we need some complexity of tenses to do the job.

We may have learned these tenses and their forms years ago, but a quick review here may help make clear how the handling of tense forms contributes to readable writing. We have three basic tenses: (1) simple, (2) progressive, and (3) perfect.

1. The *simple tenses* allow us to report an event that happens at a moment and is over: The bird *sat* on its nest (past), *sits* on its nest (present), *will sit* on its nest (future).

2. The *progressive tenses* allow us to show that an action continues over a period of time, showing the action in progress: The bird *was sitting*

(past progressive), *is sitting* (present progressive), *will be sitting* (future progressive).

3. The *perfect tenses* allow us to show an action completed or to be completed before another: The bird *had sat* (past perfect) before dawn, *has sat* (present perfect) before now, *will have sat* (future perfect) before the sun goes down. We can even put progressive and perfect together to show more detailed interaction of events: The bird *had been sitting* (past-perfect progressive), *has been sitting* (present-perfect progressive), and so on.

It may be helpful here to review a verb (*stir*, for example) in these tense forms:

	Simple Tenses	Progressive Tenses	Perfect Tenses	Perfect-Progressive Tenses
Past	stirred	was/were stirring might have stirred	had stirred might have stirred	had been stirring might have been stirring
Present	stirs/stir	is/are stirring may be stirring	has/have stirred may have stirred	has/have been stirring may have been stirring
Future	will stir	will be stirring	will have stirred	will have been stirring

Still more possibilities are available with the helping verbs *can, should, would* (*can* stir, *could* stir, *should* stir, *should be* stirring, *should have* stirred, *would have been* stirring, and the like).

We use these tenses to relate an incident with some complicated (yet clear) relationships:

> As I *awoke* this morning, a robin *was sitting* in the tree outside my window. The bird *broke* into a cheery song, and then, because I *had heard* that song before, I *knew* the day *would be* worth stirring for. I *tossed* the covers off and *was* up.

The verbs are all past tense, but the past progressive ("was sitting"), the past perfect ("had heard"), and even a predicting blend of past and future ("would be") allow us to show some actions as immediately over, others as continuing for a time, others previously completed, and still others looked forward to.

Awkward Shifting of Tenses

The readability of our work depends in part on a consistent treatment of the tenses. If we tell about the robin and its song, we may forget ourselves for an instant and let the tenses slide about unreasonably:

> As I *awoke* this morning, a robin *was sitting* in the tree outside my window. Suddenly it *breaks* into a cherry song, and then, because I *have heard* that song before, I *knew* the day *will be* worth stirring for. I *tossed* the covers off and *am* up.

The sudden shifts from the past ("awoke," "was sitting") to the present ("breaks") and back again to the present ("have heard"), then to the past ("knew"), then to the future ("will be")—all these inconsistencies force our reader to do mental flips to follow the story. Writers of readable writing don't ask readers to do mental flips of that sort. We want our readers to think, but we don't want them distracted by puzzles over grammar.

Here's a sentence with tense-shift trouble:

> If you *have lost* your job, you *might* get money from your unemployment insurance, but that money *may* not *have been* enough to live on.

The present ("have lost"), then the past ("might"), then the present-perfect ("may have been")—the inconsistency weakens the style. In revising, we can adjust the tenses, holding to either present or past:

> If you *have lost* your job, you *may get* money from your unemployment insurance, but that money *may* not *be* enough to live on.

> If you *had lost* your job, you *might have gotten* money from your unemployment insurance, but that money *might* not *have been* enough to live on.

We may, of course, with good purpose use more than one tense in a sentence.

> We *know* (present) that the team *will play* (future) as well tonight as it *did* (past) last week.

Here we are clearly and properly dealing with three different times. If we do shift verb tense, it should be because we intend to present such distinct difference in time.

Sequence of Tenses

It is often necessary to relate events in a sequence of tenses, one event happening before another, though both were in the past. A first draft may go like this:

When the van *ran* out of gas, Sidney *knew* how foolish he *was* in passing up that last station.

Although "*ran* out of gas" is past tense, Sidney's being foolish happened even before that. Clear sequence of tenses calls for the *had been* form rather than *was:*

When the van *ran* out of gas, Sidney *knew* how foolish he *had been* in passing up that last station.

A special case arises when we write of ideas that are timeless, that is, true for all times. Such ideas should be in the present tense even if a main verb is in the past:

Columbus *knew* that the earth *is* round and *can be* circumnavigated.

Jake's science project *demonstrated* that hydrogen *is* lighter than air.

Guideline

32   Stick to one tense.

Revision Practice: Time Frame

Revise this brief essay for consistency of tenses, crossing out the wrong verbs and writing in acceptable ones.

A SHREW NOT FOR ALL SEASONS

1   In his perennially amusing play <u>Taming of the Shrew,</u>

2 William Shakespeare had presented a conflict of the sexes,

3 a conflict that lost something in the nearly four hundred

4 years between the 1590s, when he writes it, and the 1980s,

5 when a modern audience has seen it. The current movement

6 toward equality of the sexes gave us a new view of the place

7 of women in the marriage contract, a view that differed

8 sharply from the one that is held by the bard's Elizabethan

9 audience.

10   The heroine, Katharina, is the shrew. Daughter of a

11   wealthy merchant of Padua, she was unruly, ill-tempered, and

12   altogether unwilling (at first) to conform to a conventional

13   idea of what a woman should be--submissive, sweet, lovable,

14   and attentive to male whims. She got along well enough

15   apparently, content to be without a husband, until from

16   Verona comes Petruchio, who was in search of a wealthy

17   wife.

18   Petruchio, tempted by her father's money as well as

19   Katharina's own saucy spirit, vows to marry her. Once alone

20   with Petruchio, she scorns him, even struck him. But

21   Petruchio is unmoved. He calmly praised her beauty. He

22   even declares that she is "passing gentle" and "sweet as

23   springtime flowers." She protests violently, but Petruchio

24   then and there declares that he would marry her whether she

25   liked it or not:

26   And bring you from a wild Kate to a Kate

27   Conformable as other household Kates.

28   In old Padua a father's will prevailed, not a daughter's,

29   and Katharina and Petruchio are to be married.

30   From that moment Petruchio sets out to humiliate

31   Katharina. He has shown up late for the wedding, and he

32   was dressed in filthy clothes. They are wed, and he drags

33   her away immediately, not staying for the wedding feast, and

34   carried her off on his broken-down horse.

35 At their home he professes to love her, but he treated
36 her miserably. He declares the food is unfit for her to
37 eat, so he throws it on the floor; she remained famished.
38 He declares the bed unfit for her to sleep in, so he does
39 not allow her to sleep. He says the clothes he had made for
40 her are unfit for her to wear and forced her to wear old
41 rags. Petruchio beats her with birch rods until the blood
42 runs on the floor. She fainted. He wraps her in the skin
43 of a dead plowhorse. Her mood begins to sink, and finally
44 she promised obedience.

45   Today's audience is unlikely to be convinced that Kate
46 is justly "tamed." Modern women will probably find that she
47 is mistreated unmercifully, even criminally, and that her
48 "taming" was coercion rather than conviction. Yet, Shake-
49 speare had shown us one thing: Petruchio had been treating
50 Kate only as she has treated the world. Once she has given
51 up her shrewish temper, she found her new husband--and the
52 world--much easier to love.

Follow-up

Some elements of the essay clearly must be treated as past tense, the reference to Shakespeare (line 2) and to the Elizabethan audience (lines 8–9), for example. But in most of the essay, you must decide for yourself whether to relate the tale in the past or in the present; then you must maintain the basic tense throughout, using its simple, progressive, and perfect forms where they are appropriate.

Lesson 33

Verb Agreement

It's the custom of English to make verbs "agree with their subjects." What we mean is that, following custom, we use a singular verb (one with the *-s* or *-es* added) when the subject of the verb is third-person singular:

One bird *sits* on the nest; the other *catches* worms.

And when the subject is plural, we use the plural verb (without the *-s* or *-es* ending):

A few birds *sit* on their nests; most birds *catch* worms.

What it boils down to is this: One *sits,* several *sit;* one *flies,* several *fly.* Verb agreement is a problem chiefly in the present tense (only *was* and *were* shift from singular to plural in the past; other verbs do not).

But our choice of verb is not always automatic, since the way we talk and write isn't always limited to plain one-subject-before-the-verb situations like "the bird flies" or "the Senate approves." We have to be aware of some complications in the subject-verb relationship, such as these:

1. *Verb before subject.* When we write the verb first, we have to think ahead to the subject:

   There *are* certainly many <u>ways</u> to do most things.

   There *have* not been many volcanic <u>eruptions</u> lately.

   Then *comes* the most difficult <u>step</u> of all.

   Into the hall *come* the <u>dancers</u> to perform.

   Subjects are always nouns or pronouns, so words like "there" and "then" and phrases like "into the hall" are not subjects.

2. *More than one subject.* Two or more subjects joined by *and* are usually treated as plural; but if the subjects are joined by *or,* the verb agrees with the one nearer the verb:

   The <u>lawyer</u> *and* her <u>client</u> *sign* the statement.

   The <u>lawyer</u> *or* her <u>client</u> *signs* the statement.

   The <u>lawyer</u> *or* her <u>clients</u> *sign* the statement.

3. *Something between subject and verb.* We make the verb agree with the actual subject, not with the noun or pronoun between:

   <u>Workers</u> in government service *earn* about the same as others. ("Workers," not "service," are the subject.)

   <u>Each</u> of the brothers *wants* a job at the plant. ("Each," not "brothers," is the subject.)

   The <u>mother</u> as well as her children *goes* to the head of the line. ("Mother," not "children," is the subject.)

   All <u>quizzes</u> in addition to the term paper *are* due next week. ("Quizzes," not "term paper," are the subject.)

4. *Negative subject.* If one of two subjects is affirmative and the other negative, the verb agrees with the affirmative:

   The <u>politicians</u> and not the government *make* the laws.

   The <u>administration</u>, not the people, *wants* this bill.

   The <u>speaker</u> rather than his opponents *supports* it.

5. *Noun complement.* When we use a verb to link subject and complement, the verb (usually *is, are, was,* or *were*) agrees with the subject before the verb, not with the noun after:

America's favorite <u>food</u> *is* hamburgers.

<u>Hamburgers</u> *are* a staple of many diets.

6. *Clause as subject.* When the whole clause is subject, the verb is singular:

   <u>What the people want</u> *is* an equal opportunity for all.

   <u>How we select officers</u> *is* a matter of department policy.

   <u>That you are among friends</u> *makes* some difference.

7. *Who as subject.* When we use *who* as subject, the verb agrees with whatever *who* stands for:

   She is one of those students <u>who</u> *take* politics seriously.

   Many students, not just one, take politics seriously; "who" stands for "students," not for "she" or "one." But:

   She is <u>the only one</u> of the students <u>who</u> *studies* the issues.

   This time, since the other students do not study the issue, "who" stands for "one."

8. *Special words.* Certain words are recognized as singular although they end in *s: news, politics, economics, mathematics.* And certain others without *-s* endings *(media, data, alumni)* are plural:

   The <u>news</u> *is* good today: <u>Politics</u> *has* regained popularity.

   The <u>media</u> *have* reported that few <u>data</u> *are* available on voter opinion.

   Two other pronouns, *that* and *which,* may be subjects; they are treated like *who:*

   Soccer is one of the games <u>that</u> *have grown* in popularity.

   This is the only one of the cereals <u>that</u> *is* salt-free.

   I love candy and cake, <u>which</u> *are* sinfully fattening.

Guideline

Make a verb singular if its subject is singular, plural if its subject or subjects are plural.

Revision Practice: Verb Agreement

Revise this essay specifically for verb agreement, crossing out any verb that doesn't agree with its subject and writing above it one that does. Refer to the eight guides to verb agreement for assistance.

EQUALITY, INTERDEPENDENCE, AND LOVE

1   Family life and its success never is simple. Among the

2   most difficult of problems of families are that involving

3   equal rights and responsibilities. Either a conventional

4   marriage or an "open" marriage face the issue of equality.

5   Every man and wife have to face that question. The media

6   today is full of reports that two sources of income often

7   becomes essential for a family's survival, so that both

8   husband and wife sometimes finds it advantageous to work.

9   When there is children to consider, the husband as well

10   as the wife ideally contribute equally to their care and

11   training. None of the children are without need for both

12   parents, so the family's life seldom become happy unless

13   each of the parents have plenty of time with the kids. And

14   all children, too, needs responsibilities. Each have to

15   feel that some measure of the family's well-being depend on

16   him or her.

17   When misunderstanding of any kind come up between

18   husband and wife, extra pressure and concern often bears

19   upon the whole family. The married couple has to learn to

20   keep their disagreements under control, since their effects

21   on children often is much greater than the parents suspect.

22   Sometimes, indeed, the children, rather than the husband or

23   wife, is the first who senses something wrong.

24   Absolute equality, of course, evade us all. A happy

25   family life mostly depend on understanding and love.

Follow-up

You should have revised one verb in each line of the essay. Can you explain each verb's agreement with its subject or subjects? In line 1, two subjects linked by "and" require a plural verb—*are*. In line 4, two subjects linked by "or" require a singular verb—*faces*. In line 5, "every man and wife" refers to the man or wife singly and must take a singular verb—*has*. In line 6, the subject "media" is plural and requires a plural verb—*are*. In lines 11 and 13, "none" and "each" are singular pronouns and must take singular verbs. In lines 22– 23, the negative subject (expressed with "rather than") should not govern the verb choice. In line 25, the subject "life" requires a singular verb—*depends*.

Writing and Revising

For detailed suggestions on getting started, writing a first draft, revising the draft, and preparing the essay for submission, refer to the Introduction. Choose one of the following topics.

Topics for Writing

1.   Recall the most terrifying experience you have ever known. Recount the when, where, how, why—all the details. As you look back on it, was your fear justified? Jot a list of your ideas and devise a thesis on the topic. Your purpose is to *relate an incident* and *argue to convince*. Number the ideas in an appropriate order and write a first draft.

2.   What do you now judge to be the most important event of your own life so far? Recall the experience, recounting details of the event and why they seem important to you. Jot a list of your ideas and devise a thesis on the topic. Your purpose is to *relate an incident* and *argue to convince*. Number the ideas in an appropriate order and write a first draft.

3.   If you've ever had a traffic citation, you know the feeling of helpless rage (at yourself, at the ticketing officer, at the whole society). Recount such an experience, giving details of its happening and of your emotional reactions. Jot a list of your ideas and devise a thesis on the topic. Your purpose is to *relate an incident* and leave a dominant impression. Number the ideas in an appropriate order and write a first draft.

4. Most persons have some experience of crime as either outlaw or victim. Recount one of your own such experiences, anything from cookie-jar banditry to witnessing a robbery or being burglarized—or worse. Jot a list of your ideas and devise a thesis on the topic. Your purpose is to *relate an incident* and *analyze cause and effect*. Number the ideas in an appropriate order and write a first draft, focusing on the emotional impact of the event on you.

Follow-up

Read your first draft carefully, considering its point of view. Make sure you have not shifted from first person to third or vice versa. Also consider the time frame of your narrative: Have you kept it consistent? Make sure your verbs agree with their subjects.

Lesson 34

Pronoun Agreement

Pronouns substitute for nouns, and consistency calls for every pronoun to agree with what it stands for, singular with singular, plural with plural:

> We should accept our *friends* for what *they* are.

> A *woman* has *her* right to any job *she* can qualify for.

> Among artistic *people* are *those* who create with *their* hands.

> *Everybody* has *his* way of pursuing what *he* needs to fulfill *himself*.

Growing awareness of the equality of the sexes has had its effects on language, some of them visible in current pronoun usage. Why, we now ask, should we think of "everybody" as male, as we seem to do in using "his," "he," and "himself" in that fourth example? In speech, many now avoid the problem by using deliberate disagreement of pronouns:

> *Everybody* has *their* way of pursuing what *they* need to fulfill *themselves*.

But that solution to the sex-bias problem produces an awkward style, not readable writing. Writers can take several other routes to smooth and socially acceptable treatment of pronoun agreement. One way is to use the plural, since plural pronouns have no gender:

We all have *our* ways of pursuing what *we* need to fulfill *ourselves.*

People have *their* ways of pursuing what *they* need to fulfill *themselves.*

Another way to avoid the problem is to avoid pronouns:

Everybody has a way of seeking what is needed for personal comfort.

Perhaps a special reminder will help here. Certain words are classed as *indefinite pronouns* because they name no definite person or thing. Most of those pronouns are always singular:

anybody	everybody	somebody	nobody
anyone	everyone	someone	no one
anything	everything	something	nothing

each	none	one
either	little	other
neither	much	another

When we use one of those words and then use another pronoun to refer to it, we use a singular:

Anybody can have *his* own glasses prescribed for *him.*

Somebody lost *his* wallet while *he* was at the park.

Each of the girls can make what *she* needs for *her* own use.

Neither does *her* best when *something* takes *its* toll against *her.*

Four indefinite pronouns (*both, few, many,* and *others*) are always plural:

Few have all *they* want, but *many* have what *they* deserve.

Both of the girls have *their* jackets, but *others* have nothing to keep *themselves* warm.

Four other such pronouns (*all, any, most,* and *some*) are sometimes singular, sometimes plural, depending on what they stand for:

When *all* is as *it* should be, *all* of us will have *our* just reward.

Any who take pride in *themselves* will like *any* of the jobs that has a challenge in *it*.

Most of the show had comedy in *it*, and *most* of the jokes had serious point to *them*.

Some use *their* spoons, because *some* of the rice has sauce with *it*.

Subject, Object

Many personal pronouns take one form when they are subjects in a sentence, another form when they are objects:

I (subject) know she likes *me* (object).

He (subject) wanted his friends to appreciate *him*(object).

When *she* (subject) came in, *we* (subject) all stared at *her* (object), and *she* (subject) ignored *us* (object).

I (subject) am sure *they* (subject) know what's good for *them* (object).

Agreement demands that pronouns paired with subjects take the subjective form; those paired with objects take the objective form:

Danny and *we* (subjects) took the bus and didn't wait for Pete and *her* (objects).

If *you* (subject) want to see my friends and *me* (objects), *they* and *I* (subjects) will be happy to meet *you* (object).

The *-self* words (*myself, yourself, herself, himself, ourselves, yourselves, themselves*) are always used as object, never as subject.* As object, "They only hurt *themselves*" is proper; as subject, "Jake and *myself* ordered lunch" is not. And there is a further caution: These *-self* words, used when an action is reflected on the doer ("I saw *myself* in the mirror"; "she caught *herself* napping"; "he asked *himself* why"), are properly used when the subject, or doer of the act, is the same person as the receiver of the act. "They gave prizes to Jay and *myself*" is wrong, since it was "they," not *I* (not "myself"), who gave the prizes. Make it, "They gave prizes to Jay and *me*."

---

*These words are often used as intensifiers following a subject: "I *myself* did not go along" or "She pitched the tent *herself*." In these uses they emphasize the subject, but the proper subject cannot be omitted.

Guideline

Make a pronoun singular if what it stands for is singular, plural if what it stands for is plural.

Revision Practice: Pronoun Agreement

Revise this essay, making all pronouns consistent (singular or plural) with what they stand for.

THE PLACE TO GO-GO-GO

1   If a friend asked me about where to go on vacation, I'd

2 tell them without hesitation--New York City. Everything can

3 be found in "the Big Apple," as my fellow New Yorkers and

4 myself call it, and anyone can have a pleasant vacation

5 there if they stay in the right area.

6   Manhattan island is the heart of New York, the chief

7 one of the five burroughs. Manhattan has all kinds of

8 culture, people from every country on earth. The visitor

9 can see Italians and Israelis, Persians and Puerto Ricans,

10 Swedes and Swiss, Chileans and Chinese, and they will be

11 amazed to find two dozen foreign restaurants within a half

12 mile. And the visitor can drop in at scores of fast-food

13 places that will stuff themselves with falafel, egg foo

14 yong, tamales, pizza, caviar, or wienerschnitzel.

15   All types of shops are within a block or two of

16 wherever the visitor is staying, so they can easily walk.

17 And if one is interested in museums, art galleries,

18 libraries, and concert halls, it's available within short

19 distance. But my friend would not have to walk unless it

20   pleased them to do so. One of the best things about the

21   city is the transportation system. The subway is the heart

22   of the system, and they are running at every hour. The

23   waiting time to board a train is never more than five

24   minutes. If someone wants to go to the other end of the

25   city, they can do so in less than twenty minutes.

26   Life in Manhattan is fast paced and around-the-clock.

27   The city never sleeps. On their big night in town, I would

28   suggest my friend should go to dinner at Tavern on the

29   Green, then walk along Central Park. After the walk, he

30   should take in a Broadway play. They are all excellent.

31   After such an evening, my vacationing friend would surely be

32   as excited about New York as me.

33   There are no other places more exciting than New York.

34   If there are, it would have to exist only in dreams.

Follow-up

When you have finished your revision, check every pronoun—every *it*, *they*, *them*, *their*, *myself*, *themselves*. Make sure that you've changed either the pronoun or the noun it stands for, making the two agree. If you are troubled by the distinction of sexes and want to avoid the masculine *he*, try using plural for the noun: "friends" (lines 1, 19, 28, and 31); "visitors" (lines 8, 12, and 16); *people* instead of "anyone" (line 4), "one" (line 17), and "someone" (line 24). The singular "subway" (line 21) can't be "they," nor can "a Broadway play" (line 30). The plural "other places" can't be referred to as "it" (lines 33–34). Have you changed "myself" to *I* (line 4)? And what have you done with "themselves" (line 13) and "me" (line 32)? Would it be right to say "as excited about New York as *me* am"?

Lesson 35
Parallelism

        Two words are *parallel* when, like a team of horses, they are linked together in some way and have the same job to do. The italicized words in this passage by George Orwell are parallels:

> So long as you are not actually *ill, hungry, frightened,* or *immured* in a prison or a holiday camp, spring is still spring. *The atom bombs are piling up* in the factories, *the police are prowling* through the cities, *the lies are streaming* from the loudspeakers, but *the earth is still going round the sun,* and neither *the dictators* nor *the bureaucrats,* deeply as they disapprove of the process, are able to prevent it.[1]

Two items in parallel are a *pair,* like "the dictators and the bureaucrats." Three or more items in parallel form a *series,* like "ill, hungry, frightened, or immured."

---

[1]George Orwell, "Some Thoughts on the Common Toad," in *The Orwell Reader* (New York: Harcourt, 1949), p. 386.

Orwell also shows us a series of independent clauses in "The atom bombs are piling up, . . . the police are prowling, . . . the lies are streaming, . . . the earth is still going round the sun."

By parallel, we mean the words in the pair or series are all in the same grammatical form and have the same relationship to the rest of the sentence. Parallel words or word groups are often joined by *and, or, but,* or *yet,* or such groups as *either/or* and *neither/nor.* In a series, the items are usually separated by commas.

If we write a pair or series whose items are not in the same form, the reader is forced to switch from one track to another for no good reason:

> Water may be unhealthful if it contains *sulfur, sediment,* or *tastes funny.*

The first two words in the series are nouns; the last is a verb. In revising we must make all three the same—all nouns or all verbs.

> Water may be unhealthful if it contains *sulfur, sediment,* or excessive *iron.*

> Water may be unhealthful if it *looks* dirty, *tastes* funny, or *smells* bad.

Sometimes revising for parallelism means only adjusting the position of connectives:

> Jeff <u>not only</u> *won* the game <u>but also</u> *a handsome trophy.*

The verb "won" and the noun phrase "a handsome trophy" don't match. We can revise by moving "not only" to another position:

> Jeff won <u>not only</u> *the game* <u>but also</u> *a handsome trophy.*

The idea is to make sure that what follows one of the connectives is in the same form as what follows the other. All items in a pair or series should be the same part of speech and have similar form.

Guideline

In a pair or series, use the same part of speech and similar structures for both or all items.

Revision Practice: Parallelism

As you read this essay, give special attention to pairs, series, and such connectives as *and, or, but, yet,* and *either/or.* Revise the essay to make elements in pairs and series consistent in form, achieving as much balance as you can.

LITTLE GIRL BACKWARD

1   The friend I see in my mirror is not the easiest to

2   either understand or be appreciated. At her best she is

3   affable, thoughtful, and tender; at her worst she has

4   unstable temperament and moods. She can be cheerful and

5   friendly at one time, then at another snap shortly at anyone

6   who speaks to her--or perhaps refusing to speak at all.

7   She shows a sentimental streak, forever talking of the

8   good old days and loves to recall her childhood. She hovers

9   between childhood and being mature, longs to be grown-up,

10 yet hesitant to relinquish her youth.

11   Easily hurt, she tends to keep her problems to herself

12 rather than sharing them with friends. Now and then she

13 freezes up when her feelings are hurt or weeping and pouting

14 when she feels rejected. She cries, sniffles, sobs at

15 movies, whether comedy or tragic. She often sheds tears

16 while listening to a friend's troubles. Often eager to

17 listen and doing what she can to help, she is at other

18 moments unwilling to listen to any tale of woe but her own.

19   When a genuine crisis strikes, she is forceful, tough,

20 and encourages others. But she often falls apart when the

21 crisis is superficial, exaggerating its importance.

22   Out in public she is quick to strike up a conversation.

23 She sees few strangers, but many new friends are met. She

24 is attractive enough to have many boyfriends, but often her

25 sudden moods discourage them, and she spends many date

26 nights undated.

27   She is a wishful thinker. She knows everything in her

28 mirror world is backward, sometimes wishing she could be the

29 girl looking in instead of the one who looks out. If she

30 were looking in, she could see the other girl growing up.

31 As things are, she looks out and sees a child, and sometimes

32 no one at all.

Follow-up

Have you balanced such uneven pairs as "either *understand* or *be appreciated*" (line 2)? Would "either *understand* or *appreciate*" be better? Are "affable, thoughtful, and tender" (line 3) balanced by "unstable temperament and moods" (line 4)? Would "temperamental and moody" be better? How have you revised "snap shortly" (line 5) and "refusing" (line 6) to balance "cheerful and friendly" (lines 4–5)? And what of "talking" and "loves to recall" (lines 7–8); "to keep" and "sharing" (lines 11–12); "freezes up" and "weeping and pouting" (line 13)? In line 15, "comedy" is a noun, "tragic" an adjective; have you put them both into one form? Does the verb "encourages" (line 20) balance against the adjectives "forceful, tough" (line 19)? Does the clause "who looks out" balance against the phrase "looking in" (line 29)? As you reread your revision, do you find the effect improved over that of the original?

Lesson 36

Consistent Images

When we write, we usually intend to share with readers our own view of a topic—or some other view that is probably new to them. To make it easier for them to see the new idea, we often compare it to one we think they will be familiar with. The two, of course, are really not alike; we point out a similarity in spite of the basic difference:

Maryellen's smile was a sunrise.

Aunt Margaret entered the room under full sail.

We've compared the smile to a sunrise, implying that the smile did for us what a sunrise might—bring light and warmth. And we've compared Aunt Margaret to a full-rigged sailing ship, implying her confident, imperious manner and intent.

These comparisons of unlikes are *metaphors*, imaginative bits of language that help us explain what we have in mind in terms of what the reader already knows about.

But metaphors must be handled carefully. They arouse images in the reader's mind, and if we cause the images to clash, we throw the reader off what we want to say and force attention to the strange way we've said it:

> Entering the room under full sail, Aunt Margaret soared to her place at the head of the table.

Here Aunt Margaret is a sailing ship that soars. The clash of images spoils the readability, and the reader laughs at us, not with us.

> Steve tugged at Nancy's heartstrings, but he struck out.

Steve apparently plays a guitar and baseball at the same time, a ludicrous idea. As we revise the metaphors, we make the two images consistent:

> Steve tugged at Nancy's heartstrings, but his tune was off key.

Metaphors, as they age and are widely used, often lose their power to arouse an image. To say that one's hopes were "crushed" now seems almost literal language; the image of the tender grape is lost. When we use such a "dead" metaphor, we may be unaware of its faded image and thus fail to notice any incongruity. And we often use clichés, neglecting to consider how they clash with one another. The best way to avoid the fault is to take George Orwell's advice: "Never use a metaphor, simile or other figure of speech which you are used to seeing in print." If we use only fresh metaphors, carefully considering how they fit our meaning, we guard against a foolish mixture of images.

Analogy is something like metaphor but more extended in application. The reader is encouraged to see several ways, not just one, in which two things are similar. Here's a brief passage from an essay about how ailing computers are fixed by technicians:

> The patient, the computer, is but a child, born only a few decades ago. The child, easily disturbed by a small increase in room temperature or by the failure of a power source, has malfunctioned. It comes to us as a sick man, with a headache in its electronic brain, indigestion in its circuitry, faulty elimination. We technician "doctors" have to cure its pains.

The writer sees the computer as a sick child coming to the doctor and within that analogy compares computer ills with human ills. But the writer has presented some confusing inconsistencies. Human beings, if born "a few decades ago," would not be thought of as children, so the analogy becomes tainted. Indeed, the writer tells us later that the computer is really a "sick man," not a child. The confusion can be cleared in revision if the writer eliminates the distracting reference to when the computer was born and avoids referring to it as a *man:*

> The patient, the computer, is but a child. Easily disturbed by a small increase in room temperature or by the failure of a power source, it has malfunctioned. Now it comes to us with a headache in its electronic brain, indigestion in its circuitry, faulty elimination. We technician "doctors" have to cure its pains.

Once we establish an analogy, we must take care to make all details consistent within it.

Guideline

When images clash, revise to make them consistent—or use literal language.

Revision Practice: Consistent Images

Revise clashing metaphors for consistency of image. When no appropriate image comes to mind, keep one metaphor and express the other idea in plain, literal language.

1. The American voter is a timid sparrow, afraid to swim against the tide.

2. Our quarterback snaked his way downfield at full gallop.

3. A friend is one who will always go to bat for you, pulling you out of life's quicksands.

4. My father is always cooking up something for the family to kick around in discussion.

5. We saw Jackie hovering about, trying to worm his way into the argument.

6. Life in the fast lane demands that you either sink or swim.

7. Someday all those political red herrings will come home to roost.

8. The officer's icy stare burned right through me.

9. The major powers should get together and cook up a nuclear freeze agreement.

10. Today a woman who is a good reporter can become an anchor on the air.

11. To allow offshore oil drilling simply opens the door to pollution of our shores.

12. The prosecuting attorney held back his trump card until his summation, then let it go with both barrels.

13. More than sixty years ago he built that little cabin in the shadow of the lake.

14. The competent investigator must weigh all evidence under the microscope of reason.

15. I marveled at how my father faced a mountain of work and sailed right through it.

16. Mankind still struggles in the dark cave of ignorance, following an unreachable star.

17. Mother always took in strays. She instinctively reached out a helping hand and took them under her wing.

18. I didn't want to be called a quitter, but what I secretly wanted to do was hang up my gloves and get out of the rat race.

19. Sometimes we sweep unpleasant experience under the rug of memory, gone with the wind.

20. In today's secular world the core of religious belief has been peeled away.

Follow-up

Do sparrows swim (1), snakes gallop (2), worms hover (5), or herrings roost (7)? Does ice burn (8), and can one cook up a freeze (9)? Was the prosecuting attorney (12) playing cards or shooting ducks? Do lakes have shadows (13)? Do we weigh things with a microscope (14)? What strange sort of apple (20) have we imagined?

Summary
Revising for Consistency

Guidelines 31–36

31. Keep to a single point of view.

32. Stick to one tense.

33. Make a verb singular if its subject is singular, plural if its subject or subjects are plural.

34. Make a pronoun singular if what it stands for is singular, plural if what it stands for is plural.

35. In a pair or series, use the same part of speech and similar structures for both or all items.

36. When images clash, revise to make them consistent—or use literal language.

Writing and Revising

For detailed suggestions on getting started, writing a first draft, revising the draft, and preparing the essay for submission, refer to the Introduction. Choose one of the following topics.

Topics for Writing

1. Relate your experience of the first day on a new job. Tell of your excitement and fears as well as of what you learned about the work. Jot a list of your ideas and devise a thesis on the topic. Select a purpose (such as *description*, *relating an incident*, or *analyzing a process*), then number the ideas in an appropriate order and write a first draft.

2. "Red tape" is frustrating. Write about your own experience with filling in forms, going through channels, and putting up with delays. Jot a list of your ideas and devise a thesis on the topic. Select a purpose (such as *relating an incident* or *arguing to convince*); then number the ideas in an appropriate order to write a first draft.

3. Is "civilization" generally a good thing? Would the world (and you) be better off if things were simpler, less "modern"? Justify your attitude. Jot a list of your ideas and devise a thesis on the topic. Select a purpose

(probably *arguing to convince*); then number the ideas in an appropriate order and write a first draft.

4. Habits take time to build; harmful ones may take forever to break. Consider a good habit that you struggled to build—or a bad one that you succeeded in breaking. Describe the struggle and show what its outcome has meant to you. Jot a list of your ideas and devise a thesis on the topic. Select a purpose (such as *definition, description, relating an incident,* or *arguing to convince*); then number the ideas in an appropriate order and write a first draft.

Follow-up

As you revise your first draft, give special attention to your use of pronouns, making sure that each agrees (singular or plural) with what it stands for. If you have used a pair or series of elements, are all the items in parallel form? Look also for images in your essay; make sure that you have not made two images clash.

Review Quiz

In this quiz you may find inconsistency of person (pers), shift of tense (st), careless verb agreement (v-agr), careless pronoun agreement (p-agr), careless parallelism (paral), and mixed imagery (mix). In the first ten items the problems have been italicized and labeled; later you must find the troubles yourself. Revise to make every sentence more readable.

1. Surfing has been an important part of my life. It helps relieve any anxiety that *you* have stored up.
    pers

2. Surfing is healthful, exciting, and *helps* relieve anxiety.
    paral

3. How can a member of a large family find a few moments to *themselves*?
    p-agr

4. The satisfaction of it only *last* momentarily.
    v-agr

5. From what I have seen on television, skiing *was* a dangerous sport.
    st

6. A politician has to get people to support *your* ideas.
    pers

7. I accepted every person for what *they* were.
    p-agr

8. Material things never bring complete satisfaction, and the few satisfactions that *it* does bring *doesn't* last.
    p-agr   v-agr

9. As each of us *travel* the river of life, *they* must *sow* seeds of happiness.
                 v-agr   p-agr   mix

10. Most of us have gone through situations covered by Murphy's Law; for example *your* horn sticks while *you're* driving through a group of
                                      pers   pers
    Hell's Angels.

11. The prevalence of certain problems in society contain an irony.

12. If we eliminate poverty, the world would be a nicer place.

13. My elderly uncle was an odd fish, very set in his eccentric ways. When we try to talk with him, he would just flutter away to be alone.

14. People's emotions and feelings are brought back to them through experience, and through experience we learn.

15. Sometimes I do things I know are right, but they aren't what I felt like doing.

16. There still exists Nazi groups that drink the fires of hatred.

17. The doctor gave me a prescription that leaves a scar on me for life.

18. They were victims of a religious cult who blindly send in donations.

19. My brother is thinking of three possible careers: dentistry, teaching, and a lawyer.

20. One of the things I fear most are that I may strike out before I reach the finish line.

21. Portia was a pillar of justice who bleats to her suitors about the terms of her father's will.

22. Adults have responsibilities that can ruin his best-laid plans.

23. It's not whether a player wins or loses; it's how you played the game.

24. Keeping a garden is both hard work and time-consuming.

25. Hand in hand with selfishness and jealousy goes a dim view of human nature.

Revising for

Appearance and Custom

Custom, then, is the great guide of human life.
David Hume (1711–1776)

Human beings had highly developed systems of spoken language long before they had devised any way of writing. Our alphabets and spellings and punctuation marks are relatively recent developments. Even after writing was invented, it was for a long time hard to read. Writers did not put spaces between words. They did not use capital letters to begin sentences, nor periods to end them. There were no commas or question marks. If Lincoln had written his Gettysburg Address as the first writings were written, it might have started like this:

> fourscoreandsevenyearsagoourfathersbroughtforthuponthiscontinent anewnationconceivedinlibertyanddedicatedtothepropositionthatall menarecreatedequal

Early writings were even harder than that to read, since no spelling system had been developed, either. In Shakespeare's time, less than four hundred years ago, words were spelled rather haphazardly, the same word often spelled several different ways on a single page. Consistent spelling is one of our most recent customs.

Such devices as capitals, spaces, and periods were developed over the centuries to make reading easier. Gradually such systems have been adopted in most cultures—different ones in different places, of course.

All language "works" because of convention. Human beings have to *agree*, or at least believe that they agree, that certain words and expressions have certain meanings. This kind of agreement doesn't really happen at a "convention," of course, but only over the centuries by word of mouth—and pen. The devices become customs within a culture, just as certain other kinds of behavior do. We observe the customs, mostly; if we didn't, we'd be too hard to live with, our speech wouldn't "make sense," and our writing would be too difficult to read.

Writing, despite all its rich possibilities, remains a meager way of representing speech. On the written page we cannot convey the sound of the voice, the intonation of a word or phrase. We cannot make a sentence mean something different by smiling as we write it, nor can we emphasize an idea by a meaningful pause or by shouting or pounding on a table. To make up for the lack of those dynamic elements of speech, we use the conventions of writing: capitals, punctuation marks, spacing, and indention.

Observing the conventions of writing is something like observing the rules of the road while driving a car. Others are depending on our doing what is customary, what they expect. When we don't do what's expected, we make life—at least reading—too troublesome.

What happens, then, to originality? Do we all become robots, writing like everybody else? No. Spelling, capitalizing, and punctuating are essential, not important; we must have them, but they are not what *makes* writing good. When we adopt and follow customary rules for spelling, capitalizing, and punctuating, we can with practice make them automatic, doing them right without conscious effort. Then we can put our best energies into what is more important, that is, what we have to say and the style we use to say it. Until we have learned the customary systems thoroughly, of course, we cannot make them automatic.

Saying It
Right: Idioms

If we have grown up speaking English, we use and understand many a phrase that would bewilder a newcomer to the language. Among our everyday expressions are quite a few that defy grammar and logic.

We just sailed easily past two examples. Since "a phrase" is obviously singular, why do we say "*many* a phrase"? And since "few" is clearly plural, why do we say "*a* few"? We can't explain why, but we just do—as a matter of custom.

Such expressions are *idioms*, rooted in customary usage. Thousands of them are in daily use, some of them grammatical and others not. We just don't worry about their "correctness"; they are accepted because we are comfortable with them. And no matter how original we'd like to be, we'd better not twist an idiom out of its old and easy pattern if we want our writing to be readable. Suppose we heard this beginning of a newscast:

Good night. This is Mudd Reasoner with the news. Scores of demonstrators walked on the White House this morning in protest to the appointment to Phil Spayce, an expert at economics, to Secretary for

Defense. Observers say the Congress is probable to confirm to the appointment in spite of public resentment to it.

The report seems all wrong. But how could we explain to a foreigner that "Good *night*" is wrong where "Good *evening*" would be right? "*Walked on* the White House" seems laughable, but "*marched on* the White House" would be right. "In protest *to*" is wrong; "in protest *of*" or "in protest *against*" is right. It shouldn't be "the appointment *to*" but "the appointment *of*." "An expert *at*" is wrong; "an expert *in*" is right. It's not "Secretary *for* Defense" but "Secretary *of* Defense." And we just don't say "probable *to*," "confirm *to*," or "resentment *to*"; we say "likely *to*," "confirm," and "resentment *against*."

As written, the news report is not in readable style because it goes against those customary patterns of usage. To make it acceptable, we must use idiomatic English:

> Good *evening*. This is Mudd Reasoner with the news. Scores of demonstrators *marched on* the White House this morning in *protest of* the *appointment of* Phil Spayce, an *expert in* economics, as Secretary *of* Defense. Observers say the Congress is *likely to confirm* the appointment in spite of public *resentment against* it.

Most of the idioms in English have developed over centuries of usage, many of them putting words together in capricious ways. Often one word entirely changes the meaning of the other. Consider:

> Thieves *make off* with our bags, and we *make after* them on foot. They *make for* the street, then *make tracks* toward the bus station. We *make out* one of them climbing into a car while the other *makes do* with a bicycle. We try to catch the second thief, but we don't *make it*. We walk back and *make as if* nothing had happened.

To write idiomatically, we have to be familiar with hundreds of customary ways of combining words. No list could ever be complete, but here are some typical idioms:

abide *by* (not *to*)

adhere *to* (not *with*)

admit guilt (not admit *to* guilt)

agree *to* something (not *with*)

agree *with* a person (not *to*)

apropos *of* (not merely apropos)

capable *of* (but able *to*)

center *on* (not *around*)

dissimilar *to* (not *from*)

equally (not equally *as*)

find fault *with* (not *toward*)

forbid *to* (not *from*)

identical *with* (not *to*)

independent *of* (not *from*)

inherent *in* (not *to*)

knack *of* (not *for*)

compatible *with* (not *to*)	lavish *on* (not *to*)
comply *with* (not *to*)	oblivious *of* (not *to*)
concur *in* an opinion (not *with*)	originate *in* (not *from*)
concur *with* a person (not *to*)	persevere *in* (not *at*)
confide *in* someone (not *to*)	preferable *to* (not *than*)
conform *to* (not *with*)	prohibit *from* (not *to*)
contented *with* (not *at*)	to separate *from* (not *out*)
deficient *in* (not *of*)	succeed *in* (not *at*)
delight *in* (not *at*)	superior *to* (not *than*)
deprive *of* (not *from*)	sympathize *with*, have sympathy *for*
desire *for* (not *of*)	take exception *to* (not *with*)
disappointed *in* (not *at*)	violation *of* (not *to*)
dissent *from* (not *to*)	visit (not visit *with*)

A few idioms often used in writing deserve special attention, among them the verbs *compare* and *contrast*. We compare one thing *to* another when we see them as similar ("He compared her smile *to* a sunrise"); we compare one thing *with* another when we want to know how they are similar or different ("Let's compare New York *with* Chicago"). One thing compares *with*, not to, another ("Her smile compares *with* a sunrise"). And we contrast one thing *to* another ("Let's contrast New York *to* Chicago"), but the one contrasts *with* the other ("New York contrasts *with* Chicago").

A good ear and long acquaintance with the language can help us write idiomatically, and a good dictionary may give some help when we have a specific question about usage.

Guideline

 Strive for customary, idiomatic usage.

Revision Practice: Saying It Right—Idioms

Revise each sentence, using readable, idiomatic English.

1. Nobody who is deficient of charisma is likely to succeed at politics.

2. Sammy was almost identical to his brother physically but didn't compare to him in attitude.

3. Almost anything is preferable than admitting to prejudice.

4. After martial law was declared, citizens were prohibited from assembling, and everyone had to conform with strict regulations.

5. Children who have been deprived from watching television often prove that they are capable to achieve higher grades in school.

6. Many who do not agree with elimination of nuclear energy are nevertheless fearful from nuclear weapons.

7. Nonconformists are people who have a desire of personal freedom and do not want to abide to traditional patterns of behavior.

8. The Environmental Protection Agency found one corporation in violation to regulations governing waste disposal, but several others were equally as guilty.

9. Our flight originated from Philadelphia, and most of us passengers were oblivious to the engine trouble until we arrived to our destination in Miami.

10. The candidate is popular because he has an easy knack for getting by with people.

Revise the following paragraph, using acceptable idioms:

Almost inherent with childhood is the desire of being independent from parental influence. Children, forced to comply to parents' decisions, feel angry at the parents, even though silently. They are seldom able to confide to their parents, and the suppressed anger builds. Over the years the young come to delight at taking exception with their parents' way of looking toward life. As the young grow, they often become resentful to all authority. It is hard for them to avoid to consider the ways of age inferior than those of youth. Parents, their authority challenged, are disappointed at what "the kids have come to." Often the parents blame on the schools. The schools,

meanwhile, blame on the parents. Many social problems center

around this genuine generation gap.

Follow-up

Check your revisions against the list of idioms shown earlier. For convenience,
underline the changes you have made.

Spelling
the Words

Good spelling and good manners usually go unnoticed, but both bad spelling and bad manners draw scorn. Whether true or not, the idea that the careless speller is also a careless thinker does prevail, and we'd best avoid the blemish lest it be taken as a disease.

Spelling is one aspect in which "correctness" remains an almost universal requirement. We may cut grammatical corners; we may twist syntax to our purposes on occasion; but if we misspell a word, it stands out like a wart on the nose and easily distracts readers from all the fine things we have to say.

Oddly enough, misspelling does not often cause writing to be misunderstood. Readers will get the message even if we write like this:

> As everyboddy nose, are sistem of English speling dosen't make much sence.

The trouble is that readers will get more message than we want them to get. They will understand not only what we say but also what we don't say; namely, that we are ill schooled in literacy and possibly in other things as well. So, though spelling is one of those unimportant aspects of writing, it remains essential, and we writers can avoid it only at our peril.

Attempts to adopt a simplified spelling system based on how words are pronounced are doomed by a simple fact: Words are correctly pronounced differently by different people. And too many words are pronounced alike and need to be distinguished in print—write? Rite. What can be made of a Bill of Rites? Even when we think our spelling is silly, we will probably go on using those strange *gh*'s and never go gentle into "nite."

Spelling by the Book

Dictionaries are generally useful guides to spelling, but we must know how to use them. Most dictionaries show first the preferred spelling of a word; if variant spellings are often seen, the dictionaries will probably show them too. *Funk & Wagnalls Standard College Dictionary*, under *tranquillity*, shows "Also *tranquility*." It is always best to use the first-listed spelling of a word, since that is the one preferred by most writers and publishers (according to the dictionary's careful surveys).

Using a dictionary is difficult if we don't know how a word begins. Is it *sigh-* or *psy-*? Is it *phys-* or *fiz-*? Is it *co-* or *cho-* or *ko-* or *quo-*? What we must do is look up all the possibilities until we come to the right one. If we are too lazy to look, then we are too lazy to write. If we cannot even guess at the possibilities, then we are probably not ready to write.

Spelling by the Rules

Dictionaries tell us how words are spelled *as a rule*—that is, most of the time, though not always. And that is what the "rules" tell us, too. The rules are not commandments; they are descriptions of how most careful writers spell. It pays to memorize a few rules and save having to memorize thousands of words. Here are the chief rules:

Silent E's. Memorize these few words: *judgment, mileage, ninth, wholly.* In other silent *e* words, drop the *e* if it follows *u* (*truly, argument*) or if the added ending begins with a vowel (*believable, dining, severity,* and so on). If the added ending begins with a consonant, keep the silent *e* (*safety, requirement, strangely, useful,* and so on). Special note: If the silent *e* follows a soft *c* or *g* (as in *notice* or *manage*), keep the silent *e* if the added ending begins with *a* or *o* (*noticeable, manageable, courageous*).

Final Y's. Memorize these few words: *daily, gaily, paid, laid, said.* If the added ending is *-ing*, keep the final *y* (*trying, flying, complying,* and so on). If the final *y* follows a vowel, keep the *y* (*player, destroyed, royal, employable, conveyance,* and so on). Otherwise, change the final *y* to *i* before adding an ending (*tried, reliance, accompaniment,* and so on).

Doubled consonants. Memorize these few words: *tranquillity, programmer* (but many use just one *m* in *programming*). If a word is pronounced with stress on the final-consonant syllable, double that consonant before a vowel (*planned, beginning, occurred, preferred, unforgettable,* and so on). If the word is not stressed on the final-consonant syllable, do not double (*reference, traveler, marvelous, benefiting,* and so on). Do not double the consonant before another consonant (*dimly, hatless, deferment*).

IE *and* EI. Memorize these few words: *friend, seize, either, neither, leisure, weird,* and *financier.* In others, if the syllable is *not* pronounced as long *e,* spell it *ei* (*weigh, neighbor, eight, freight, height, their,* and so on). If the syllable is pronounced as long *e,* spell it *ie* except right after *c* (*believe, field, chief, mischief, briefly; receive, conceive, ceiling,* and so on). If the two letters are not in the same syllable, it's usually *ie* (*science, drier,* and so on).

-ANT, -ANCE; -ENT, -ENCE. Most such words are spelled *-ent* and *-ence,* so use that spelling if in doubt. But do not remain in doubt; use a good dictionary.

-ABLE, -IBLE. Most such words are spelled *-able,* so use that spelling if in doubt. But do not remain in doubt; use your dictionary.

Taken all at once as we have just taken them, these spelling rules seem like a lot to remember. But taken one at a time with considerable practical application, they can keep us from thousands of misspellings. They are worth spending some time with.

Once good spelling becomes a habit, we save ourselves much embarrassment and much time. Until then, revising for spelling may require a special read-through of an essay, a deliberate search for words we're unsure of.

Guideline

Attend to spelling, using a good dictionary to check words you are not sure of.

Revision Practice: Spelling the Words

Check the spelling in this brief essay, revising as you go. Problem words in the first two paragraphs (some right and some wrong) are underscored.

```
                    THE ARMS AROUND US

1        A global nuclear war could bring an end to mankind.

2   A recent artical on the Soviet Union and it's arsonal of

3   weapons said that a 100-megaton bomb could incenerate
```

4   everything within three hundred miles of its <u>detonation</u>

5   point. Anything that was left would <u>probally</u> soon die from

6   <u>raddiation</u> in the <u>atmostphere.</u>

7   I'm not an <u>antinucular</u> enthusiast, though I do <u>beleive</u>

8   in <u>deterence.</u> I think any nation should be <u>stoped</u> from

9   world <u>expantion</u> and <u>dommination.</u> And it would no doubt be

10 <u>advantagous</u> to all of us to <u>reduce</u> the stockpiles of <u>atommic</u>

11 weapons. If we <u>elimanated</u> ours and the Soviets <u>they'res</u>,

12 the result would be a <u>tremendus</u> <u>benifit</u> to all mankind.

13   The trouble, of coarse, is there are so many arguements

14 on both sides of the question of defencive and ofensive

15 weapons. Are we building up our "nukes" to protect our

16 country or to attact theres? And are the Soviets useing the

17 threat of nucular war to keep there sattelite countries in

18 line and frighten other nations into submision? Niether

19 side has come out with any genuine proposeals for arms

20 controll and inspection of military sights, so at the moment

21 the prolifferation of military hardware is virtualy

22 uncontroled.

23   The main thing that seams to be holding back arms

24 limmitations is mutuel fear. Each side feels that the first

25 step must be taken by the other; another words, we human

26 beings misstrust one another. Perhaps the only sollution is

27 to continuelly search for a sceintific breakthrough that

28 would bring us a way of stoping nucular missles before they

29 can reach us, a way that could be safly used without danger

30 to any people.

31   If we could do that, and if the Soviets could do

32 likwise, their would be no further need for spending bilions

33 on military weapons. Then we could all get on with the main

34 job of our social lives--becomming civilized.

Follow-up

One problem of spelling is that we often think one word and write another that "sounds" the same. Did you check for the difference between "its" and "it's," "seams" and "seems," "sight" and "site," "coarse" and "course," "their" and "there" and "they're"? Did you check "advantagous" and "becomming" against the silent *e* rule and "uncontroled" against the doubled-consonant rule? You should have found and corrected fifty-five misspelled words in the essay.

Lesson 39

Using Abbreviations

Whatever is written to be readable should avoid all but conventional forms of abbreviation. Needless abbreviating is a mark of discourtesy, saying to the readers that we have saved a few seconds of time at their expense. Perhaps the most common offender in handwritten work at college is the ampersand (&) or plus sign (+) used for *and*. These marks are useful in notetaking and in speeding the work of preliminary drafts, but they should not appear in drafts to be read by others.

What do we mean by "conventional" abbreviations? We mean those that are more common in print than their spelled-out forms: Mr., Mrs., Dr., St. (for Saint), and the academic degrees (B.A., B.S., M.A., M.S., M.D., Ph.D., and so on). Certain others are more often used in both speech and print than are the spelled-out forms (A.M., P.M., B.C., D.C. (for District of Columbia), FBI, CIA, YMCA, CBS, NYU, UCLA, and so on). But even some designations of that last sort are better spelled out than abbreviated. In writing for readers it is generally better to write *United States* for U.S., *United Nations* for UN, and *television* for TV.

In scholarly writing the habit of using such abbreviations as *i.e., e.g., et al.,* and *viz.* has now given way to the use of more readable spelled-out forms in

English *(that is, for example, and others, namely)*. Other Latin terms have generally been eliminated *(ibid.* and *op. cit.* being cut in favor of repeating an author's name with a page number). A few abbreviations that do remain in use are the handy *p.* and *pp.* for *page* and *pages.* (The much-seen *pg.* is simply wrong.)

Names of days and months are best spelled out in an essay or scholarly thesis, though *The MLA Style Sheet,* followed in most scholarly writing, calls for *Jan., Feb., Mar.,* and so on, in footnotes and bibliographies. In other words, the style used in the footnotes and bibliography (for reference rather than for reading) permits abbreviations not acceptable in the paper itself.

We should never write A.M. or P.M. unless it follows a specific hour written in figures (11 A.M., 5:30 P.M.), and even then it is usually better to write "eleven o'clock in the morning" or "5:30 in the afternoon").

Names of cities, states, nations, and continents are almost always spelled out in writing essays, though journalists often abbreviate U.S., U.K., and U.S.S.R. The words *street, avenue,* and *boulevard* should be spelled out.

Some abbreviations become *acronyms,* pronounced as words though each of their letters stands for another word (NATO, NASA, OPEC). The first time such an abbreviation is used in an essay, the name should be written in full so that its meaning cannot be mistaken: North Atlantic Treaty Organization first, NATO later.

Even OK is better spelled *okay*—but should seldom be used in formal or scholarly writing.

In writing about literature, history, science, or the arts, it is customary to use well-known names as their owners did. George Bernard Shaw often referred to himself as G.B.S., but it would never do to write his name as George B. Shaw. The given names of T. S. Eliot are almost never written in full. And in writing about such persons we almost never use *Mr., Mrs.,* or *Miss.* It is not proper to write "*Miss* Dickinson" in reference to the poet Emily Dickinson; simply "Dickinson" will do. Still, it may be useful, in an unusual case, to refer to Elizabeth Barrett Browning as "*Mrs.* Browning," since "Browning" would not distinguish her from her husband, Robert Browning.

Guideline

Abbreviate only when the spelled-out form would not be acceptable.

Revision Practice: Abbreviations

Revise these sentences, using abbreviations only where they are customary in formal writing.

```
1. My sister + I had an appointment with the Dr. at 2 p.m.
```

2. Our neighbor, Mister Lederman, & his wife both once worked in a TV commercial.

3. My job with the telephone Co. lasted only from Apr. to Sept.

4. One of my closest friends is finishing a Doctor of Philos. thesis at the Univ. of Tenn.

5. That morning I had several things to do; e.g., confer with Prof. Miguel about my paper on Mr. Picasso's blue period.

6. One high ct. decided the gov't was not responsible for any damage claimed by people who lived near Three Mi. Island.

7. This year the local theater group will produce Wm. Shakespeare's Romeo + Juliet during the Oct. festival.

8. We heard two fellows in Central Pk. arguing about the no. of sts. that have been canonized by the Catholic Church.

9. The Gk. philosopher Aristotle died in 322 Before Christ.

10. It seems likely that Mr. Tolstoy took less time to write War & Peace than most of us do to read it.

11. When in N.Y. last Aug., we took a tour of the UN Bldg. on the Ave. of the Americas.

12. When I moved from Chicago to Phila., I continued to read Mike Royko's col. in the newspaper.

13. Doctor Martin L. King, Junior, left the rest of us to work toward realization of his dream.

14. Most of the good music on radio is on the Frequency Modulation stations.

15. The assassin of R. F. Kennedy could be released from prison in just a few yrs.

16. Several flights out of the L.A. airport were delayed because of fog, and the psgrs. were waiting impatiently for flights to the E. Coast.

17. In the 3rd game of the St. L.-Mont. series the umpire threw both mgrs. out during the 1st inning.

18. We were asked to write at least 6 pp. for the exam. After two hours, I was only on pg. four.

19. For many years John Wooden was coach of the University of California at Los Angeles bsktball team.

20. That Fri. night I missed the convention because I had an accident and wound up in the County Hosp. with 2 broken ribs.

Follow-up

Check each abbreviation against the advice given earlier. Some abbreviations are conventional (*Mr.* is never spelled out, and *Doctor* is used only when not with a name). In most writing, numbers should be spelled out if they can be written as one or two words (*sixty, ninety-seven, two hundred, five thousand,* and so on) except when they designate dates, years, addresses, times of day, or page numbers.

Writing and Revising

For detailed suggestions on getting started, writing a first draft, revising the draft, and preparing the essay for submission, refer to the Introduction. Choose one of the following topics.

Topics for Writing

1. Are you one of those who "need people," or can you be called a "loner"? What benefits and drawbacks do you find in each? Do you really prefer to be as you are in this respect, or would you prefer to change? Jot a list of your ideas and devise a thesis on the topic. Select a purpose (such as *definition, description,* or *analyzing cause and effect*); then number the ideas in an appropriate order and write a first draft explaining your attitudes.

2. The human urge toward security is strong, yet we are often drawn toward danger. When you have a choice, do you prefer to "play it safe" or to experience the thrills of danger? Jot a list of your ideas and devise a thesis on the topic. Select a purpose (you may *argue to convince* your readers that your preference is best); then number the ideas in an appropriate order and write a first draft.

3. Guitar playing, typing, auto repair, computer programming, cooking—nearly everyone has a manual-mental skill of some kind. Tell

about one of your own, how you first learned it, and what it has meant in your life. Jot a list of your ideas and devise a thesis on the topic. Select a purpose (such as *relating an incident* or *arguing to convince*); then number the ideas in an appropriate order and write a first draft.

4. In American society today the word *benefits* often means things one can get free from a government agency or from an employer. What "benefits" do you think are most worthwhile? Are some benefits really detrimental to the individual? How? Jot a list of your ideas and devise a thesis on the topic. Select a purpose (such as *definition* or *arguing to convince*—or a combination); then number the ideas in an appropriate order and write a first draft.

Follow-up

Unless you are already adept at using English idiom, there is no quick way for you to check your first draft for naturalness of expression. If any usage seems unnatural, it may be helpful to ask several friends about it (people who you think speak good English). Your dictionary may also be of help concerning idioms; consult entries under words that seem questionable in your essay. And refer to the list of idiomatic usages in Lesson 37. Check your manuscript for spelling; a little extra time spent with the dictionary may noticeably improve the appearance and appeal of your work. Wherever you have used abbreviations, check them against the suggestions presented earlier and follow Guideline 39.

Lesson 40

Guiding
the Way:
Punctuation

Punctuation marks are to reading what street signs and signals are to driving; they help tell us where we are, when to go, when to make a turn, when to slow down, and when to stop. When the marks aren't where they should be, we can easily get lost—and frustrated.

To write readable stuff, we have to know what the marks mean and where to use them. Sprinkling them on like pepper from a shaker will not do. There's no good way but to learn the system.

In general the system of punctuation is geared to sentence structure and is designed to group and separate parts of sentences.

There is only one mark that most written sentences must have: a period. If a sentence isn't marked by an ending period, it must be a question (?) or an exclamation (!). All three of these end markers are something like boulevard stops. They should never be used more than one at a time.

From here on the system gets more meticulous, so we'll take up the marks in turn.

282

About Commas

Commas are used for grouping and for separating. The words that appear between two commas, like these right here, are grouped—and they are also separated from the rest of the sentence. Sometimes the commas set off a single word. Among some of the groups (or single words) that are usually set off between commas are:

- Groups that add information but aren't absolutely needed, such as these:

Jimmy, *the camp counselor,* taught the young campers how to find the right wood for a fire.

Mozart, *despite his short life,* was among the most prolific of composers.

Most of the workers, *who had been laid off for more than six months,* eagerly returned to their jobs.

My most persistent interest, *although I had many minor ones,* had always been music.

Each of those sentences can be read and will make full sense with or without the group set off between commas. The groups are nonessential (or *nonrestrictive*). Such groups, of course, would be set off by only one comma if they appeared at the beginning or end of the sentence:

Despite his short life, Mozart was among the most prolific of composers.

My most persistent interest had always been music, *although I had many minor ones.*

- Groups that interrupt a thought, such as these:

Our favorite sparrows, *we knew,* would return in the spring.

Cheerful spirits, *after all,* live longest.

Our bus, *as a matter of fact,* was waiting for us.

"Tell us," *she said,* "whether you had fun at the fair."

Word groups that are needed—that is, could not be cut from the sentence—should not be set off between commas:

Frederick *the Great* lived *until he was seventy-four.*

Mozart's opera *The Marriage of Figaro* is still a world favorite.

The few workers *who had not gone on strike* were held in scorn.

He never smoked a cigarette *after he learned to read the package.*

Those sentences would not be clear—or would not be true—without the word groups shown in italics. Those groups are essential (or *restrictive*) and should *not* be set off between commas.

Certain groups (or single words) that begin a sentence are always to be set off by a comma:

- Introductory modifiers:

Perfectly composed, she sat without a glance to either side.

Shaking with fright, my sister could hardly say a word.

When the alarm went off, it seemed a part of my dream.

- Introductory interjections:

Well, we may never know who put the bikini in the fire.

Oh, yes, I did get the assignment done on time.

All right, let's try digging the tunnel with a spoon.

Brief prepositional phrases that begin a sentence are ordinarily *not* set off:

In the late afternoon the winds came up.

Under the apple tree they spread their picnic.

For no good reason they had taken the early train.

Commas are used to separate certain independent clauses linked in one sentence:

My roommate had left on vacation, and the rest of the floor was vacant.

We broke the glass, but the fire extinguisher was rusted.

Either we learn to listen, or we spend much time alone.

Commas are used to separate items in series:

On the platform were *the speaker, the governor,* and *the party's new candidate.*

The waiter *slipped, fell,* and *broke all the dishes.*

He is *often out of sorts, usually out of money,* but *never out of chutzpah.*

Newswriters have long held that the comma before *and* in such a series is unnecessary, apparently on grounds that the comma and the conjunction do the same work. The point is arguable, except that the job of the comma is to separate and the job of *and* is to join—clearly not the same. We need to do both. Consider how ambiguity may arise from the omission of the comma:

> The primary goal . . . is to understand just how fires start, spread and kill their victims.
>
> *Newsweek*

Do fires "spread . . . their victims"; no, clearly there should be a comma after "spread" to avoid the misunderstanding. Some other examples:

> Hurriedly he washed his face, shaved and combed his hair.

> The two men had robbed banks, repeatedly raped and terrorized the whole town.

If we want to omit the comma, we must at least make sure we have no likely misunderstanding.

About the Semicolon

In rank as a separator, the semicolon is stronger than a comma, weaker than a period. Its chief use is to separate two main ideas that are related but not joined by a conjunction:

> Art is long; life is short.

> Old soldiers never die; they just fade away.

The semicolon also separates two main ideas that are joined by adverbs such as *therefore, however,* or *on the other hand* (note that the adverb is also set off by a comma):

> Weak lies are seldom believed; *therefore,* speak up.

> The lamp flickered out; *meanwhile,* so did I.

> We're all doomed; *in fact,* the day may have passed without our knowing it.

When a number of commas appear in a sentence, the semicolon is often useful to mark a point of greater separation:

> With the party were Stephanie, my cousin; Wilt, an insurance agent; two children, both unruly; and a panting basset hound that no one seemed to own.

About the Colon

The colon is something like a pointer; it announces a coming example, restatement, or explanation:

A writer can't go wrong who gets in all the information: *who, what, when, where, why, how,* and *so what.*

We had reason to be annoyed: We had been deceived.

The candidate had a problem: how to get blood money out of a rather turnipy town.

The colon should *not* be used after a verb to introduce objects of the verb, as in "we visited: the zoo, the city hall, and the museum."

About the Hyphen

The hyphen is a joiner; it puts two or more words together as a compound idea:

He saw his *twenty-third* year as a *cooling-off* period.

Our party favors a *pay-as-you-go* fiscal policy.

The hyphen is also used after certain prefixes:

The *ex-governor* hadn't enough *self-confidence* to run for the *vice-presidency.*

With certain other prefixes the hyphen is used when the main word begins with the letter that ends the prefix—or when the main word begins with a capital:

The *anti-imperalist* attitude shouldn't be interpreted as *pro-Palestinian* or *anti-Semitic.*

Words beginning with *non* take no hyphen unless the main word begins with a capital:

Holding to *noninterference,* he was *nonpartisan* and *noncommittal* until the *non-Chinese* policy was discussed.

When we use a hyphen for splitting a word between lines, we must follow the strict rules of syllable division.

About the Apostrophe

The apostrophe has two uses: (1) to indicate omission of letters in contractions and (2) to indicate the possessive. The apostrophe should *not* be used to make ordinary nouns plural; write *two buses*, not *two bus's*.

In contractions the apostrophe goes where letters have been left out:

We're too smart to go where we *shouldn't* be seen when *it's* impossible to know *who's* watching.

In writing the possessive form of a noun, we follow a simple (but often abused) system:

1. If the noun is plural and ends in *s*, add only the apostrophe: the *girls'* club, ten *singers'* voices, all *members'* dues, his *parents'* car, the *Joneses'* dog, *states'* rights.

2. For all other nouns, form the possessive by adding *'s:* a *girl's* purse, a *singer's* voice, one *member's* dues, Dr. *Jones's* office, the *state's* capital, the *men's* dorm, our *children's* safety, the *bus's* windows, the *dress's* neckline, Sam *Clemens's* life, the *media's* responsibilities. The system really *is* that simple: After a plural noun that ends in *s*, add apostrophe only; elsewhere, add *'s*.

About the Dash

The dash separates, groups, emphasizes, and lends suspense or irony. It is a mark of informality. We should not toss it in for lack of knowing what mark to use but should reserve it for special needs, as for a moment of suspense or an instant of delay before an afterthought:

Dad seemed to know what I was thinking—always.

She was a picture of health—perfectly framed.

Light-verse poet Richard Armour wrote this about the dash:

It's used to gain emphasis, vigor, a touch
Of surprise—and it's also—by some—
Used too much.

About Quotation Marks

Quotation marks are used to enclose directly quoted material, as in dialogue:

"Hold on to the rope," he shouted, "and pull yourself up."

They should never be used to enclose material that is indirectly quoted or in any way changed from an original:

He shouted *that I should hold on to the rope and pull myself up.*

Occasionally quotation marks are used to emphasize a word or phrase, possibly to give it special meaning:

Nothing is more annoying than a "good idea" that interferes with your plans.

When we quote something within another quotation, we use single quotation marks:

"I see a vast difference," the professor said, "between 'possible' causes and 'probable' ones."

When we use closing quotation marks, they always belong *outside* a comma or period, as in the sentence above.

About Parentheses

Almost always used as a complementary pair, parentheses enclose material that we want to insert as an "aside" to the main thought:

Even if prejudice were based on truth (it seldom is), it would still be prejudice.

Parentheses can also be used to enclose organizing devices, such as numbers for items in an outline or a list within a paragraph.

It is wrong to use two different kinds of punctuation to do one job. If we use parentheses or dashes, we do not use commas also for the same purpose. These are mistakes:

Sam closed his eyes, (he was always doing that), and looked bored.

We were eager to try the stunt,—an exciting adventure.

In such cases, omit the commas:

Sam closed his eyes (he was always doing that) and looked bored.

We were eager to try the stunt—an exciting adventure.

Guideline

40 Use punctuation marks carefully to guide your readers through ideas, following the standard conventions.

Revision Practice: Guiding the Way—Punctuation

Punctuation has been omitted from this brief essay, but we have underlined places where punctuation *may* be appropriate. If you find that no mark is necessary, leave the spot blank; if you find a mark necessary, put it in.

SHIFTY

1   My roommate__ Sylvester__ was nicknamed __Shifty__ and

2 he deserved it__ We met__ and became roommates in a unique

3 experience__ that I later came to rue__

4   Sylvester was rooming down the hall with another

5 student__ who had left for the Christmas break__ and the

6 rest of the floor was deserted but for me__ He knocked on

7 my door__ and I granted his request to borrow some steak

8 sauce__ __later to find he had taken both bottles__ He went

9 back to his room__

10   Not more than twenty__seconds later__ I heard him

11 yelling__ I thought he was trying to outshout the Tom Petty

12 record he had on his stereo__ The yelling went on__ then he

13 was pounding at my door again__ and continuing the vocal

14 din__ I opened the door__

15   Smoke had filled the hall__ __My room__ he shouted__

16 __It_s my room__ I had a quick vision of steak sauce going

17 up in flame__

18   I ran to the end of the hall__ took the metal rod__ and

19 smashed the glass to sound the alarm__ Smoke thickened__ as

20 I unrolled the fire hose__ carrying the nozzle toward

21 Sylvester_s_ room__ __Turn it on__ I shouted__ and he did__

22   Aimlessly__ I pointed the gushing water into the room__

23 flooding everything__ Flames subsided__ but smoke continued

24 to billow__ By this time a dozen students had appeared from

25 the other floors__ all shouting__ as Sylvester told how it

26 happened__

27   An hour later__ he became my roommate__ moving in with

28 what was left of his possessions__ a wrinkled Clint Eastwood

29 poster__ burnt on one edge__ and the stereo with melted Tom

30 Petty record__

31   After that__ nothing in my room was mine__ He

32 rearranged my furniture__ brought my television out of the

33 bedroom and set it up at the end of __his__ couch__ A few

34 days later all the alligators had been trimmed off my

35 shirts__ and my lunchroom pass was missing__ it turned up

36 later on the dean_s_ desk__ bearing my signature__ but

37 Sylvester_s_ photo__ When I was called in__ I had to

38 explain__ who I was__ and that I had absolutely not eaten

39 three lunches a day__ for nearly a week__

40   When semester break came__ I left that place__ Shifty

41 presented to me a plastic baggie with six alligator

42 appliqués in it__ and said__ __he was sorry__ I was leaving_

43 Two friends helped me move my things to a borrowed pickup

44 truck__ Shifty shouted __that I should come back next

45 semester__

46   __You should live so long__ I said__

47   __What__ he called__

48   __I said__ __So long__ I said__ and I started up the

49 truck and never looked back__

Follow-up

If you can explain each mark of punctuation by reference to the suggestions given earlier in this section, you probably have firm control of conventional punctuation. Make sure that questions end with question marks, exclamations with exclamation points, and all other sentences with periods. Some of the blanks should have no punctuation; some may require two—possibly three— punctuation marks. Did you find single quotation marks necessary in line 48?

Remember that commas and periods always go inside, not outside, quotation marks. A question mark or exclamation point goes inside quotation marks if it is a part of what's quoted. (Did you use parentheses in line 9?)

Lesson 41

Capitalizing

By their contrasting size, capital letters draw attention and are used to bring special notice. If overused, they lose this power—and that is why we almost never write ALL CAPITALS for more than a few words. In English, capital letters are used to begin certain words:

1. First words of sentences.

2. The personal pronoun *I*.

3. First words and other words of titles—except *a, an, the,* and prepositions and conjunctions shorter than four letters.

4. Proper names of people (Christopher Columbus); specific geographical areas and places (the Far West, the South, Europe, Seattle, Fifth Avenue); time periods (the Renaissance, the Roaring Twenties, October, Friday); specific holidays (Easter, Labor Day); races, nations, nationalities, and languages (Caucasian, Egypt, Nepalese, Spanish); institutions (the Methodist Church, the University of Kansas, the Rockettes); trade names (Volkswagen, Chevron); specific academic

courses that are numbered or lettered (Chemistry 1, History 6, Psychology B); but general studies other than languages are not capitalized (chemistry, history, psychology).

5. Titles of rank or office used before names (Queen Elizabeth, Senator Kennedy, Admiral Jones).

6. All references to a specific deity (God, Buddha, Allah, Jehova, He, Father, the Creator).

7. Proper epithets and personified abstractions (Smokey the Bear, Magic Johnson, the North Star, Father Time, blind Justice, elusive Truth).

Also capitalized are the initials popularly used for any of the above or for certain other terms (USA, NBC, PLO, YWCA, TV). Words that should not be capitalized include names of the seasons (spring, summer, autumn, winter) and points of the compass (north, south).

Other than *I* or proper nouns, the first word after a colon or within quotation marks is capitalized only if it begins a full sentence, and the first word after a semicolon is not capitalized.

Guideline

Capitalize words according to conventional usage.

Revision Practice: Capitalizing

Revise this essay using proper capitalization.

```
1                         deadwood roots

2        on a winter morning in may--a tuesday it was--i was

3    born in deadwood, south dakota.  right in the badlands of

4    the usa, my home town is yet one of the most picturesque

5    places in america.  within eyesight of my early home were

6    the sculptured faces of washington and lincoln at mount

7    rushmore, and my mother and father several times took me to

8    the nearby spot where wild bill hickok died.

9        in that part of the midwest the people have a fierce

10   sort of pride and a hardy nature tuned to hard work and
```

11 freezing winters. my uncle harley still works a farm in

12 those badlands, and i go back now and then to visit--

13 usually in summer, for i moved west and i'm a californian

14 now, and no longer happy in the cold winds that come down

15 out of canada from the north pole.

16   my college major is geology, and i've made a special

17 study of the area around deadwood. and in my art classes i

18 have painted several watercolors of the dakota landscapes.

19 no, i'm not a chauvinistic dakotan, but i would not change

20 my heritage.

21   today i give thanks to god for at least two things:

22 that he permitted me to be born in deadwood, giving me a

23 great love for its past--and that he got me out of there

24 before i fell in love with those harsh, forbidding seasons.

Follow-up

All proper names are capitalized, as is the title (which contains no prepositions or conjunctions). Words like "mother" and "father" (line 7) are not capitalized unless used as names, never when preceded by a possessive like "my." But words like "uncle" (line 11) are capitalized if they precede a proper name. All geographical area and place names (lines 3, 4, 5, 6–7, 9, 12, 13, 15, 17, 18, and 19) are capitalized, but directions (line 13) are not capitalized. Studies named in general (lines 16 and 17) are not capitalized, nor are the names of seasons (lines 2 and 13). All references to God (lines 21–23) are capitalized.

Setting Up the Page

The legibility of a typed or handwritten paper depends on its appearance on the page and contributes in some measure to the more important matter of readability. And, in college work and professional writing, there are other practical reasons for making a piece of writing look good on paper.

We have already shown that spaces between words are an aid to reading. But there is another space too: space between sentences, space between paragraphs, and space around the whole body of writing on the page. Unused space can be as important in making an impression on the eye as can the used space in making an impression on a reader's thoughts. Let's begin, then, by discussing space.

About Margins

Good pictures are often enhanced by careful framing. An essay on paper makes an effective first impression when it has margins wide enough to form a frame. The frame, of course, is on all sides—top, bottom, left, and right. As a general rule, each of the four margins should be at least one inch, the top margin perhaps a bit more.

Other than aesthetic appearance, the main reason for those margins in college work is to allow the instructor some space for writing comments and suggestions. In professional writing, the main practical reason for the marginal space is to allow copy editors to mark directions to typesetters. No matter how crowded a first draft may be, its revision to be submitted to readers should always have margins wide enough for appearance, for suggestions, and for editing.

About Spacing

Typed manuscripts should always be double-spaced. Professional work must always be typed, and single-spaced material is simply unacceptable; so too in college work, in most places. Even the handwritten paper, wherever it is accepted for college, will usually be improved in appearance and in practicality (for marking changes or edits) if it is double-spaced.

Standards usually call for a single space between words, two spaces between sentences within a paragraph. The first line of each paragraph is indented about one inch, or five typing spaces.

About Titles

The title of a paper, if typed, is usually written in ALL CAPITALS and is centered on the page. At least two spaces, often three or four, should be left below the title before the beginning of the essay itself. If the paper is hand-written, the title should follow standard rules for capitalization.

The title usually appears on the first page only. In college the instructor may require the writer's name on every page, perhaps with some designation of the assignment.

About Page Numbers

The first page of a manuscript needs no number. Subsequent pages should each be numbered in order (usually with a number only, not with *p.*). The figure may appear between hyphens (-2-, -3-, and so on). That number is most handy when it appears at the upper right on the page.

The end of a manuscript may be marked so that a reader will be sure there is no more to come. The mark ordinarily used in professional work is #, the printer's symbol for "space" or "end." That mark may be used in college work as well and is usually centered below the last line of writing.

About Handwriting

Handwriting is, in one sense, a private and individual act—to each his own. But since it is also a social act, generally intended to communicate, it is subject to certain social requirements, chief among them being the courtesy of legibility. No one has a "right" to write illegibly if the work is intended for others' eyes.

Handwritten work, even if not the clearest, is usually made more legible by double-spacing—and that method is recommended at all times, since it also contributes ease to the editing process. When a manuscript is double-spaced, new materials can be written in without making a mess of the paper.

It should go without saying (but often does not) that pencil work is considered unacceptable for a submitted draft.

Guideline

Before you submit a manuscript, make the appearance of each page enhance your readable style.

Revision Practice: Setting Up the Page

Complete the Review Quiz on pages 299–301. Make sure that your submitted draft follows manuscript standards set by the instructor or the editor who is to receive it. If no such standards have been issued, use those set forth here.

Summary
Revising for Appearance and Custom

Guidelines 37–42

37. Strive for customary, idiomatic usage.

38. Attend to spelling, using a good dictionary to check words you are not sure of.

39. Abbreviate only when the spelled-out form would not be acceptable.

40. Use punctuation marks carefully to guide your readers through ideas, following the standard conventions.

41. Capitalize words according to conventional usage.

42. Before you submit a manuscript, make the appearance of each page enhance your readable style.

Writing and Revising

For detailed suggestions on getting started, writing a first draft, revising the draft, and preparing the essay for submission, refer to the Introduction. Choose one of the following topics.

Topics for Writing

1. If you have observed prejudice in action (political, religious, racial, or personal), write an essay relating details of how, when, and where it appeared and who was involved. Jot a list of your ideas and devise a thesis on the topic. Select a purpose (such as *relating an incident, arguing to convince*, or *analyzing cause and effect*—or a combination); then number the ideas in an appropriate order and write a first draft, focusing on the event's emotional impact on you.

2. Is shyness an advantage or disadvantage to the shy? Write on that question, illustrating your point by reference to some real person (possibly yourself). Consider what is the opposite of shyness also—and try to give it a name. What would be the ideal state between the extremes? Jot a list of your ideas and devise a thesis on the topic. Select a purpose (such as *definition, arguing to convince*, or *analyzing cause and effect*—or a combination); then number the ideas in an appropriate order and write a first draft.

3. The "unalienable" rights of human beings, says our Declaration of Independence, are "life, liberty, and the pursuit of happiness." Are any of those rights being limited or denied in your community, state, or nation today? If so, to what extent—and who is doing the denying? Jot a list of your ideas and devise a thesis on the topic. Select a purpose (such as *analyzing cause and effect, relating an incident*, or *arguing to convince*—or a combination); then number the ideas in an appropriate order and write a first draft.

4. What is your most satisfying accomplishment so far in your life? Jot a list of your ideas and devise a thesis on the topic. Select a purpose (such as *relating an incident, analyzing cause and effect, description, analyzing a process*, or *arguing to convince*); then number the ideas in an appropriate order and write a first draft.

Follow-up

Revise your first draft to make it as readable as you can, drawing on all you have learned in using this book and by completing your essays and revisions. Check for punctuation and use of capitals and make your submitted manuscript as presentable as you can.

Review Quiz

The following essay has many departures from customary usage, errors that mar its readability. Revise the essay, making all necessary changes in idiom, spelling, abbreviation, punctuation, and capitalization. Also make sure to set the essay up attractively on your pages, using acceptable margins and other spacing.

```
1                    FOR US THE BELL TOLES

2         At the turn, of this centery, telephones seemed like a

3    luxury because people weren't realy use to them, but today

4    the phone is an absolute neccesity.  Our country operates

5    around the Telephone System so much that if we were suddenly

6    to loose all our telephones, we would surly come grinding at

7    a halt.

8         We all depend on the telephone everyday.  Its the

9    fastest most convienent form of communication.  We can talk

10   to practicly anyone in the World from the safty of our own

11   home just by dialing a number. How could any of us afford to

12   see all the people we have to communicate with if we had to

13   talk with them face to face?  We might just use the mails

14   but, that would be far to slow in these fast paced days.

15        And what of people who want to talk with us when weed

16   just as soon avoid them?  When they turn up at the door were
```

17 stuck with them but when they call on the phone, we can

18 always hang up, (or pretend we have to run to take something

19 out of the oven. We can do the same thing with people

20 trying to sell things it is hard to get rid of them if they

21 have a foot in the door; If there on the phone, we can just

22 hangup.

23 Telephones have life and death usefullness in emergencys.

24 Dial the Police, dial the Dr., dial the Hospital or make our

25 one phone call from jail we are all glad to have the phone

26 at such times

27   Businesses and the Stock-Market which have to comm-

28 unicate all day long, in order to keep functioning would

29 absolutly fall flat on their deficits without the telephone.

30 Some people have made fortunes by wheeling and dealing with

31 associates they have never seen in person in fact if they

32 had to be in the same room they might not find it so easy to

33 make the deals.

34   Sure there are inconvienences. We all get alot of

35 wrong nos. and our fare share of obseen calls and bothersome

36 insurance salesmen. There are even the monthly bills from

37 the dastardly Telephone Co. But we never no when the phone

38 may ring and we'll find that wev'e won the sweep steaks.

39   i think that the few drawbacks of telephones will never

40 begin to outwiegh our absolute need for them. they have

41 given us the freedom as the comercial says to reach out and

touch someone", as we often want too do.   When our phones

43   stop functioning so will our country, and alot of the best

44   part of our personal lifes.

Follow-up

Recheck to make sure you have corrected thirty-one misspellings and thirteen errors of capitalization. You should have added punctuation in lines 8, 16, 17, 19, 24, 25, 27, 31, 32, 41, and 43. You should have corrected punctuation errors in lines 18, 28, 42, and 43. Did you use semicolons in lines 20 and 31, and a dash in line 25? Three words were abbreviated that should be spelled out (lines 24, 35, and 37). Is the hyphen in line 27 properly used? What of the division of *communicate?* Should the beginning of line 23 be indented? Check the spelling of "sweep steaks" in line 38.

Index

Summary of Guidelines
for Readable Writing

Revising for Substance

1. Select a *topic* that interests you and is likely to engage the minds of others. Limit that topic to what you can cover in a short essay.
2. Choose an appropriate *purpose* to guide your approach.
3. Give your central idea a personal twist. *Challenge* the reader's mind.
4. Make ideas concrete by *example, illustration, comparison,* or *contrast.*
5. *Define* essential terms. *Describe* people, places, processes, and physical objects.
6. Make sure what you say is well founded and *reasonably* worded.

Revising for Order

7. As you revise a draft, make sure the essay has an effective beginning, middle, and end, with its ideas arranged in an order that suits your purpose.
8. Arrange details so that the reader can "see" or understand them in a reasonable order.
9. In an essay of analysis, present categories, parts, steps, or reasons one by one, so that each makes clear sense in itself and in relation to the whole.

Revising for Economy

10. Trim wasteful words. Make every word do all it can.
11. Trim flabby phrasing and empty modifiers.
12. Cut useless repetition. Trim wasteful "there are," "who," "that," and, "which" clauses. Watch for wordy, passive voice and overloaded sentences.

Revising for Emphasis

13. Make your title and first paragraph challenge your readers. Introduce your topic, suggest your thesis, and establish your tone.
14. Be sparing in your use of hedging, apology, passive voice, and euphemism—and never use any of these to hide important truth.
15. To add emphasis to a passage, consider repetition of words, rhythms, and sounds, as well as symmetry of forms.
16. Stress important elements by form or position. Play down minor ideas, using minor forms.
17. Make every paragraph cover just one phase of the essay's topic.
18. Bring your essay to a full-circle ending that echoes (but does not merely repeat) the essay's central point.